Venice and Its

Thomas Okey

Alpha Editions

This edition published in 2024

ISBN : 9789362927859

Design and Setting By
Alpha Editions
www.alphaedis.com
Email - info@alphaedis.com

Contents

PREFACE

THE History of Venice is the history of a State unparalleled in Europe for permanence and stability. For centuries Venice occupied that position of maritime supremacy now held by Great Britain, and time was when an English king was fain to crave the loan of a few warships to vindicate his rights in France. The autonomy of the Venetian Republic so imposed on men's minds that it was regarded as in the very nature of things, and even so acute an observer as Voltaire wrote in the *Dictionnaire Philosophique*, less than three decades before her fall: "Venice has preserved her independence during eleven centuries, and I flatter myself will preserve it for ever."

In the course of our story we have freely drawn from the old chronicles, while not neglecting modern historians, chiefest of whom is the Triestine Hebrew scholar, Samuele Romanin. Indeed, all that has been written on Venetian history during the past forty years does but increase our admiration for the imperturbable industry and sagacious judgment of the author of the *Storia Documentata di Venezia*, to whom our heaviest debt is due.

The history, criticism and appreciation of Venetian architecture and Venetian painting are indissolubly associated with the genius of Ruskin, and notwithstanding some waywardness of judgment and spoilt-child philosophy, his writings are, and ever will be, the classic works on the subject. Among more recent authorities we are indebted to the publications of Berenson, Bode, Burckhardt, Ludwig, Morelli, and Saccardo.

For purposes of description we have divided the city and outlying islands of the Venetian lagoon into twenty sections, arranged rather with regard to their relative historical and artistic importance than to strict topographical considerations, although these have not been lost sight of. In our quality of *cicerone* we have drawn from an acquaintance of the city at various times extending over a period of twenty years: more detailed and practical information may be sought in the admirable guide-books of Baedeker, Grant Allen, Gsellfels and Murray.

A pleasant duty is that of expressing our gratitude for personal help and counsel to, among others, Mr Horatio F. Brown, Signor Cantalamessa the courteous Director of the Accademia, Mr Bolton King, Signor Alfredo Melani, and Mr René Spiers.

In order not to burden our pages with many notes we have limited references to such passages as seemed specially to call for them, exigencies of space having straitened a wide subject within close bounds. If, however, the perusal of this slight and imperfect sketch may lead intending travellers to turn to richer springs—and in that hope we have appended a list of the main sources[1] from which we have drawn—our pleasant labours will be amply rewarded. It is with travel as with other modes of observation. The eye will see what the mind takes with it, for as the Spanish proverb quoted by Dr Johnson runs: "He who would bring home the wealth of the Indies must carry the wealth of the Indies with him."

SKETCH MAP of ITALY & the EASTERN MEDITERRANEAN

PART I.
THE STORY

CHAPTER I

The Foundation at Rialto

"Venice seems a type
Of life—'twixt blue and blue extends, a stripe,
As life, the somewhat, hangs 'twixt nought and nought."
—*Browning.*

OF the original home of the earliest settlers in that province of North Italy known to the Latins as Venetia, little can be told with certainty. Historians and antiquarians are pleased to bring them, under the name of Heneti or Eneti, from Paphlagonia, and explain some characteristic traits they subsequently developed—the love of colour and of display, the softness of their dialect—by their eastern origin. They were an independent, thriving and organised community when the Roman Empire first accepted their aid in the fierce struggle against the invading Gauls, and so they continued to be until they were absorbed as a province of the Empire. The land they cultivated, "mervailous in corne, wine, oyle, and all manner of fruites," was one of the richest in Europe. Its soil was formed by ages of alluvial deposit brought by the rapid streams that drain the southern slopes of the Alps.

The traveller who enters Italy by any of the Alpine passes will not fail to note the contrast between the northern streams and the more torrential water-ways of the south, which, however, being soon checked by the deposit they bring, grow slack and fray out into many and varying channels, through which the waters find their way with small, at times almost imperceptible, flow into the sea. So lazily do the rivers discharge that the north-east shores of the Adriatic are formed of sandbanks, shoals and islets, which for nigh a hundred miles from Cavarzere to Grado constituted the *dogado* of Venice. The famous Venetian lagoon is confined to some thirty miles north of Chioggia, and is divided into the *Laguna morta*, where the tide is scarcely felt, and the *Laguna viva*, where the sea is studded with numerous islands and islets protected by the *lidi*, a long line of remarkable breakwaters formed by the prevailing set of the current to the west, with narrow openings or *Porti* through which the shallow tide ebbs and flows. This natural barrier has made the existence of Venice possible, for the islands on which the city is built afforded a refuge safe alike from attack by sea or land. The colonisation, development and defence of these lagoons and islands by settlers from the mainland make up the early history of Venice. Some misapprehension exists as to the nature of these settlements. The picture of terror-stricken and despoiled fugitives from the cities of Venetia escaping from hordes of pursuing Huns or Lombards to seek a refuge in the barren and uncertain soil of mud-banks and storm-swept islands is true in part only. In many cases the movement was a deliberately organised migration of urban communities, with their officers, their craftsmen, their tools, their sacred vessels, even the very stones of their churches, to towns and villages already known to them. Among the settlers were men of all classes—patrician and plebeian, rich and poor. "But they would receive no man of servile condition, or a murderer, or of wicked life."

ON THE LAGOONS

Some islands were already inhabited by a hardy race of pilots and fishermen: others by prosperous Roman patricians, with their villas, farms, gardens and orchards. Grado was a busy commercial settlement with rich vineyards and meadows, and joined to the mainland by a causeway that led to Aquileia. Heraclea was rather a mainland than a lagoon city; Torcello is said to have been a fashionable Roman watering-place, and Roman remains have been found at S. Giorgio Maggiore. Much of the ground was covered with pine forests, the haunts of game and other wild creatures. For a long time the islands were not regarded by the settlers as abiding places. Again and again many of them returned to their old homes on the mainland when the invaders' force was spent. It was only in 568 that the Lombards, more cruel, or perhaps more systematic in their oppression than Marcoman or Hun, finally determined the Venetians to make the lagoons their permanent home.

Who of us northmen that has reached the descending slope of an Alpine pass, it may be through mist and sleet and snow, to gaze upon the rich and luscious plains of Lombardy or Venetia smiling with vine and fruit and corn; who that has felt the warm breath of sun-steeped Italy caressing his face as he emerges from northern gloom, but will feel a twinge of envy which is akin to covetousness, and which in strong and masterful races quickly develops into lust of conquest?

In the fifth century of our era the Roman Empire decaying, like most giants, at the extremities, lay defenceless before the inroads of those forceful, elemental peoples who from north and east swept down the passes to ravage the garden of Italy and to enslave her inhabitants. In 452 Venetia became the prey of God's scourge—Attila. Aquileia, now a poor village just within the Austrian frontier, but then a Roman city of the first rank, was plundered. Altinum, a city famous for its strength and wealth, resisted for a time but soon its inhabitants and those of Padua, Asolo, Belluno and other mainland cities forsook their homes and migrated to the lagoons.

The earliest settlements were twelve: Grado, Bibbione, Caorle, Jesolo (now Cavallino), Eraclea, Torcello, Burano, Rivoalto (now Venice), Malamocco, Poveglia, Cluges Minor (actual site now unknown, but not Sotto Marina, as sometimes stated), Cluges Major (now Chioggia). Of these, Grado was occupied by the Aquileians; Rivoalto and Malamocco by the Paduans; Eraclea by the Bellonsese; Torcello and Burano by the Altinese. To the pious imagination of chroniclers these migrations were not without divine admonition. In 568 the terrible Lombards were threatening Altinum, whose inhabitants entreated the help of heaven with tears and prayers and fastings; and, lo! they saw the doves and many other birds bearing their young in their beaks flying from their nests in the walls of the city. This was interpreted as a sign from God that they also were to expatriate themselves and seek safety in flight. They divided into three bodies, one of which turned to Istria, another to Ravenna. The third remained behind, uncertain whither to direct their steps. Three days they fasted, and at length a voice was heard saying: "*Salite alla torre e guardate agli astri.*" (Ascend the tower and look at the stars.)

S. FOSCA AND THE DUOMO, TORCELLO

PONTE S. GIUSTINA

Their good Bishop Paul climbed the tower, and to his gaze the very stars of the firmament seemed to set themselves in a constellation that figured forth the fateful group of islands in the lagoon before him. His flock, following this warning from heaven, went forth, headed by their bishop and clergy bearing the sacred vessels and relics, and passed to an island high and fertile, which they called Torcello, from one of the twelve towers of their old city. The very hierarchy of heaven, from Our Lord and His Blessed Mother to St Peter and the Baptist, even to Giustina, the martyred little maid of Padua, appeared to Mauro, the priest, in a vision, as he paced the sea shore, and in sweet voices bade him build here a church and there a church in their honour. The immigrants therefore had come to make the lagoons their permanent home. Their new city was organised. In process of time churches were built; trade guilds were formed; painters and mosaicists enriched the buildings. The marble seat on the grass-grown piazza of Torcello, to this day called Attila's chair, was probably the official seat of the tribune when he administered justice to the people.

It will be seen that no definite date can be assigned to the foundation of Venice, though Sanudo is very sure it was in "the year ccccxxi., on the xxv. of March, which was a Friday, that day on which our father Adam was created, when about the hour of nones the first stone of St Giacomo di Rivoalto was laid by the Paduans." The great diarist gives a charming picture of the earliest Venetians trading in fish and salt with their little barks to the neighbouring shores: "They were a lowly people, who esteemed mercy and innocency, and, above all, religion rather than riches. They affected not to clothe them with ornaments, nor to seek honours, but when need was they answered to the call."

There is little doubt that originally the settlers were subject to the Consuls at Padua, but in 466 they were strong enough to meet at Grado and to elect their own tribunes, one for each of the twelve communities. A passage in a famous letter of Cassiodorus to these *Tribuni Maritimi* in 523 affords the first glimpse in history of the lagoon folk. The secretary of Theodoric the Great writes urging them not to fail to transport the tribute of oil, honey and wine from Istria to Ravenna, and expatiates on their great security and the wonderful habitations that he has seen, like sea-birds' nests, half on land, half on sea, or like the cyclades spread over the broad bosom of the waters. Their land is made not by nature but by man, for the soil is strengthened by flexible withy bands, and they oppose frail dykes to the waves of the sea. Their boats are tied to posts before their doors like horses are on the mainland. Rich and poor live in equality. They flee from the vice of envy, to which the whole world is enslaved. Instead of plough and scythe they handle cylinders. In their salt they produce a merchandise more desired than gold, so all the fruits of the earth are at their command.

THE CUSTOMS HOUSE.

About 530, when Narses the Eunuch began the great campaign which wrested the Italian dominions of the Emperors from the Goths, the Venetians gave him effective aid by transporting an army of Lombard mercenaries from Aquileia to Ravenna. As a reward Narses sent some Byzantine masters, who from the spoils of the enemy built the Church of St Theodore at Rivoalto on a plot of ground known as the *Broglio* or garden where now stands the Basilica of St Mark.

Scarcely, however, were the Goths defeated, when in 568 Alboin and his Lombards menaced the land. Longinus, who succeeded Narses in the exarchate of Ravenna, came to Venice and asked her aid as subject to the Emperor. He was given an honourable and festive welcome, but the Venetians had bought their freedom at a great price and stoutly refused to admit his claim. They declared that the second Venice which they had made in the waters was a mighty habitation and their very own by right of creation; that they feared no power of Prince or Emperor, for it could not reach them.

They, however, furnished a ship and sent an embassy with Longinus to Constantinople, and in return for valuable trading rights, agreed to acknowledge the suzerainty of the Emperor if no formal oath were exacted.

In 584 the lagoon folk had so expanded that an additional tribune was chosen for each community. Of these *Tribuni majores* was formed a federal council, the original tribunes now serving as heads of local administrations.

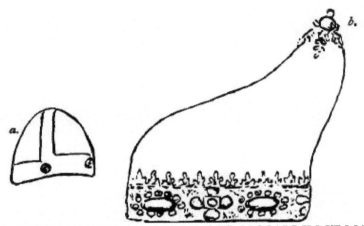

a. EARLY DUCAL CAP FROM AN OLD MOSAIC IN ST MARK
b. DUCAL CAP OF DOGE MORO, 1462-1471, FROM THE PORTRAIT IN S. GIOBBE

The golden age so lovingly dwelt upon by the early chroniclers was of short duration. Already, before the institution of the new tribunes, family and local feuds, the ambition of the tribunes and jealousy of the people, led to bloody affrays in the *Pinete* (pine forests) with which the *lidi* were clothed. Anarchy threatened the state; bands of Lombards under the Duke of Friuli plundered the churches of Heraclea and Grado. The crisis was met by the public spirit and wisdom of the Church. A general meeting (*Arengo*) was called by the Patriarch of Grado at Heraclea. Two vital problems came to the front—the organisation of self-defence and the maintenance of public order. The whole Assembly having invoked the name of Christ, the great churchman stood forth, and after reviewing the political situation, proposed that all the tribunes should be relegated to purely local offices, and a *Capo* or chief elected for life. His new polity was approved and in 697 Pauluccio Anafesto was chosen first Doge and invested with sovereign powers. Thus was constituted the Dogeship of Venice which, save for a short interruption of six years, endured for eleven centuries. The Doge could nominate, degrade or dismiss all public officers, convoke or dissolve the *Arengo* and the synod. The appointment of Patriarchs and Bishops was subject to his veto. The military authority, entrusted to a Master of the soldiers, was subordinate to him; foreign affairs were in his hands, though the approval of the people was required to declare war or conclude peace. He could impose taxes; his feudal dues and rights of *corvée* were extensive. His state was regal. When he went abroad, girt with a sword and surrounded by his guards, a state umbrella was held over him, lighted tapers were borne by his side, trumpets blared and banners waved. He sat enthroned in an ivory chair, holding a sceptre, and arrayed in a silk mantle with a fringe of gold fastened by a gold clasp over a tightly fitting tunic trimmed with ermine; he wore red hose and a high biretta richly jewelled, which was subsequently shortened by constricting the middle so as to form two lobes, one of which soon disappeared, and the familiar horned cap of the later Doges was evolved. A close cap of fine linen was worn beneath, so that when the biretta was raised his head should be covered as a mark of dignity. The Doge was no *fainéant*. He rose before the dawn, and having heard mass went forth to judge the people and transact the business of the day. On solemn occasions he gave his benediction. The blessing of God was invoked upon him in the litany. The election, more or less democratic until the abolition of the *Arengo* in 1423, was made by the whole people, who were summoned from Grado to Cavarzere. Their chosen one was acclaimed and carried shoulder high to the church, which he entered barefoot, and there swore to govern according to the laws and to work for the good of the people. The result of the election was communicated to the Pope and the Emperor; to the latter usually by the Doge's son in person.

Anafesto had a difficult task. The young state lay between two mighty powers: Lombards or Franks and Pope in the west, the Byzantine Emperor in the east. Only by vigilance and prudence could she escape subjection. And these rival interests were active within her borders—aristocratic Heraclea leaning towards the Eastern Empire; democratic Malamocco and Jesolo towards the Western kingdoms and the Pope. One of the first acts of the new Doge, after securing internal peace, was to conclude a treaty with Luitprand, King of the Lombards, by which the boundaries of the Republic were defined, and in return for an annual payment, valuable rights of wood-cutting and horse-breeding and trading were conceded. But political jealousy dies hard. Two powerful families revolted in 717, and the Doge perished in a civil broil in the Pineta of Jesolo.

During the reign of the third Doge, Orso of Heraclea, the Venetians were called to meet a new danger. The rise of the Iconoclasts in the early eighth century, and the zeal of their protagonist, the Emperor Leo III., had set east and west aflame. Leo's attempt to enforce the decree against the use of images in the western Church was met by an invitation to the Lombards from the Pope to attack the seat of the eastern power in Italy. War was the very breath of their nostrils, and they were not slow to respond. Ravenna was besieged and captured and the Pentapolis occupied.[2] The Exarch Paul fled to the lagoons and appealed to Orso for help. The fugitive enlarged on the danger to Venice of the advancing Lombards, now at their very door. The Doge agreed to furnish a fleet, and by successful strategy Ravenna was surprised and recaptured and the Exarchate restored. The gratified Emperor rewarded the Venetians by conferring the title of Hypatos (knight) on their Doge, who adopted it as a family name.

This imperial policy was, however, bitterly resented by the popular party. A civil war ensued which lasted two years, and ended in the defeat of the Heracleans, the murder of the Doge, and the banishment of his son. Another experiment in statecraft was now made. The Dogeship was abolished, and the Master of the soldiers appointed head of the State for a term of one year. This new departure proved disastrous. After six years of civil discord, the last of the Masters, a Heraclean, was captured and blinded by the opposite party. An *Arengo* was called, this time at Malamocco, and a compromise effected. Deodato, son of Orso, a Heraclean, was made Doge at Malamocco, whither the capital was now transferred. But Heraclea and Jesolo were rivals, fierce as ever, for the ducal chair. The internecine strife went on with its savage incidents. Assassination, blinding,[3] or banishment were the price of defeat. At length, by the election of Maurizio Galbaio in 764, "noble by race, nobler in deeds," the distracted state was ruled with wisdom and firmness, and faction for a time was silenced.

BASIN OF S. MARCO.

The epoch-making victory of Charles of the Hammer over the Arabs at Tours had drawn the eyes of all men to France, and to a mighty race of princes destined to change the face of Europe. The restless Lombards in 752 had reoccupied Ravenna and the Pentapolis, and the Pope turned to the new Carlovingian dynasty for help against them. Pepin answered to the call, wrested the cities from their hands, and gave them to the Pope, who thus became a temporal sovereign. Twenty years later the papacy was again constrained to summon help. Charlemagne, Pepin's son, crossed the Alps by the Great St Bernard pass, fell like a thunderbolt of war on the Lombards, and in 774 their dominion was finally crushed by the capture of Desiderio, their King, and Pavia, their royal city. Romanin argues from the silence of the chroniclers that the Venetians took no active part in the siege of Pavia, but from an old inscription in Venetian, on a thin plate of hammered lead,[4] preserved in the British Museum, we learn that on the invitation of Charlemagne, the Venetians sent a fleet of twenty-four galleys, with four nobles who knew the art of war (*saveva far la guara*) up the Po to the siege, and had the honour of guarding the captive King. Venice had indeed watched every phase of the struggle, seizing, as was her wont, any opportunity that offered for extending the trading privileges so vital to her existence. By secret information to the Church from her merchants at Constantinople, she had nipped a plot to recover the Exarchate, now for ever lost to the Greek Emperors. But in 781 Pepin, son of Charlemagne, had been crowned King of Italy by the Pope; the power of the Franks was growing apace, and their alliance with a territorial Pope alarmed the Heraclean party. They believed a wiser policy was to form an alliance with the weaker Empire far in the east against the Franks. In 778 Doge Maurizio Galbaio was permitted, on the plea of infirmity, to associate his son Giovanni with him, and on the death of Maurizio, the son stepped into his father's office, thus effecting a subtle change in the nature of the Dogeship, by no means pleasing to the democratic party. The Franks were not long in making their power felt. Venetian merchants had acquired some territory near Ravenna, and many trading centres in the neighbouring cities. They were incorrigible slave traders. Pope Zacharias, a generation before, had been moved to compassion on seeing in Rome groups of Christian slaves,[5] men and women, belonging to Venetian merchants, destined to be sold to the pagans in Africa. He paid their price and set them at liberty. Charlemagne had recently published an edict against the traffic in slaves, and now called on Pope Hadrian to take action. The Venetians were expelled from Ravenna and the Pentapolis. In 797 the new see of Olivolo which had been created a few years before to meet the growing needs of the population, became vacant, and the new Doge preferred Christophorus Damiatus, a young Greek to the bishopric. The Patriarch of Grado, around whom the Frankish party centred, refused to consecrate one whom he regarded as a nominee of the Byzantine Emperor, and excommunicated Bishop and Doge. The Doge's answer was swift and terrible. He despatched his son Maurizio with a fleet to Grado; the city was attacked; the Patriarch captured, thrown from the tower of his palace, and dashed to pieces. To allay popular indignation, Fortunatus, a nephew of the murdered Patriarch was appointed in his stead. The new prelate soon showed of what stuff he was made. With infinite resource and indomitable purpose he set himself to avenge the insult to the Church, and, but for the premature discovery of the plot, would have wrought the destruction of the Doge and his party. Fortunatus fled to the court of Charlemagne, who was now created Holy Roman Emperor, and harbouring no tender feelings towards the rebellious children of the lagoons. Obelerio, tribune of Malamocco, and the other heads of the conspiracy found safety at Treviso, whence they stirred their partizans to action with decisive effect. The Doge and his son were exiled to Mantua; Obelerio was proclaimed Doge in 804; the triumph of the Frankish party was complete. The Heracleans, however, soon rallied. In their civil fury they fell upon Jesolo, and almost wiped it out. The Doge immediately led a punitive expedition to Heraclea, and wreaked a similar vengeance on that hot-bed of Byzantine faction. The situation was now felt to be unbearable. By general consent a meeting of the whole *dogado* was called, and it was decided that in order to make peace, the remaining populations of Heraclea and of Jesolo should be transported to Malamocco.

Fortunatus meanwhile was watching events at Istria. Under the sun of Charlemagne's favours he had waxed rich and powerful. He possessed four ships, and traded under royal patronage wherever the new western Emperor's power reached. By skilful diplomacy he effected his recall to Grado, and placed a Frankish partizan in the see of Olivolo. But the Heracleans had lost their home, not their ideals and policy. They appealed to the Byzantine Emperor, and a Greek fleet sailed up the Adriatic. Fortunatus once again was a fugitive. The Doge and his party protested a loyalty to their suzerain, which in 809 was translated into acts by the despatch of a fleet to aid him to recover the exarchate for the Greeks. It was unsuccessful, but none the less irritating to the Pope and Emperor, who now determined to subdue the Venetians and incorporate them into the Holy Roman Empire of the West. The immediate cause of the rupture is not known, but when the princes of the earth are bent on war a pretext is seldom hard to find. A great empire, aiming at universal dominion, is ill at ease with a sturdy freedom-loving state on its borders, and the far-reaching arm of the invincible Carlovingians was stretched forth to grasp, as they thought, an easy prey.

In the stress of a common danger, faction was silenced. Obelerio and his brother Beato, whom he had associated with him a year after he was proclaimed Doge, advised that the Venetians should agree with their adversary before it was too late, but a wave of popular indignation swept them from power, and Angelo Participazio, a Heraclean by birth, and one of the tribunes of Rivoalto, was made head of a provisional government of national defence. The churches were filled with earnest, determined men, entreating with fasting and prayer the divine aid in their hour of need; a call was made on every citizen at home and abroad to hasten to the defence of the fatherland. Provisions were accumulated, ships built, fortifications raised, channels blocked by chains and sunken hulks, guide posts drawn.

CLOISTERS OF S. GREGORIO

Meanwhile, King Pepin had summoned his allies, and a fleet sailed up to the lagoons. On the mainland the advance of the Frankish armies was irresistible; north and south they closed in on the Venetians. Grado soon fell; Brondolo, the Chioggie, and other cities were captured; fire and sword wasted their settlements. The *porti* of Brondolo, Chioggia, and Pelestrina were forced, Malamocco[6] the capital threatened. At this crisis the momentous decision was taken to abandon Malamocco and concentrate at Rivoalto (Rialto), the compact group of islands between the mainland and the *lidi*.

FISHING BOATS

On the *lido* of Pelestrina, south of S. Pietro in Volta, where the steamer to Chioggia now calls, is the little fishing village of Porto Secco. Here in olden times was a *porto* called Albiola. North of this passage was the city of Albiola on the *lido* which stretched towards Malamocco. South began the *lido* of Pelestrina. It was here that, according to tradition, a stand was made. The Frankish host of horse and foot gathered on the *lido* of Albiola, waiting for their fleet to force the *porto*, which was deep enough to allow of the passage of the transports. Opposite, on the *lido* of Pelestrina, stood the Venetians near their boats, which were armoured with ramparts of sails, cordages, and masts, behind which their archers did much execution. For nigh six months the desperate fight was waged. "Ye are my subjects," cried Pepin, "since from my lands ye come." The Venetians answered, "We will be subject to the Emperor[7] of the Romans, not to thee." Malamocco was at length captured, but was found to be deserted. Rough rafts and pontoons were constructed to thread the maze of shallow channels that led to Rivoalto, but the light, waspish boats of the Venetians drove them on to the shoals by the canal Orfano, where they were caught front and rear, and those who escaped suffocation in the water and the mud were quickly cut down by their enemies. The summer heats came; the arrows of the sun, more deadly than Venetian arms, wrought havoc among the Franks, whose forces wasted away, and the

Carlovingians were baffled. A Greek fleet threatening his rear, forced Pepin to come to terms. He promised to withdraw, to restore the captured territory, and to reaffirm all the ancient trading rights and privileges in his dominions in return for an annual payment. The Venetians emerged from the struggle a victorious and a united people centred at Rialto, and the State of Venice was now firmly rooted in the lagoons.

CHAPTER II

St Mark the Patron of Venice—The Brides of St Mark—Conquest of Dalmatia—
Limitation of the Doge's Power

"But I must tellen verilie
Of St Marke's . . .
. . . holy shrine
Exalt amid the tapers' shine
At Venice."
—*Keats.*

AN immediate outburst of creative energy was the result of the victory. Angelo Participazio was chosen Doge and according to precedent associated his son with him. He set himself to enlarge, fortify and embellish Rialto. The ravaged settlements of the Chioggie, Brondolo, Pelestrina and Albiola were rebuilt, and a new Heraclea, called *Città nuova*, rose on the ruins of the old capital. Dykes were built, rivers diverted and canals bridged. A ducal palace was erected near the Church of St Theodore, and a church to S. Pietro at Olivolo. The Chapel and Convent of S. Zaccaria were founded and endowed by the Doge to contain the body of S. Zaccaria, father of the Baptist, and other relics given to the Venetians by Leo the Eastern Emperor.

CLOISTER OF S. FRANCESCO DELLA VIGNA

There was an old tradition among the early settlers at Rialto that St Mark on his way from Alexandria to preach the Faith in Aquileia was caught in a violent storm and forced to land on one of the Rialtine islands where now stands the Church of S. Francesco della Vigna. As he stepped forth from his bark an angel saluted him saying: *"Pace a te Marco Evangelista mio"* (Peace to thee Mark my Evangelist), and announced that one day his body should find a resting-place and veneration at Rialto. Traditions like prophecies have a way of bringing their own fulfilment, and in the brief reign of Angelo's son Giustiniani (827-829) some Venetians trading with the infidels in defiance of imperial prohibition succeeded in stealing the Evangelist's body and carrying it to Venice. The story of "how the precious body of Monsignor S. Marco came to Venice" is thus told by Da Canale. "Now at this time there was a ship of the Venetians at Alexandria on which were three valiant men. The one called Messer Rustico of Torcello, the other Messer Buono of Malamocco, the third Messer Stauracio; which three valiant men had great hope and devotion to bring the body of S. Marco to Venice, and they so got round (*s'en alerent tant autour*) the guardian of the body that having won his friendship they said to him, Messer, if thou wilt come with us to Venice and bear away the body of Monsignor S. Marco thou shalt become a rich man. And when he, who was called Theodore, heard this he answered: Sirs, hold your peace, say not so, that may not be in any wise, for the pagans hold it more precious than aught else in the world, and if they espied us would surely cut off our heads. Then said they, wait until the blessed Evangelist command thee. And it came to pass that there entered into the heart of this worthy guardian a desire to bear away the body, and he came back to them saying: Sirs, how can we take away Monsignor S. Marco without the knowledge of any man? And one answered: Right wisely will we do it. And they went hastily by night to the sepulchre where the body was and put it in a basket and covered it with cabbages and swine's flesh, and they took another body, laid it in the tomb in the very same cloth from which the body of Monsignor S. Marco had been taken and sealed the tomb as it was before. And the valiant men bore the body to the ship in that same basket as I have told of, and for dread of the pagans slung it to a mast of their ship. What shall I tell you? At that very moment when they opened the tomb so sweet and so great an odour spread through the midst of the city that all the spiceries in Alexandria could not have caused the like. Wherefore the pagans said: Mark is stirring, for they were wont to smell such fragrance every year. Nevertheless there were of them who misdoubted and went to the tomb and opened it and seeing the body I have told of in St Mark's shroud were satisfied. And some there were who came to the ship and searched it about, but when they saw the swine's flesh by the mast did straightly flee from the ship crying, Kanzir! Kanzir! which is to say, Pork! Pork! Now the wind was fair and strong, and they set sail for Venice and on the third day came by Romania (Greece). And a mighty wind arose by night when the mariners were sleeping, and the ship was driving on to the rocks; but the precious Evangelist awakened the master mariner and said to him: Look that thou set down the sails, for we are making for the land. And the master awakened the shipmen and they struck the sails. And if anyone will know the truth let him come to Venice and see the fair Church of Monsignor S. Marco, and look in front of this fair church, for there is inscribed all this story even as I have related it, and likewise he will gain the great pardon of vii. years which Monsignor the Apostle (the Pope) granted to all who should go to that fair church."

The Doge and clergy welcomed the body with great ceremony, the traders were forgiven their unlawful voyage, and St Mark became the patron of the Republic instead of St Theodore. A modest little chapel was begun on land acquired from the nuns of S. Zaccaria in the Broglio, which was still a grass-grown field planted with trees bounded by the Canal Battario, which flowed across what is now the Piazza of St Mark. In the next reign the body, which had been temporarily placed in the ducal palace, was solemnly transferred to its shrine in the new chapel of St Mark and Stauracio appointed Primicerio or President of the Chapter.

In 829 Giov. Participazio, the third of the dynasty, began his uneasy tenure of eight years. Obelerio plotted to regain his lost power in Venice, but was foiled and executed, and his head exposed on a stake. A more successful rival was the Tribune Caroso, who worked on popular suspicion of the hereditary tendencies in the reigning family, and drove Giovanni to exile in France. Caroso's tyranny, however, was a bad exchange for the milder rule of the exiled Doge. The usurper was overthrown and blinded, and Giovanni recalled. But the same jealousy on the part of the people which made Caroso's *coup d'état* possible again manifested itself. The Doge was seized as he was returning on St Peter's Day from the church at Olivolo; his hair and beard were shaven, and he was forced to retire into a monastery at Grado.

Pietro Tradonico, the chosen of the democracy in 836, was much occupied with the pirates who, from their rocky fastnesses in the creeks and bays of the Dalmatian coast, swooped down on the rich Venetian argosies as they sailed the Adriatic. By a first expedition he reduced their chiefs for a while to submission; a second was less happy in its results.

The tide of Saracen invasion was met at Caorle and rolled back, and two great ships of war were constructed to guard the *porti*. Amid the stress of war the arts of diplomacy were not neglected. A treaty still exists, dated 840, between Lothair, "by Divine Providence Imperator Augustus and the most glorious Duke of the Venetians," for a period of five years: their relations in peace and war are defined; mutual restitution of runaway slaves is promised, and traffic in the subjects of the contracting powers prohibited; the inviolability of ambassadors and of correspondence assured. Pietro had the honour of welcoming the first royal tourists (855) in the person of King Louis II. of Italy and his consort, who spent three days at Venice. The defeated

Participazi were, however, biding their time. In 864 the people's Doge was assassinated when leaving the Church of S. Zaccaria after Vespers and his body lay on the ground until nightfall, when the pious nuns gave it sepulture in the atrium of their church. The chroniclers record the great wisdom and piety of Orso Participazio, who succeeded the murdered Doge. He cleared the seas of pirates, and sought, by calling a synod of clergy and laity, to purge Venice from the iniquitous traffic in slaves, which continued to stain her commerce. Rialto was made healthier by drainage and building; Dorsodura peopled. The growth of the arts of peace may be measured by the fact that the Venetians were able at this time to make a present of twelve bells to the Greek Emperor. Orso died full of years and honours in 881, and was buried in S. Zaccaria. During the short reign of his son Giovanni a descent was made on Comacchio, a city on the mainland north of Ravenna, whose growing power and commerce roused the jealousy of Venice. The Venetians had long memories, and the help given to Pepin was now avenged by the devastation of the city and the country even up to the walls of Ravenna. In 887 Pietro Candiano, a devout Christian, and a wise and brave prince, was elected, and after a reign of five months met a soldier's death fighting against the pirates. Pietro Tribuno, who succeeded him, was called upon to face a new danger. In the spring of 900 the Hungarians came down the usual track of the barbarian invaders by the Fruilian passes—"that most baneful gate left open by nature for the chastisement of the sins of Italy"—and ravaged the land. They were held too cheaply by Berengarius, King of Italy, and flushed with victory, spread terror even to the lagoons. The preparations made to resist Pepin were renewed. Rialto was fortified and a castle built on the island of Olivolo, which is called Castello to this day. By the way of the Franks the terrible barbarians overran the outer cities of the *dogado*, and made for the *Porto* of Albiola. The Venetian fleet met them, happy omen, at the very spot where Pepin's might was crushed. A fierce fight ensued, and the battle was again to the islanders. The Hungarians were scattered, and fled, never to return; Pietro was hailed by Berengarius preserver of the public liberty, and was honoured by the Eastern Emperor. Two years later the foundations of the old Campanile were laid in a spot where a great elder tree flourished. At the death of the Doge in 912 the Participazii returned to power.

Orso Participazio II. (912) was a saintly and righteous prince who retired to a monastery after a peaceful reign of twenty years, during which the Venetians obtained from the Emperor Rudolph a confirmation of the right to coin their own money. How great was the expansion of their trade is illustrated in the reign of the next Doge, Pietro Candiano II. (932), who, by the simple expedient of a commercial boycott, brought the arbitrary feudal lord of Istria to his knees. In 942, after a short and uneventful term of power by the rival dynasty, Candiano's son Pietro became Doge.

S. MARCO, FROM PIAZZETTA DEI LEONI.

S. PIETRO IN CASTELLO, FROM S. ELENA

A romantic incident in the ever-recurring battles with the Narentine (Slav) pirates may be referred to this reign. On the feast of the translation of St Mark it was the custom for the marriageable damsels of Venice to repair to S. Pietro in Castello, bearing their dowries with them in caskets, to be formally betrothed to their lovers and receive the benediction of the Church. Informed of this anniversary, some pirates concealed themselves in the thick bush which then covered part of the island, and during the ceremony forced their way into the church, seized brides and dowries, and regained their boats. The Doge, who was present, hastened from the church, and called the people to arms. Some vessels belonging to the Cabinet-makers' Guild, whose quarter was near the Church of S. Maria Formosa, were offered to the Doge. The avengers set forth in pursuit, and came upon the pirates dividing their booty in a remote part of the lagoon of Caorle, afterwards called *porto delle Donzelle*, defeated them, and returned in triumph to Rialto with brides and dowries, the Cabinet-makers having greatly distinguished themselves. To commemorate the rape and rescue of the brides of St Mark, the Doges were used on the day of the Purification to proceed in solemn state to the Church of S. Maria Formosa to render thanks to the Virgin. Twelve poor girls, the *Marie*, were dowered and took part in the procession, together with the chief guilds of Venice. Simple in its origin, the celebration became more and more sumptuous, till at length so great was the burden on the private resources of the families whose lot it was to provide for the *Marie*, that in 1271 the number was reduced to four. Later, a tax was imposed on every family to meet the cost of the eight days' *festa*. In 1379 the funds were swallowed up in the financial demands of the Genoese wars, and all that remained of the old magnificence was the annual visit of the Doge to the church, and the offering made to him by the parish priest of oranges, muscat wine, and gilded straw hats. The origin of the Doge's attendance at this church, and of the quaint offerings, is traced to a legend that the Cabinet-makers, in acknowledgment of their prowess, asked of the Doge the favour of an annual visit. To the Doge's objection, "But if it be too hot," they answered, "We will give you refreshment"; and to the further objection, "But if it rain," they answered, "We will furnish you with hats." The custom lasted till the end of the Republic. Da Canale gives a graphic description of the festival as it was celebrated in the thirteenth century. On the vigil of the feast of the translation of St Mark, a company of noble youths came by water to the ducal palace, and having distributed banners to some children, formed in line two by two, accompanied by trumpeters and players of cymbals, and by other youths bearing trays of silver loaded with sweets, silver vessels filled with wine, and cups of gold and silver. The clergy followed, arrayed in Calamanco cloth of gold, chanting a litany, and the whole procession went its way to S. Maria Formosa, where a number of dames and damsels were met, to whom wine and sweets were presented. On the last day of January the procession was renewed with greater splendour. Over five hundred banners were distributed, and more than a hundred lads bearing crosses of silver took part. Following the priests came a clerk, dressed as the Virgin, in Damascus cloth of gold, borne in a richly decorated chair on the shoulders of four men, gonfalons resplendent with gold waving around. The Doge, surrounded by the Venetian nobility, stood at a window of the ducal palace, while three of the clergy chanted the usual lauds of his greatness and power. The Doge then joined the procession, which wended its way to S. Maria Formosa. Here stood another clerk dressed as the angel Gabriel, who sang the "Hail Mary" as the figure of the Virgin appeared. The ceremony being ended, twelve great banquets were held, at each of which one of the *Marie* was present, clad in cloth of gold adorned with jewels and pearls innumerable, and wearing a crown of gold set with precious stones. On the day following, a gorgeous aquatic pageant, more than a mile and a half in length, with the Doge in his *mastro nave*, the clergy and the *Marie* made the tour of the Grand Canal, and "if you were there you could see the whole waters covered with boats filled with men and women, so that no one could count them, and a throng of dames and damsels at the windows and on the banks, apparelled so richly that none in Venice might surpass them." Regattas, balls, and music followed; the whole city gave itself up to joy and gladness.

A GIRL OF CASTELLO.

Pietro Candiano's reign of seventeen years set in storm and calamity. His son and colleague, Pietro, rebelled, and sought to drive his father from the throne. There was a sharp fight on the Piazza; the rebellion collapsed and the

Venetian Absalom was only saved from death by the entreaties of his aged father. He was excluded from the succession and banished, but only to turn pirate and harry his countrymen. The scourge of the plague and sorrow for his son's impiety embittered the last days of the old Doge, and in 959 he died a broken-hearted man. But scarce was he laid to rest when a splendid fleet, gay with banners, bore a deputation of nobles and clergy to Ravenna to invite the proscribed pirate to become lord of Venice: the pressure of a powerful family and the fear of civil discord had led to the recall of the only prince who seemed strong enough to rule the troubled state. He began by blinding and exiling the Bishop of Torcello, guilty of simony, and by calling a synod to deal again with the persistent abomination of the slave trade at Venice. There was no concealment. Slaves, chiefly young girls from twelve to sixteen years of age, bought in the ports of Russia and Circassia, were openly sold by auction at Venice and the deed of sale drawn up by a notary. Doge, clergy and people met in St Mark's and the disgraceful traffic was again prohibited under severe penalties. Another scandal of Venetian commerce was challenged by the Greek Emperor, who in 971 sent an embassy to Venice threatening to burn cargo and crew of any vessel found trading in munitions of war with the Saracens. It was decided that no arms, or iron, or wood for naval construction should be sold to the infidels, exception being made of utensils of carved wood, such as goblets, platters, basins.

But the demons of Pride and Ambition still lurked in the unquiet breast of the Doge. He forced his wife to take the veil at S. Zaccaria that he might marry Gualdrada, sister of the Marquis of Tuscany, who brought him a rich dowry of money and lands. He affected a state of Imperial magnificence, surrounded himself with mercenaries and dragged his subjects to fight for his feudal rights on the mainland. The indignant populace rose in revolt and attacked the palace. Foiled in their purpose by the devotion of the Doge's foreign guards, the insurgents fired the adjacent houses and drove the doomed prince to seek safety by a passage that led into the atrium of St Mark's. Here he was met by a company of Venetian nobles to whom he prayed: "And have you, too, my brothers, willed my destruction. If I have sinned in word or deed, grant me life and I will remedy all." There was an angry shout of, "He is worthy of death," and a dozen weapons were plunged into his breast. His infant son was spitted on a spear in its nurse's arms; the hated mercenaries were slain. The bodies of father and babe were cast to the shambles, and only redeemed by the entreaties of a saintly monk who removed them for burial to the abbey of S. Ilario.

S. MARCO FAÇADE.

In a city built mainly of wood, fire is a disastrous weapon. Their vengeance glutted, the revolutionists turned to count the cost, and were sobered. The churches of St Theodore, St Mark and S. Maria Zobenigo, the ducal palace, three hundred houses and a large number of factories were destroyed. It was a subdued assembly that met in S. Pietro on August 12th, 976, and elected Pietro Orseolo, a rich patrician descended from an ancient Roman family of the earliest settlers in Torcello. Threats of Imperial vengeance hung over the Republic, and Gualdrada's claims for compensation had to be met. For this, and to rebuild the city, a subsidy of a *decima* was voted to be imposed on the property of each citizen. Artificers were brought from Constantinople and plans for a new St Mark's[8] and a new palace made. The Doge dedicated nearly all his patrimony to the building; founded a hospital for the sick poor near the Campanile, and spent much time as well as money in works of charity. He soon grew weary of the cares of state, and an opportune visit of the Abbot of St Michael's in Aquitaine to Venice confirmed his desire to enter a cloister. He asked for time to prepare. The abbot promised to return and claim him. A year later, on a September night, the abbot and two friars repaired to the monastery of S. Ilario, where they were met by the Doge, his son-in-law and a friend, disguised as pilgrims. Horses were in waiting; they were ferried across the lagoon, and at full speed the party rode for France. On the morrow the Venetians awoke to find their beloved prince fled and the ducal chair vacant. The Candiani who had never ceased intriguing to regain power were ready, and their nominee, Vitale Candiano, was raised to the Dogeship, to retire after fourteen months, sick and disillusioned, to die in a monastery. Pietro Memo succeeded him in 978, a feeble prince, whose reign was dishonoured by the rise of the Caloprini and Morosini factions that in the end nearly compassed the destruction of Venetian liberties. It was the old strife renewed with increased bitterness. The Morosini being partisans of the Orseoli favoured the Byzantines: the Caloprini standing for the Candiani leaned on the western powers. For the first and last time in her history Venice saw her children traitorously inviting a foreign sovereign to enslave their fatherland. The Caloprini, having assassinated Dom. Morosini, fled to the court of Otho II., and impiously laying bare the weak places in their country's defences, called him to conquest. The Emperor was nothing loth. Venice was a standing challenge to the Empire; the only state in Western Europe that stubbornly refused to be absorbed in the feudal system. His subjects were forbidden to trade with the Republic; her food supplies were cut off; her enemies goaded on to attack her; the Caloprini faction in Venice stirred to rebellion; ships of war collected to blockade if not to attack the islands. It was the gravest danger that had ever threatened Venice, for the foes were partly those of her own household. But the stars, which watched over her birth, seemed now in their courses to fight for her salvation. The mighty arm of the Emperor was raised to crush the little state, when the angel of death touched him and it fell impotently to his side.

At this epoch arose to guide her destinies one of the greatest princes that ever sat in the ducal chair. Memo, suspected of complicity in a more than usually atrocious assassination, was deposed and forced to enter a monastery, and in 991 Pietro Orseolo II. began his eventful reign. By his consummate statesmanship the Republic soon found herself at peace with east and west and able to deal with the problem of the Adriatic pirates. The Doge at once abolished the feeble expedient of paying blackmail to their chiefs, and on a renewal of their depredations chastised them into respect. The unhappy borderland along the Dalmatian coast, nominally under the lordship of the eastern Empire, but actually eluding control by east or west, was dotted with a number of small trading communities—Zara, Trau, Spalato, and Ragusa— continually harassed by Slav and Saracen pirates from the sea and by Croats on land. The defeated pirates in their rage now united with the Croats and turned on the Dalmatians, who appealed to Venice, the only power which seemed able to protect them. The Doge at once grasped the importance to Venetian commerce of a protectorate over Dalmatia. The greatest fleet that had hitherto sailed from Venetian waters set forth with banners consecrated by the Church to police the Adriatic. The voyage was a triumphant procession. Chief after chief submitted. At Zara and elsewhere the Venetians were magnificently received: the last stronghold of the pirates, impregnable Lagosta, yielded to the splendid courage of the Venetian seamen. Slavs and Croats were cowed and hostages given for future good behaviour. The woods of Curzola now made Venice independent of Italy for timber. It was the first stage in her development as a European power. The title of Doge of Dalmatia was added to that of Doge of Venice and a ceremony instituted which a hundred and eighty years later became the famous *Sposalazio del Mare* or Wedding of the Adriatic. On the morning of Ascension Day a State barge covered with cloth of gold bearing the clergy of the Chapter of St Mark's in full canonicals and furnished with a vessel of water, a vase of salt and an aspersoir of olive branches, sailed to the Canal of S. Nicolo del Lido to await the Doge's barge, called later the Bucintoro. On its arrival two Canons intoned the litany and the Bishop rose up and solemnly pronounced in Latin the words, Deign, O Lord, to grant that this sea be calm and peaceful to us and to all that sail upon it; thus we pray. O Lord hear us. The Bishop blessed the water and, having reached S. Nicolo, drew near to the Doge's barge before the procession advanced into the open Adriatic. The Primicerio then prayed: Purge me, O Lord, with hyssop, and I shall be clean; the Bishop aspersed the Doge and his suite, and poured what was left of the water into the sea. Such was the origin of the famous *festa* of *La Sensa* of which we shall hear more later.

The fame of the Doge's exploits had fired the imagination of the young and ardent Emperor Otho III., who made a mysterious voyage by night to the great Orseolo at Venice and disguised in mean attire went about the strange city marvelling at the glories of its architecture. The new ducal palace had just been completed, a stately embattlemented edifice, in which was constructed a small chapel rich in precious marble and gold and furnished with an organ of wondrous craftsmanship. A romantic affection sprang up between the two potentates which was cemented by the Emperor standing god-father and giving his name to one of the Doge's sons. The friends parted, after much intimate converse, embracing each other and in tears.

Honours too from the East were lavished upon the Doge. Responding to an appeal from the Greeks he led a fleet to Bari, which was invested by the Saracens. Signs and wonders in the heavens heralded his coming, and after three days of hand-to-hand fighting the siege was raised and a Greek army delivered from destruction. The Byzantine Emperor showed his gratitude by bestowing the hand of his niece on the Doge's son Giovanni, and joyous festival was held at Constantinople in honour of the alliance. But whatever pride may have been engendered in the Doge's breast by this almost more than mortal success was soon chastened by failing health, affliction at home, and the desolation wrought by plague and famine in the city. Rich in piety and charity this noble and heroic servant of the people declined to his end, and at the early age of forty-eight was laid to rest in S. Zaccaria.

VINE PERGOLA ON THE GIUDECCA

The story of the enriching of this church with the body of S. Tarasio is too characteristic to be passed by. We tell it in Sanudo's words. In the year 1019 some Venetian merchants, with whom was a certain priest of Malamocco, disembarked at a promontory called Chiledro. The priest and two companions went into a deserted monastery and heard a voice crying *Tolle hoc corpus sanctum et defer tecum* (Take this holy body and bear it away with thee).

He looked around and finding no monument prayed to God for guidance, and soon discerned an altar inscribed, "This body of S. Tarasio shalt thou find wrapped in a cloth." He then turned and saw a cave in which lay the body with four lights burning before it. Now the said priest was sorely hurt in one of his hands, which he carried in a sling, and having entered the cave he at once became whole. As he raised the body, which weighed nought, so light it was, a voice proceeded from it saying, *Tolle me quia tecum venire præsto sum* (Take me, for I am ready to come with thee). They carried the body to the ship, three miles distant, and lo, there came some monks running apace and crying, "Cruel men, give us back our father. Ye shall not depart hence if ye restore him not to us, for once on a time a strange people came and stole a tooth of the saint and never could they depart until they had returned the same to us." But the Venetians caring nought for such words set sail for Venice, and, though the ship was heavy laden, she sailed light as a bird over the sea, so precious a treasure she bore.

Otho Orseolo, who succeeded his father in 1008, by overweening ambition, drew on himself the ill-will of the people. God-son of an Emperor, brother-in-law of the sainted King Stephen of Hungary, he promoted one of his brothers to the patriarchate of Grado (next to the dogeship the most important position in the state), and another to the See of Torcello. The Patriarchs of Aquileia and of Grado had long been at bitter enmity, and more than once had fought out their quarrels with all too secular weapons. During the Lombard dominion the Patriarchs of Aquileia were tainted with the Arian heresy, whereas those of Grado remained orthodox and claimed jurisdiction over the whole of the lagoons. Moreover, the growing power and wealth of the latter aroused the jealousy of their rivals. The Aquileian Pastor was generally a German by race and sympathies, and subject to the Empire, while the Patriarch of Grado was subject to Venice.[9] The Pastor of Aquileia now organised the popular discontent, and drove his rival of Grado and the Doge to exile in Istria; but the horror wrought in Grado by this warlike churchman, who added perjury to ferocity to accomplish his vengeance, brought about a reaction in the Doge's favour, and he was recalled, only, however, to wreck himself again on the iron-bound determination of the Venetians never to be subject to a feudal prince, and he was again exiled. For Venice was founded by citizens of the Roman Empire, with traditions of municipal freedom and imperial dominion to whom the feudal system of the German conquerors of Italy was alien and hateful. His successor, Dom. Centranico, elected in 1026, was unable to rule the storm, and after an ineffectual reign of six years was shorn of his beard and sent to Constantinople. Again the Venetians turned to the twice-exiled Doge. An honourable embassy was sent to invite Otho to return, only to find him beyond the reach of earthly honours. In the political confusion another Orseolo usurped power for a day, and was chased to Ravenna by the people, whose hatred of the Orseoli was now so fierce that the whole family were ostracised and laws enacted which finally blocked any tendency in the dominant families to form a dynasty.

Under Dom. Flabianico, who was raised to the ducal chair in 1032, an *Arengo* was called, and after the acts of the Doges for the past three hundred years, their ungovernable ambitions and tragic ends had been recapitulated, it was decided to abolish association and hereditary succession. Two ducal councillors were appointed to assist the Doge in the discharge of the ordinary duties of his office. In extraordinary matters of grave public importance he was compelled to *invite* the more prominent and experienced citizens to his council. By these two momentous constitutional changes that paring away of the Doge's powers was begun which in the end made of him little more than a figurehead, and gave free play to the evolution of the most capable and powerful oligarchy in history. It is easy to trace in the two *consiglieri ducali* the beginnings of the Ducal Council, and in the "Invited" (*Pregadi*) the Senate, or meeting of the *Pregadi*. The object of the reformers were effected. During the reigns (a period of thirty-eight years) of Flabianico and of Dom. Contarini, the fury of ecclesiastical jealousy alone disturbed the state.

That the choice of the Doge was still democratic in form is clear from an interesting description by an eye-witness, Dom. Tina, of the election of Doge Dom. Selvo in 1071. An immense multitude of citizens came in boats and armed galleys to an assembly on the island of Castello; and while the clergy and the monks from the Abbey of S. Nicolo, founded on the *Lido* in the previous reign, were praying in St Peter's for divine guidance, a mighty shout rose from the people, *Noi volemo dose Domenigo Selvo e lo laudiamo* (We desire and approve Dom. Selvo for Doge). Selvo was seized by a company of nobles and borne shoulder high to his barge, where he bared his feet that he might enter St Mark's in due humility. Tina, who was on Selvo's boat, intoned the Te Deum; a thousand voices joined him and a thousand oars dashed the waters into foam. From all the churches bells pealed as the Doge alighted and was carried to St Mark's, where the clergy met him and such psalmody and acclamation were raised that the very domes of the chapel seemed like to burst with the noise. The Doge entered and prostrated himself to the ground, giving thanks to God and to St Mark for the honour conferred upon him. Having taken the insignia of office from the altar he proceeded to the palace, followed by an immense concourse of people, who in accordance with usage looted the palace of its furniture and received largess from the new Doge.

Selvo's popularity was not, however, shared by his consort, a Greek princess, who shocked the simpler tastes of the Venetians by her oriental luxury. Not only was she said to bathe in dew and scent her robes with costly perfumes, she was of *tanta delicatezza* that she would not touch her food with her fingers, but made use of certain two-pronged instruments of gold to carry it to her mouth. The outraged Divine Majesty, say the chroniclers, punished her by the infliction of a loathsome disease and she sickened into such corruption that none could be found to tend her.

CHAPTER III

Expansion in the East—Reconciliation of Pope Alexander III. and the Emperor Barbarossa—The Wedding of the Adriatic

"All the golden cities
Overflowing with honey
. . .
Say, lords, should not our thoughts be first to commerce."
—*Blake.*

ONE of the most remarkable figures of mediæval history is that of Robert Guiscard, son of a poor Norman knight, who with a handful of military adventurers carved out for himself a great duchy in South Italy, founded a race of kings, defeated the Emperors of East and West, and in his colossal ambition aimed at nothing less than uniting in his person the divided Empire of the Romans. Alexius Comnenos, the Greek Emperor, hard pressed at Durazzo by the puissant duke's forces, appealed to Venice for help and promised valuable trading privileges in return. She responded to the call, and in 1081 a great *armata* of sixty-three sail under the command of the Doge appeared before the besieged city and by masterly strategy and strenuous fighting defeated the Normans. But Duke Robert was not easily crushed. In 1084 Alexius was constrained to pay the inevitable price of further commercial favours for another naval contingent from Venice. Doge Selvo with a fleet of great ships and 13,000 men fell upon the Normans near Corfu. Victory inclined to the Venetians at first, but in the end they were overwhelmed by Robert's fierce onslaught. The huge towering galleons of the islanders were involved in hopeless confusion, and as the Normans pressed on to cut down the Venetian sailors, Robert tempted them by promising to spare the lives of those who would enter his service. "Know, Duke Robert," answered the devoted Venetians, "that if we saw our wives and children slain before our eyes we would not break troth with Alexius." Robert, admiring their loyalty, suffered them to be held for redemption. Selvo reached Venice in November with a remnant of his shattered fleet and a loss of 6000 men. Before a month was past he was deposed by a popular rising whose chief instigator, Vitale Falier, lifted himself up to the ducal chair. Unhappy Doge Selvo's memory is, however, enshrined in St Mark's, for he it was who set himself to adorn the edifice with marble incrustations, columns of porphyry and other precious stones, mosaic and painting.

The naval supremacy of Venice was essential to her existence, and one of the first acts of Falier was to collect a fleet more powerful than any that had yet left the lagoons. In the spring of 1085 the shame of defeat was wiped out by a great victory over the Normans on the scene of the former engagement. In a few months plague had quenched for ever the fiery spirit of Duke Robert, and Alexius had leisure to reward the Venetians. The Doge's title of Duke of Dalmatia was formally recognised and that of Augustus added. Trading franchises and exemption from customs were granted in all the parts of the Eastern Empire. Lands and factories were assigned to them, a Venetian quarter was founded in Constantinople. The first grip of the young Republic was laid on the capital of the Greeks and never relaxed until she had overthrown their empire and fixed herself there—victorious and dominant.

SHRINE OF THE HOLY CROSS, S. MARCO.

In 1094 the new Church of St Mark was ready for formal consecration; but it was a casket void of its treasure. For since the great fire of 976 all traces of the Saint's body had been lost and great was the affliction of Doge and people. It was decided to institute a solemn fast and procession, and to supplicate the Eternal Majesty to reveal the hidden relic. On the 25th day of

June, while the procession of Doge, clergy and people was slowly pacing St Mark's, a great light shone from a pillar near the altar of St James, and part of the masonry falling away, a hand was thrust out with a ring of gold on the middle finger and a sweet fragrance was diffused throughout the church, "nor could any draw this ring off" (says Sanudo[10]) "save Giov. Delfino, counsellor to the Doge, whose descendants a few years ago gave it to the Scuola di S. Marco. The body being found, the whole city was filled with joy and gave thanks to the eternal God for having restored so great a treasure. On the 8th of October the said church, which of old was called St Theodore, was consecrated in the name of St Mark, and in the presence alone of the Doge, the bishop, the primicerio and the procurator of St Mark, the body was placed (as it is famed) in the high altar of the said church. And Bernardo Giustiniani maketh mention in his history that he being once procurator, it was told him in great secrecy where the said body lay, and that in very truth it was in the said church."

On the 6th of May 1811 the body was rediscovered in a marble tomb in the crypt, with a few coins, a gold ring minus its jewel; a *lamina* with the date October 8, 1094, and the name of Vitale Falier.

A great festival was instituted to commemorate the discovery, and the fame of the miracle drew many pilgrims to Venice, among whom was Henry IV., Emperor of the West, who combining piety with statecraft, paid his devotions to the Saint and courted the favour of the Republic, whose help, or at least neutrality, he needed in his wars with the papacy to avenge the humiliation of Canossa.[11] The Emperor was magnificently received, and after admiring the beauty of the architecture and the wonderful site of the city he left, having added many privileges to those already enjoyed by the Venetian merchants in his dominions.

In 1096 Vitale Falier died, and on Christmas day was buried in the portico of St Mark's. The people, whom the devastation wrought by tempest, earthquake and famine[12] had made unjust, ran to the church and cast bread and wine at the tomb, cursing and saying: "Sate thee now, who in life wouldest not provide plenty for thy people."

Towards the close of the 11th century harrowing stories of the atrocities committed by the Saracen conquerors of Palestine on Christian pilgrims, and the impassioned oratory of Peter the Hermit had fired the West with a desire to cleanse the Holy Land from the pollution of the infidel. Wave after wave of unorganised enthusiasm broke against the forces of nature and the military prowess of the Saracens, until at length the epic story of the conquest of Jerusalem by the organised Chivalry of Christendom rang through Europe. The Venetians, who aimed at something more solid than the gratification of religious emotion, looked on unmoved, until an appeal came to the maritime states of Italy to furnish transport for the crusaders and pilgrims who were flocking to the East. Doge Vitale Michieli, in 1096, called an assembly in St Mark's. He appealed to the religious zeal of the people and dwelt on the unwisdom of permitting their rivals of Pisa and Genoa to forestall them again and increase their power in the East. Commercial interest and state policy left them no choice. A fleet was manned and after solemn mass at St Mark's the expedition set sail, bearing the consecrated banner of the Cross, under the command of the Doge's son Giovanni and the Bishop of Castello. But the Greek Emperor, ever fearful of the whole movement, incited the Pisans to attack the Venetians, and a fierce battle between the rival armaments at Rhodes disgraced the Christian host. The Venetians were victorious and continued their voyage. A call was made at Myra, where lay the body of St Nicholas, patron saint of mariners, which the Bishop had long coveted for the Abbey of St Nicolo on the Lido. Having learnt from his spies that the city was almost deserted, the worthy prelate proceeded to the church accompanied by some sailors, and demanded of the custodians where the body of the saint was. They replied that they knew not, and indicated an old tomb, saying that some relics were there and some had been removed, and the Bishop might have what he could find. The sailors working day and night broke open the tomb and found nought save some oil and water. Whereupon the Bishop, waxing very wroth, put the four custodians to the torture, who cried: "Wherefore dost thou afflict us, verily in the altar of St John are two bodies of saints." The altar being opened two chests were found with inscriptions saying they contained the bodies of St Theodore the Martyr and St Nicholas the Less. The spoilers were about to depart when a sailor, by "divine inspiration," turned back to look again at the rifled tomb, and lo, an odour of such great sweetness came forth that surely, he said, there must lie some relic of great worth. The sailors dug deeper and came upon a third chest with an inscription in Greek saying: "Here rests the great Nicholas, who wrought wonders on land and sea." The chests were carried abroad with great devotion, and the fleet went its way to the Holy Land. The Venetians assisted in the capture of Caifa, and on St Michael's Day returned laden with the saint's body and much spoil. Meanwhile their interests in the West had not been neglected. For help afforded to the Countess Matilda in Ferrara the usual reward of trading privileges in that city was given.

In 1104, in the third year of the reign of Ordelafo Falier, a Doge, "young in years but old in wisdom," came a summons from Baldwin, King of Jerusalem, for a naval contingent. A fleet of more than a hundred sail was despatched, which, after contributing to the victory of Jaffa and to the capture of Sidon, swept the sea of pirates. The Venetians exacted important concessions—a quarter of the conquered city; their own church, bakery and mill; a market-place; exemption from customs, taxes and dues; the right to use their own weights and measures; and a yearly tribute in money from the king. They were also to be subject to their own laws.

But at home evil days had fallen upon Venice. An awful tempest and inundation wrought havoc in the city. Houses and factories were levelled to the ground; the ancient capital Malamocco was engulfed in the sea. Scarcely had the unhappy citizens recovered from their terror when two disastrous fires consumed a great part of the city. Thirty churches were destroyed, and the ducal palace and St Mark's injured. Abroad, the King of Hungary attacked their protectorate of Dalmatia, and the fleet was recalled from the East. It had done what was expected of it. A certain Friar Peter being at Constantinople heard that the body of St Stephen, the proto-martyr, was in a church there, and "found means to obtain it." The fleet was in the harbour, and the sacred treasure put on board, not without opposition from the Greeks, who were with difficulty restrained from attacking the bearers. A great procession went forth to meet the fleet as it neared Venice, and the Doge himself transferred the holy burden on his shoulders to the ducal barge. Many churches contended for the possession of the relic, which at length was conferred on the rich Benedictine Abbey of S. Giorgio Maggiore, founded in the year 982.

The Bishop of Castello, who had been sent to Constantinople to plead for help in the reconquest of Dalmatia, was no less successful. As a token of the Emperor's favour, he returned with the right hand of St John the Baptist in a vase. Two armaments were sent to recover Dalmatia. In 1117, when the Venetians were wavering before a fierce attack of the Hungarians outside Zara, the Doge spurred forward to hearten them. His horse stumbled on a dead body: the enemy closed on him, and he was slain—the second Doge who had met a soldier's death.

THE SQUERO, S. TROVASO

Ordelafo Falier is remembered in Venice to-day by two monuments: one of art—the famous *Pala d'oro* in St Mark's; the other of civic utility—the scattered *squeri* or shipyards were concentrated by him in the great Arsenal, whence issued the mighty vessels innumerable that for centuries maintained the naval supremacy of Venice. It was this *Arzanà*, now the *Arsenale Vecchio*, which Dante saw and immortalised in the famous description of the fifth of the Malebolge:—

"Quale nell'arzanà de' Viniziani
bolle l'inverno la tenace pece
a rimpalmar li lor legni non sani,

che navicar non ponno, e in quella vece
chi fa suo legno nuovo, e chi ristoppa
le coste a quel che più viaggi fece;

chi ribatte da proda, e chi da poppa;
altri fa remi, ed altri volge sarte;
chi terzerudo ed artimon rintoppa."[13]

The first duty of Dom. Michiel, 1118, was to make peace with the King of Hungary, that he might be free to devote himself to Eastern affairs. The King of Jerusalem was a prisoner in the hands of the Saracens and a stirring appeal from the Pope for Venetian help was read in St Mark's. A year was spent in building and equipping a fleet of forty great galleys, twenty-eight transports, and many smaller craft. It was a magnificent spectacle when the vessels, painted with many colours and bright with banners, set forth bearing a gallant army of knights and footmen, their armour flashing in the sun, the banner of St Mark and the consecrated standard of the Cross waving proudly from the Doge's ship. But the captive king was to linger yet another year, for the Doge had pressing affairs nearer home. The Greek Emperor Johannes must be chastised for his unfriendly attitude. The fleet anchored before Corfu and spent the winter in an attempt to capture the island. Having wreaked what damage they could and having "invoked the divine assistance," they resumed their voyage in the spring. After devastating Chios, Lesbos and Rhodes they reached Cyprus, where news came that a Saracen armament was off Jaffa. The fleet at once pressed forward and fell upon the infidels. The Doge's galley went straight for the Emir's ship and sank it. Confusion seized the enemy and a memorable victory was won. The slaughter was terrible. For years the mariners of Jaffa declared the sea to be infected with the corpses of the Saracens. The Doge was met at Jaffa by the clergy and barons of Jerusalem and borne in triumph to the holy city, where he was acclaimed as the champion of Christendom. Being urged to further service the Doge replied that nothing was nearer the hearts of the Venetians than to increase the Christian dominion in the East, and that the piety and religion which had always distinguished them was burning to express itself in deeds. In the name of the King and his barons it was agreed that of the captured cities and all spoils one-third should be the portion of the Venetians, one-third of the King, one-third of the Patriarch of Jerusalem, and that the cost of the war should be met in thirds. The trading privileges granted in Sidon were confirmed and were to be extended to all future conquests. A hot discussion arose as to whether Tyre or Ascalon should be the objective of the next expedition. It was decided to cast lots, and a boy drew from the urn the word "Tyre."

The capture by the Venetians and Franks of Tyre, mother of Carthage, "the mart of nations made very glorious in the heart of the seas," is one of the epics of history. The besiegers attacked with desperate courage. The flower of Saracen chivalry garrisoned the city. The warriors of Damascus and fleets from Egypt fought in vain to raise the siege. In the alternations of the struggle murmurs were heard among the Franks of impending desertion by the Venetian fleet. The Doge, when the report came to his ears, had a plank knocked out of the side of each ship and borne before him to the Frankish camp. With grave words he rebuked the slanderers and offered to leave those material pledges of Venetian loyalty. Towards the end of the siege money failed: the Doge cut coins of leather, promising to exchange them for good ducats when the fleet returned to Venice. After five months' resistance, famine wore down the courage of the Saracens. Honourable terms of surrender were granted and the banners of the King of Jerusalem and the standard of St Mark floated over the captured city. Venice had planted her foot in Syria. The fleet turned westward, but its work was not yet done. Johannes had expelled the Venetian traders from the ports of the Empire, and the Greeks were to be taught another lesson. The course of the avengers through the eastern seas was marked by the ravaged cities of the Greek islands spoiled of their wealth and bewailing their captive sons and daughters. The Doge paused in his work to recover the Dalmatian fiefs from the King of Hungary, and cities reduced to heaps of smouldering ruins bore witness to the power of Venice to vindicate her sovereignty. Reinforced from Dalmatia the victorious fleet turned again on the Greeks, who hastened to make peace and agreed to the Doge's terms. Great was the rejoicing in Venice when the triumphant Doge returned bringing the bodies of St Isidore from Chios and of S. Donato from Cephalonia, and such spoil of Eastern magnificence as had never yet been seen there since she rose from the sea. But before we follow him to his retreat and death in the Monastery of S. Giorgio Maggiore, where to this day may be seen a partially obliterated epitaph to the "Terror of the Greeks and the Glory of Venice," we may record one domestic innovation worthy of grateful remembrance. Few things are more charming to the wayfarer in Venice than the little shrines of the Virgin and Child decked with flowers and lighted by night with an oil lamp in the nooks and corners of the city. Though no longer needed for their original purpose of illuminating the ways, they are still tended by the piety of the people. It was to Michieli that this provision was due. To aid the watchmen in ridding the dark and tortuous lanes of the thieves that infested them, and to light the city, the clergy were ordered to provide for the public safety by erecting and maintaining the shrines, and were empowered to levy a rate to meet the cost.

From the retirement of Dom. Michieli to the election of Vitale Michieli II. in 1156, two Doges, Pietro Polani and Dom. Morosini, presided over the growth of the lagoon state. In spite of troubles with the Adriatic pirates, the Hungarians in Dalmatia and the Paduans, new markets for Venetian commerce were won by the familiar process of squeezing the rival Cæsars of East and West. It was a time of building. The Campanile was finished, many churches were erected, and a hospital was founded for the mothers and widows of seamen fallen in the service of the state.

Political theories that no longer correspond to realities are dangerous in proportion to the character and genius of those whose imagination they seize upon. Actually the Roman Empire had fallen to pieces, but so faithfully had the Romans wrought that it was regarded even by the northern invaders as an integral part of civilisation. The Church accepted and sanctified it, and the Holy Roman Empire continued to exist in theory until the wit of Voltaire and the big battalions of Napoleon destroyed the sham for ever. In the poetic mind of Dante, with his passionate aspiration for peace and righteousness, it became a beautiful but ineffectual ideal of a kingship over kings; an Emperor curbing the warring factions and states of Christendom and coercing such as threatened to break the common peace, so that the golden days of the *Pax Romana* might be seen of men again. But the times were making for nationality and not for empire, and the attempts of the great emperors to realise their theoretical power were foredoomed to failure.

S. MARCO—INTERIOR—CHAPEL OF S. CLEMENTE.

Such an attempt was made by Frederick Barbarossa. Reports came to his ears of a rebellious and factious spirit in the south. The burgesses of the Italian cities were growing restive under the imperial vicars. Milan had attacked and wasted Lodi: the feudal princes both of Church and State were scandalised by common burghers and mechanics rising to hold public offices, and even exercising the profession of arms. Twice the Emperor descended the Alps to bring the Italian communes to subjection. For a time he was successful, but a new era was dawning in Italy. The Lombard cities banded themselves in a league whose soul was the Pope, and swore to make no peace with the Emperor until their communal rights and privileges were secured. Venice, true to her policy of facing both ways, at first held aloof; but later, fearing her turn might come next, promised naval and financial aid to the league. The struggle continued until 1176, when the flower of German chivalry, including the emperor himself, bit the dust before the stout burghers of the Lombard League at Legnano. Frederick, to punish the Venetians for their support of the League and of Alexander III. against his own nominees for the papal chair, moved their arch enemy the Patriarch of Aquileia to attack Grado. He was defeated by the Doge and taken captive to Venice. With twelve of his canons he purchased liberty by undertaking to pay a yearly tribute of a fine bull, twelve pigs, twelve loaves of bread, and a quantity of wine. A quaint ceremony marked the reception of the tribute. The Doge with a train of nobles repaired to the ducal palace, where he struck down certain wooden castles with a wand. Then in the presence of the Doge and his suite a bull-fight took place in the Piazza; the pigs were beheaded, cut in pieces, and distributed among the nobles. At later celebrations a youth by an ingenious contrivance flew down from the top of the Campanile to the balcony of the ducal palace and presented a nosegay to the Doge. In Leonardo Loredano's time the number of recipients had so increased that it was decided to distribute the pigs among the monasteries, and the bread and wine were given to the prisons.

In 1171, a few ships, all that remained of a fine merchant fleet in Constantinople, sailed up the lagoons and roused the Venetians to fury by the recital of a wanton attack on their countrymen in the East. All the Venetians in the ports of the Empire had been seized by order of the Emperor Manuel, cast into prison, and their property confiscated. The Emperor had been secretly gathering his forces, and by leaning on the Genoese felt strong enough to pay off old scores. An irresistible wave of popular indignation swept the state into a war with the Eastern Empire. To meet the cost a forced loan of one per cent. on property was levied, a national bank formed, and state bonds were issued for the amount of the loan bearing interest at four per cent. These securities were quoted daily on the Rialto according to the fluctuations of the market, and formed the first funded debt in Europe. In six months the Doge set forth with a magnificent fleet and the flower of Venetian manhood; but he wasted precious time in a punitive attack on Ragusa, and while besieging the capital of Negropont, the ancient Eubœa, weakly agreed to treat with the Emperor. The subtle Greeks temporised with the Venetian envoys, one of whom, Enrico Dandolo, we shall hear of again. Winter came, and a terrible pestilence wasted the Venetian forces. So great was the mortality that the Giustiniani perished to a man, and the last scion of this noble house was permitted to leave the cloister in order to marry the Doge's daughter and save his name from extinction. Having raised up several sons, his wife retired to a convent and he to his cell at S. Nicolo del Lido to fulfil his interrupted vow. Before a year was past the unhappy Doge and all that remained of the expedition returned to Venice. The city became infected with the plague, and the angry people turned upon the Doge, who fled for refuge to S. Zaccaria, but was cut down before he reached the threshold.

The hasty inception and calamitous issue of this ill-omened war profoundly impressed the aristocracy of Venice. They determined that neither popular passion nor ducal ineptitude should again sway the policy of the state. The supersession of the democratic element and the further curtailment of the ducal privileges were effected by an elaborately-conceived constitution, which gave the shadow of power to the people and the substance to the aristocracy. Each of the six wards (sestieri) of the city was to elect two representatives, who were each to appoint forty of the chief citizens of their respective wards to form a great Council of four hundred and eighty members. The Council sat for a year, and when its term was completed, it, *not the wards*, nominated the twelve who were to appoint the Council for the following year. The Council was to elect the officers of state, including the Doge, who was chosen by eleven of its members delegated for that purpose. Further to control the Doge the two privy councillors instituted in 1032 were increased to six.

The constitution of 1172 narrowly escaped a baptism of blood. When the new Doge, Sebastiano Ziani, was presented for popular approbation a riot ensued, but the people were duped by an empty formula—*Quest' è il vostro doge se vi piace* (This is your Doge if it be your pleasure), and debauched by a more abundant distribution of largess and a more gorgeous pageant.

The state of the finances no less than affairs on the mainland impelled the Republic to come to terms with Manuel. To strengthen her hands an alliance was sought with the Normans, and again we find Enrico Dandolo an ambassador, this time at the Court of Sicily. Barbarossa was now wearying of the struggle with the papacy. Like Henry IV., he found his legions powerless against a feeble old man armed with the impalpable weapons of the spiritual power. He had set up three schismatic popes, seized the very seat of Peter at Rome, and driven Alexander III., a wanderer and a suppliant, to the Courts of Europe. The indomitable old pontiff at length found his way to Venice, *all' unico domicilio di libertà*, and an attempt at reconciliation was made. A splendid naval procession went to meet him: a seat of honour was prepared for him in the ducal barge between the Doge and the Patriarch, and apartments were assigned to him in the patriarchal palace at S. Silvestre. Soon it was reported that the Emperor himself was at Chioggia, and after many negotiations terms were agreed upon.[14] A bitter morsel the Emperor was forced to swallow. The uncompromising Pope would abate no jot of his claims—the Emperor must solemnly recognise him as the true and only successor of Peter, God's vicar on earth, supreme over Cæsar.

**S. MARCO AND THE DOGE'S PALACE, WITH THE
LOGGETTA IN THE FOREGROUND**

Sunday the 24th of July 1177 was a superb day for Venice. The whole Piazza
was alive with princes and peoples of many nations. Two tall masts lifting up
the banners of St Mark stood at the landing-stage by the Piazzetta. The day
before, the Emperor, who was not permitted to land at Venice, "until he had
set aside his leonine ferocity and put on the gentleness of the lamb," was
brought in great pomp from Chioggia to Lido and passed the night at the
Abbey of S. Nicolo. In the early morning the Pope, having received at St
Mark's the formal abjuration of the schism by the Chancellor of the Empire,
solemnly absolved the Emperor from the ban of the Church. The Doge and
a great procession then set forth and brought the Emperor from Lido seated
in the ducal barge between Doge and Patriarch. When he disembarked a
procession was formed headed by the Doge, the Patriarch, and the clergy
bearing banners and crosses, behind whom walked the Emperor. Having
reached the Piazza he saw the Pope enthroned in full canonicals and
surrounded by a throng of cardinals, archbishops, bishops, and clergy
awaiting him in front of the atrium of St Mark's.[15] "Touched by the Holy
Spirit" he cast off his purple cloak, bowed his neck, and prostrated himself
at the Pope's feet, "venerating God in Alexander." The pontiff then arose,
stretched forth his hand, raised the Emperor, gave him the kiss of peace and
blessed him. The air shook with the pealing of bells and the singing of the Te
Deum by the Germans. The doors of St Mark swung open, the Emperor,
giving his right hand to the Pope, led him to the altar, and having received
his benediction returned to the Ducal Palace. The next day at the request of
the Emperor a solemn mass was sung in St Mark's by the Pope. The Emperor
laid aside his mantle, took a wand, expelled the laity from the choir and led

the aged Pope to the altar protecting him from the crowd. Himself sat in the choir amid the clergy, and devoutly and humbly listened to mass. At the sermon the Pope noticing the Emperor close by the pulpit ordered the patriarch of Aquileia to translate the sermon from Latin into German. The *credo* having been sung, the Emperor approached the Pope's feet and made his oblations. At the end of mass the Emperor took the Pope's hand, led him to his white horse and held the stirrup while he mounted. The Pope permitted him to go no further, dismissed him, and gave him his blessing. The successful accomplishment of this reconciliation added great lustre to the Venetian state. Never had she stood so high in the eyes of Europe. Nor were more solid gains lacking. Making the best of both worlds she received valuable privileges both spiritual and political before Pope and Cæsar left her shores. Many were the legends that clustered round this dramatic scene. Stories were told in later days of the fugitive Pope arriving in Venice, in mean attire, wandering about the tortuous ways until overcome by fatigue he lay down and slept on the bare ground near the Church of S. Apollinare. When rested he wandered on until he was received in the monastery of the Carità, where he served six months as a common scullion. A Venetian who had been on a pilgrimage to Rome recognised him. The Doge was advised and the Pope led to the palace in great pomp. To this day near the Church of S. Apollinare an inscription marks the legendary spot where "Alexander III. reposed when fleeing from the violence of Frederick the Emperor." Frederick then bade the Venetians, so runs the fable, deliver up the fugitive or he would plant his eagles in St Mark, where they had never been before. To which the Doge retorted that the Venetians would not wait for him, and on learning that a fleet of seventy-five ships under the Emperor's son, Otho, was under sail for Venice, set forth with thirty-four galleys, attacked the imperial fleet, captured forty vessels, sunk two, and made Otho prisoner. In the great scene before St Mark's the Emperor was imagined lying prostrate on the ground, the Pope placing his heel on the imperial neck and saying: "I will tread on the asp and on the basilisk." To which the Emperor objected: "Not to thee but to Peter"; to be quickly answered by the Pope: "Both to me and to Peter."

THE PIAZZETTA AND COLUMN OF S. MARK.

COLUMNS OF SS. MARK AND THEODORE

The festival of La Sensa was celebrated during the Pope's stay at Venice. The pontiff on that occasion handed a consecrated ring to the Doge saying: "Receive this as a pledge of the sovereignty which you and your successors shall have in perpetuity over the sea." Henceforth the ceremony was held with added magnificence, and became the greatest of the many pageants for which Venice was so famous. On his gilded barge, the Bucintoro, commanded by three admirals and many captains of the fleet, and impelled by the arms of one hundred and sixty shipwrights from the arsenal, four to each oar, stood the Doge surrounded by the Patriarch and clergy, the great officers of state and the foreign ambassadors, the standard of St Mark waving over their heads. A great procession of gilded galleys and gondolas bright with flags followed the Doge to the island of St Helena where a collation of peeled chestnuts and red wine was offered by the Bishop of Castello and his clergy, while the Doge presented damask roses in a silver cup. One he took himself and distributed the others to his suite. The Bucintoro then swept through the Porto of the Lido into the open Adriatic. The patriarch blessed the ring and handed it to the Doge who cast it into the sea pronouncing the formula: "Sea, we wed thee in token of our true and perpetual dominion over thee." From the musicians' gallery on the barge rang out a joyous theme, and the Doge returned to the Molo after having heard mass at S. Nicolo. In the evening a banquet was given at the palace to the admirals and the hundred masters of the arsenal, the chief magistrates and the ambassadors. A great fair was held and the city gave itself up to a week's festivities. Such with some modifications in detail was the famous wedding of the Adriatic, which ended only with the Republic herself in 1797.

Among the spoil from Syria were three huge granite columns, one of which had fallen into the canal during unloading: the other two lay on the shore, and no one could be found to raise them. A proclamation was made that any *onesta grazia* would be granted to the master who should erect them on the piazzetta. Many had tried and failed when Nicolo Barattieri, a Lombard engineer, offered his services. He is said to have stretched stout ropes, soaked them in water and fixed them to the pillars.[16] As the ropes dried and contracted the columns "with great art and some little assistance" were slowly elevated and were surmounted with the familiar bronze and marble statues of the Lion of St Mark and St Theodore. The former was cast and erected in 1178, the latter carved and erected in 1329. When asked to name his reward, Nicolo begged permission to set up gaming-tables between the columns. His request was granted, but orders were given that all public executions should henceforth take place there, and the "two red columns"[17] have a gruesome interest in subsequent Venetian history. Two attempts, one in 1559, another in 1809, were made to recover the third pillar. The same ingenious master is said to have erected the first wooden Rialto bridge in 1173.

On Ziani's retirement the method of electing the Doge was again modified. Instead of the eleven, four members of the Great Council were chosen who nominated an electoral college of forty. Only a single member might be taken from any one family, and the forty elected the Doge by an absolute majority of votes.

When the papal summons came to Venice in the reign of Ziani's successor, Mastropiero, for a naval contingent in the service of the third Crusade, she held too great a stake in Syria to remain wholly indifferent. Manuel promised satisfaction for the spoliation of the Venetians in 1177 by the payment of a large indemnity, and the long struggle with the Hungarians for the recovery of Zara and the Dalmatian protectorate was intermitted. A fleet was sent to the east which bore a brave part in the relief of Tyre and the famous two years' siege of Acre. But Venice fought in conjunction with her rivals of Pisa and Genoa, and it was not until the barons of France, during the organisation of the fourth Crusade gave her the opportunity of demonstrating her naval supremacy and controlling the movement for her own ends that she put forth all her strength.

Enrico Dandolo, now an old man of more than four score years, was made Doge in 1193. On his election he was made to subscribe to a *Promissione ducale* (coronation oath), an ingenious instrument designed in the interests of the aristocracy, which defined and limited his powers. Dandolo had inherited the Dalmatian trouble, and was occupied with stubborn Zara, which for the fourth time had resisted the efforts of the Venetians to recover it from the King of Hungary, when a wail of distress from the hard-pressed Christians in Palestine reached the ears of the great Pope Innocent III. and the fourth crusade was launched.

CHAPTER IV

Enrico Dandolo and the Capture of Constantinople

"August pleasant Dandolo
Worshipping hearts about him for a wall,
Conducted blind eyes hundred years and all
Through vanquished Byzant, where friends note for him
What pillar, marble massive, sardius slim,
'Twere fittest to transport to Venice' square."
—*Browning.*

THE fourth crusade afforded Venice an opportunity of rising to a commanding position in Europe. She seized it with resolution yet with the cautious deliberation so characteristic of her temper. Amid the fervent enthusiasm of the crusaders she kept a cool head, ever intent on directing the movement to the attainment of her secular policy—the extension of her commerce and of her dominion in the East.

The story of the Conquest of Constantinople has been told for us by one who played a leading *rôle* in the drama, Jeffrey of Villehardouin, Marshall of Champagne, who was one of the six envoys sent by the organisers of the crusade to Venice to treat for the transport of the army to the East. He was a man of simple piety and singleness of purpose, a heroic soldier and capable administrator, but like his fellows no match for the shrewd old Doge who then directed the policy of the republic. It is difficult to say how far the almost cynical exploitation of the crusaders' enthusiasm, charged upon Venice by some historians, was redeemed by nobler motives. The policy of making the best of both worlds is not a modern invention, and states as well as individuals are moved by mixed impulses. To the Doge and his councillors it may well have seemed that the expansion of the Venetian Republic and the cause of Christendom were not incompatible. Certain it is that this, the finest armament that ever set sail to wrest the Holy Land over seas from the infidel, was diverted by Venetian policy to an attack on the possessions of a Christian prince, himself a crusader, and after wasting a precious year melted away in a wanton conquest and spoliation of the capital of Eastern Christendom, and in the attempt to maintain there a Franco-Venetian Empire.

In February 1201 the envoys reached Venice and laid their request before the Doge. A delay of three days was asked. On the fourth day they entered the ducal palace, *qui mult ere riches et biaus* (which was very rich and beautiful), and found the Doge seated in the midst of his Council. They prayed his help on behalf of the high barons of France who had taken the cross to revenge the shame of Jesus and to reconquer Jerusalem, for no people were so mighty on sea or so powerful to further their cause. They entreated him in the name of God to have pity on the land beyond the sea and on the shame of Jesus Christ, and lend them warships and transports. "This," replied the Doge, "is a great thing you ask," and begged eight days' interval for reflection. In due time the terms on which help would be forthcoming were stated. Venice would furnish transports for 4500 horses and 9000 esquires, ships for 4500 knights and 20,000 footmen, with provisions for nine months. The sum asked was 85,000 marks in silver of the standard of Cologne. The terms were to hold good for one year from the day of the departure of the Armata, "to do the service of God and of Christianity in whatsoever place it may befall." The Republic would add on her own part fifty armed galleys on condition that of the conquests "which we shall make on land or sea we shall have the one half and you the other." The envoys requested a day's delay. They took counsel by night and in the morning came before the Doge and agreed to the terms. "The Doge summoned the Senate and Great Council, and by his great wisdom and clear wit disposed them to do his will and praise his purpose. Then he assembled in the Chapel of St Mark 10,000 of his people and bade them hear mass and pray God for counsel concerning the envoy's request, and so did they most willingly. When mass was ended the Doge begged the envoys to come before the people and humbly entreat them to agree to the conditions. There was great curiosity to see the barons, and they were much gazed at. Jeffrey spoke for them, and said: 'Sirs! the highest and most powerful among the barons of France have sent us before you. They crave that ye may take pity on Jerusalem, which is in bondage to the infidel, and that for God's sake you be willing to aid therein to avenge the shame of Jesus Christ, for they know no other nation so mighty as yours on the sea, and they command us to fall at your feet and not to rise again till you have granted their prayer and had pity on the Holy Land *oltremer*.' Then the six fell upon their knees with many tears at the feet of the multitude, and the Doge and all his people burst into tears of pity and cried aloud with one voice—'We consent, we consent.' Great was the tumult, so that the very ground did shake. When the noise was calmed and that great pity assuaged, the good Doge ascended the pulpit and said: 'Sirs! behold the honour that God hath shown you, in that the best nation in the world has scorned all the other nations and chosen your company to effect together a thing of such high import as the deliverance of our Lord.' All the fair words the Doge spoke to them I cannot relate."

S. MARCO—INTERIOR, WITH PULPIT

Sealed contracts were exchanged with more weeping and genuflexions, the parties to the contract on either side swearing on the bodies of the saints to well and loyally keep their bond. It was secretly agreed that Babylonia (Old Cairo) should be the objective of the expedition. Publicly it was given out that it was bound for beyond the sea. On the Feast of St John, 1202, the Frankish host was to assemble at San Nicolo on the Lido, and the vessels were to be ready. Every detail was specified; the amount of bread and wine per man, and corn per horse. A court of arbitration was formed to settle matters of dispute that might arise. But selfish and worldly motives swayed the actions of too many among the warriors of the cross and whole armies were foresworn. A rich and powerful detachment set sail from Bruges after swearing on the gospels to join at Venice, but engaged transports at Marseilles and Genoa.

Walter of Brienne,[18] with many another great knight, went off to Apulia to subdue the inheritance of his wife and promised to meet the army at Venice.

"But adventures befall as it pleaseth God," and at the trysting-place they were found wanting. Many others, including the Bishop of Autun, broke their oaths.

Great was the consternation of the leaders of the crusade. The Venetians had honourably, indeed generously, done their part. Never had such a fleet been beheld by Christian men. But the crusaders were too few to fill it or to meet the payment due. The barons spared neither entreaties to their erring companions nor their own possessions and credit. Time went on: the day for meeting their obligations was past; the Venetians demanded payment; 30,000 marks were still wanting, perchance to the secret satisfaction of the Republic, for the Venetians had no keen desire to dislocate their remunerative trade with the East. The Sultan of Egypt was their good friend. Commercial privileges had been granted them while the crusaders were gathering at Venice. Two envoys, Marino Dandolo and Dom. Michieli[19] set sail for Egypt, and in May 1202 had concluded a secret treaty between the Republic and the Caliph, by which in return for increased and substantial commercial privileges the Venetians implicitly agreed to divert the fleet from any attack on Egypt.

The Doge was not slow to make the most of the crusaders' hard case. For the fifth time Zara had revolted and was held for the King of Hungary. The Frankish leaders were eating their hearts out at the delay; inaction was demoralising their forces. The Doge offered a compromise. The contract had been broken, and legally the amount paid was forfeited, but if the barons would help the Venetians to subdue Zara on the way, the *Armata* might sail and payment of the balance of money be deferred. The papal legate, Peter of Capua, indignantly declaimed against the bargain, but the barons were in a cleft stick. They could do no other than accept, and the chance of winning from the spoils of Zara enough to pay the balance of their debt was a potent factor in their decision.

All was now ready; the people were assembled in St Mark's on Sunday, the barons being present, and says Villehardouin *ere mult gran feste* (there was a very great festival). "Before Mass began the Doge ascended the pulpit and said: 'Sirs, ye are companions of the best nation in the world for the highest emprise that ever man attempted. I am old and feeble and have need of repose, nor am I whole in body; but I perceive that none can guide nor command you so well as I who am your lord. If ye will grant that I take the sign of the cross and watch over you and direct you, and that my son remain in my stead to guard the land then will I go to live or die with you and the pilgrims.' When the people heard him they all cried out, 'We beseech you in God's name that ye do even as ye say.' Then great pity melted the hearts of the people of the city and of the pilgrims, and many tears were shed for this valiant man who had so much cause to remain at home, being old, and though his eyes were beautiful he saw not, because he had lost his sight through a wound. But he was of exceeding great courage. He left the pulpit and fell on his knees before the altar, and the cross was sewn on the front of a great silken biretta that it might be seen of all. Then the Venetians began to put on the cross in great numbers, for up to that day few were they who joined."

S. MARCO, CHOIR.

At length on the octave of the Feast of the Holy Incarnation of Jesus Christ the host took ship and set forth. Never did so great a fleet sail from any port. "Ah! dear God," exclaimed Jeffrey, "how many a good steed was there, and great ships charged with arms and gallant knights and squires and banners so fair."

It was indeed a gorgeous and thrilling spectacle. Three chief Venetian galleys, the *Peregrina*, the *Paradiso* and the *Aquila* towered above the rest of the fleet. The vessels were one mass of glittering steel and magnificently coloured banners, that of St Mark, a golden lion on crimson ground, waved proudly in the wind. The air trembled at the blast of trumpets. In swelling chorus the host burst forth into the *Veni Creator Spiritus*, and the mighty fleet turned its prows—for Zara.

On the way a punitive call was made at Trieste, which agreed to pay tribute to Venice. Another call was made at Omago and an oath of allegiance exacted. Zara was reached on St Martin's Eve, the 10th of November. The stronghold so impressed the Marshal of Champagne that he exclaims: "How shall such a city be taken except God be with us!" On the 18th, after a stubborn fight the city yielded, pillage followed and half the booty went to each ally. The Pope was scandalised. He had tried to tamper with the French: he now demanded the restitution of the pillage of a city that belonged to a Christian king and crusader. The barons excused themselves as best they might; the Venetians boldly told the papal nuncio that the Holy See had no concern with the affairs of the Republic.

The season was now far advanced, and the fleet wintered at Zara. The chief of the Crusaders, Boniface, Marquis of Montferrat, who had stayed at Venice, took up his command after the capture. The problem of the fate of the expedition faced the allies. Already a bloody fray had embittered the feeling between Venetian and Frank. Boniface, too, was tempted by his own ambition. He claimed the kingdom of Salonika, and hoped to subdue it with the help of the *Armata*.

And events seemed to beckon away from duty. The sickening drama of bloodshed and treachery that stained the palace of the Greek Emperors during the Comnenian dynasty had, in 1185, reached the point when Isaac Angelos Comnenos, having stabbed his kinsman Andronicus (himself a usurper), was enthroned at Constantinople. But a throne whose steps are drenched with blood affords but a slippery foothold. In 1195 Isaac in his turn was dethroned, cast into prison, and his sight destroyed by his brother Alexius Angelos, who unaccountably spared Isaac's son Alexius. He was a bright lad twelve years of age when his father fell, and was forced by his uncle to attend the court and exalt the usurper's state. He escaped, and after many vicissitudes reached the court of Philip of Swabia, who had married his sister Irene. The fleet was on the point of leaving Zara when the young Alexius arrived to implore the help of Boniface on behalf of himself and his father Isaac. King Philip promised in his nephew's name tempting rewards. The moment was well chosen, Boniface with an eye to Salonika lent a willing ear to his plaint: Dandolo, too, apart from the 100,000 marks to be gained by another year's hire of the fleet, had politic reasons for giving the wronged prince a sympathetic audience. Egypt would be safe from attack, and the Venetians had an old score to settle with the Greeks, for a large part of the indemnity promised by the Emperor Manuel for the wanton spoliation of the Venetians in 1171 was still unpaid. Isaac, first repudiating, then yielding to threats, had promised to pay the 200,000 marks due. When Alexius Angelos seized the throne the account was still unsettled. He, too, was evasive, though ready enough to grant commercial favours. The young Alexius, therefore, was told that the leaders would receive him at Corfù, whither the fleet was bound.

But what of the unhappy infidel-ridden land over the sea? Many of the more conscientious knights, mindful of their high purpose and of the holy zeal with which they had set forth, loudly demanded to be led to Syria. The Pope, who had just received news of the most wretched state of the Christians in Palestine, wrote warning the crusaders that they had taken the cross not to avenge the wrongs of princes but of God: he refused his benediction, and menaced them with the curses of heaven. But it was of no avail, present gain was more potent than a far call to duty. At an opportune moment the young Alexius arrived. The chivalrous natures of the crusaders were wrought upon: the recalcitrant knights were swept away in a wave of enthusiasm for the wronged prince's cause.

After much negotiation the start was made from Corfù on the eve of Pentecost 1203. "There were all the transports and galleys of the host and many a merchant ship. The day was fair and clear; the wind gentle and mild; the sails were set to the breeze. And Jeffrey de Villehardouin doth truly witness, who never lied in one word to his knowledge, and who was present at every Council, that never was so fair a sight. And verily it seemed that the fleet must subdue the land, for so far as the eye could reach nought could be seen save the sails of ships and of vessels, so that men's hearts did much rejoice." Once again the avenging host set forth, and not against Saracen or Turk but against the capital of Eastern Christendom.

To follow the incidents of the capture and re-capture of Constantinople would take us too far. Venetian and Frank fought with desperate courage. Dandolo by his local knowledge (for he had already been ambassador there), by his iron will, his ready wit and dauntless spirit became leader. It was a stupendous venture. The apparently impregnable city of a million souls was girt by a double rampart of walls and towers, and a moat wide and deep. The attacking force could have barely exceeded 20,000 men. Dandolo was the hero of the siege. At a critical moment the brave old sea-dog was seen erect in his armour on the prow of his galley, the gonfalon of St Mark unfurled before him. His men had wavered; with entreaties and threats he urged them on. The galley was driven ashore and the old fellow[20] leapt on to the beach, the gonfalon being borne before him. From shame and humiliation the

Venetians followed. Twenty towers soon fell into the hands of the Venetians. Meantime news came that the French were in danger. Alexius Angelos at the head of sixty squadrons was about to fall upon them. Dandolo, with characteristic chivalry, let the prize fall from his grasp and hastened to relieve his allies. The very rumour of his coming was enough to scare the craven heart of the Greek prince. He returned within the walls, and having gathered a great treasure of gold and jewels, sought safety and won disgrace by flight. Isaac was led from a dungeon to a throne: his wife recalled to his side: his son restored to him. But his joy was tempered by a hard and one-sided bargain. Fulfilment of the promise made by Philip in the name of young Alexius at Zara was demanded by the allies.

Twenty thousand marks were to be paid to the Venetians; the Greek Church was to recant her heresy and submit to Rome: 10,000 men were to be raised for the Holy Land. Young Alexius as he entered the city in triumph by his bearing and presence won the hearts of the people. But the bond lay heavily on the restored family. Holy vessels and images of the saints were seized and melted; private fortunes were impounded. Yet sacrilege and extortion combined did no more than meet in part the demands of the allies. Disaffection began to show itself. Young Alexius, fearing lest the departure of the crusaders would leave him at the mercy of his fickle subjects, urged his deliverers to winter at Constantinople, and promised to pay the Venetians for the extended hire of the fleet. The more restive barons, chafing at the delay, were overruled by the authority of the Doge. The young Prince gained his purpose. Boniface was bribed by the promise of 1600 pieces of gold to head him (now joint-Emperor with his father) on a tour of the provinces to test the loyalty of his subjects and attempt the capture of his uncle. But his popularity at the capital, already waning, was quenched by the fanatical license of the Latins, who, in destroying a mosque and in spoiling the Jews, wrought the destruction by fire of a whole quarter of the city. On his return, young Alexius had to choose between his subjects and the hatred of the Latins. He was weak and angered both. The allies sternly demanded the execution of his bond. Their envoys with almost incredible daring penetrated to the very throne-room of the palace, passing lines of sullen and angry Greeks eager to leap at their throats. They saw Isaac enthroned, between his wife and son and surrounded by all the luxury and pomp of an Eastern court. In a peremptory voice they delivered their ultimatum, strode proudly from the imperial presence, leaped on their horses, and rode to camp. They were but six, three Venetians and three Franks, who braved the fierce passions of a treacherous populace and the armed retainers of a despotic court. The rage of the Greeks at this insult reacted on the restored family. Alexius Ducas, dubbed Murzuphles from his black and shaggy eyebrows, led the revolt. The Venetian fleet was saved from destruction only by the vigilance of a sentry and the address of the sailors.

The instrument of the popular vengeance was a Prince of far different calibre from his namesake. His unscrupulous ambition was served by energy, resolution and capacity. He first fawned on the young Alexius, then seized his person and saw him strangled. At once grasping the sceptre, the opportune death of Isaac spared him another crime. He sent an envoy with a plausible story to the French camp and an invitation to the chiefs of the army to dine at the palace, but the sagacity of the Doge saved them from the fate that awaited them had they accepted.

After some parley the second siege of Constantinople was decided upon. A plan of operations and the principles on which the booty was to be shared were arranged. It was a tougher job than before. Murzuphles was a resourceful leader; the Greeks were hot with the passion for revenge. Early on the morning of the 9th of April 1204 the assault began. The French made desperate though unsuccessful efforts to scale the walls. But stout old Dandolo heartened his Venetians by an oration thus given by Da Canale:—

"Sirs, marvel not that the French have failed to take the city, for though they be brave men and wise they are not used to climb ships' ladders as you are. Remember what your forefathers did at Tyre, and through Syria and Dalmatia and Romania, where verily no fortress could withstand their onslaught. I know well that ye be of such lineage that no city can be defended against you. And I promise you, by the faith I hold in God, that I will share among you the great treasure within the city; and to the first who shall plant the ensign of Monsignor S. Marco on the walls I will give 1000 perperi; to the second, 800; to the third, 500; to the fourth, 300; to the fifth, 200; and 100 to every one who shall mount the walls. Now, be valiant, that the blood of your forefathers, whose issue ye are, may be proven in you, so that by the help of Jesus Christ and of S. Marco, and by the prowess of your bodies, ye be masters of the city and may enjoy the riches thereof."

On the 12th the second assault was made, and after varying fortune, by a happy change of wind, the huge galleys, the *Pellegrino* and the *Paradiso*, the flagships of the bishops of Soissons and Troyes, firmly locked together, were brought under one of the principal towers of the city. The ladders just reached the summit. Two whose names are preserved to us, Pietro Alberti of Venice and André d'Artoise of France, were the first to win a foothold; their fellows swarmed up, and the tower was won. Meanwhile three gates were battered down. Panic seized the Greeks, and the besiegers rushed in. They stood by their arms all night, and in the morning the enormous riches of the city lay before the victors. It was forbidden to slay, but free scope was allowed to rapine. The sack of the town began, and lasted through Holy Week. "Humanity reddens with shame," says Romanin, "and the mind recoils from telling the story of the horrors committed." The Crusaders' lust was unrestrained even by the sanctity of virgin vows. Nothing was spared. Palaces and houses were ransacked; churches and sanctuaries stripped; priceless statues were melted down; pictures torn to shreds. The Latin Christians wrought more havoc in those few days than Hun, Sclav or Arab had done in as many centuries. The Venetians, says Romanin, *che animo più gentile aveano* (who were a more cultured people), exerted themselves to save as many as possible of the wondrous works of art from destruction.

It had been decided that all the loot should be placed in three churches set apart for that purpose, but large spoils of jewels and of smaller objects of value were secreted by individuals. The worth of the French plunder, after deducting the 50,000 marks due to the Venetians, amounted to the magnificent sum of 400,000 marks. All over Western Europe the monasteries and churches were enriched by reliquaries and precious stones, some of them finding their way as far as Norfolk. The plunder of the city, says Jeffrey, exceeded all that has been witnessed since the creation of the world. The four famous bronze horses of St Mark's formed part of the Venetian spoil. It is related that a hind foot of one of the horses was broken during the transit, and Morosini, the owner of the galley that was freighted with them, begged permission to retain the foot as a memorial. The Senate agreed, and had another foot cast and fitted to the horse. "And," says Sanudo, "I have seen the said foot at the front of Morosini's house in S. Agostino, whence it was afterwards removed to the corner of a house in the SS. Apostoli."

Two master passions dominated the Venetians—to possess living commerce; and dead saints. As a centre of hagiolatry, Venice now became second to Rome. She acquired the bodies of St Simeon the Apostle and of St Lucy, part of the wood of the Holy Cross, some of the Holy Blood, part of the body of St John the Baptist, the arm of St George the Martyr, and the famous image of the Virgin, which still remains the object of Venetian devotion in St Mark's.

The political results were incalculable, for the chief bulwark of the Cross against the growing power of the Crescent was shattered. Six electors were appointed by each of the allies to choose an Emperor. Dandolo by his commanding genius was the obvious choice, but he refused the proffered honour and threw his weight on the side of Baldwin, Count of Flanders, who became the first Latin Emperor of the East. Of the territorial spoils St Mark took indeed the Lion's share. One-fourth formed the Emperor's domain; another fourth was shared among the Frankish lords, Boniface's reward being the sovereignty of Crete and of Salonika. To Venice went one-half—a rich possession, including the Morea, the Ionian islands, the islands of the Archipelago, a large slice of Thessaly, among other cities those of Adrianople, Trajanople and Durazzo, the province of Servia and the coasts of the Hellespont. But the Lion of St Mark had a greedy maw. Like the *Lupa* in the "Inferno," after a meal he was hungrier than before. Crete, the largest and most fertile of Mediterranean islands, was a trading centre of tempting value and covetous eyes were set upon it. Boniface was approached, and for a sum of 10,000 marks the island was transferred to Venice which at one bound rose to be the dominant power in the Levant. To the title of Doge of Venice, Croatia and Dalmatia was now added that of Despot and Lord of one-fourth and one-half of the Romanian Empire. A Venetian—Tomaso Morosini—was appointed to the Partriarchate of Constantinople, and the Chapter filled with his nominees.

But to carve out territory on a map is one thing: effective possession another. Adrianople was recalcitrant. In April 1205, while the united forces of Baldwin and Dandolo were attempting to subdue it, the King of Bulgaria, once spurned by the haughty Latins, appeared with a powerful army to raise the siege. The Latins, attacking with their usual impetuosity, were snared by the enemy's light cavalry; the Emperor and many knights taken prisoners; the main body put to flight. Jeffrey gives a graphic picture of the disaster. The old Doge, infirm but unbroken in spirit, advised a retreat to Constantinople and led the van. The retreat was successfully accomplished but the Latins were in evil plight; their Emperor was a prisoner; Boniface slain; the whole country swarming with the Bulgarian light horse; an Armenian reinforcement wiped out. And now the great Doge, their chief counsellor and leader, worn by disease and privation, died. His long span of life was but two years short of a century. He was buried in June 1205, with due pomp and honours, at St Sophia in a private chapel belonging to the Venetians, "for even the church was divided."

The magnificent tomb erected to perpetuate his memory was destroyed by Mahomet II. and the old hero's breast-plate, helmet, spurs and sword were afterwards given to Gentile Bellini, who brought them back to Venice on his return from the Turkish court. To this day a marble slab remains in the south gallery of the great mosque of S. Sofia with the inscription—Henricus Dandolo. His best epitaph, is the simple phrase of Jeffrey, *mult ere sages et proz* (he was very wise and brave).

SUNSET ON THE ZATTERE.

It was on the 20th of July that a post galley brought the sad news to Venice that her greatest Doge lay dead. Pietro Ziani, a wealthy noble, experienced in Venetian statecraft, was chosen to second him. The Republic had now in fact become an empire. From the mother city along the Gulf of Trieste over Dalmatia, Croatia, the Morea, the islands of Corfù, Crete and the Archipelago from Greece to Constantinople, even up to Syria, the standard of St Mark was planted. Most of the islands were granted in fief to such of the leading Venetian nobles who engaged to secure and maintain effective possession. Crete was made a great feudal colony. Many vassals of the Greek Empire swore allegiance to their new masters and promised tribute. But the cost of empire was soon felt. A new loan was raised. A fleet of forty-three galleys and thirty ships was placed under the joint-command of Premarino and of Dandolo's son Renier, for the seas were swarming with Genoese pirates and a heavy task remained to consolidate and occupy the new possessions. The fleet sailed eastwards and in its way captured the Genoese corsair Liovecchio, an old enemy of the Republic, and twelve galleys; another, Arrigo Bellapolo, with five galleys, met the same fate. The Venetians swept the sea. Da Canale describes them as swooping down like hawks on their quarry. They reached Corfù, hanged Liovecchio and planted a garrison there. Crete, ever a stubborn and rebellious vassal, gave more trouble. Renier Dandolo was slain, and many a stout Venetian bit the dust or died a sailor's death ere the dominion of Venice was made good. The Latins meanwhile had recovered themselves at Constantinople, but their empire was a shadow; the real masters were the Venetian governor and his ubiquitous officials. Baldwin I. did not long survive his captivity. The story of Joseph and Potiphar's wife was enacted in his person and that of the Bulgarian queen. He met a horrible death at the hands of the abused king and his successor and brother, Henry of Flanders, held unquiet possession of the Empire for ten years, continually fighting against stubborn vassals. Henry's sister, Yolande, and her consort, Peter of Courtenay, next sat on the unstable throne. Their son Robert, a feeble prince, succeeded. His incapacity and the anarchic state of the Empire, raised the most vital problem that ever Venetian statesmen were called to face. Events seemed inevitably tending to one solution—that they who were masters in fact of the new Latin Empire should proclaim themselves so in name. Doge Ziani called a meeting of the Great Council and put forward a proposition, fraught with tremendous issues, that the seat of the Government should be transferred from Venice to Constantinople. The orations made by Ziani for and by the venerable Angelo Faliero against the revolutionary motion are given at great length by the chroniclers. A curious passage in the speech attributed to Faliero recalls Macaulay's famous New Zealander: "A few years hence perchance," cried the old statesman, "some Venetian traveller calling at these islands will find our canals choked, our dykes levelled, and our dwellings razed. He will see a few pilgrims wandering amid the ruins of our rich monasteries, a scanty and fever-stricken population; and a foreign ruler will be sitting in this very hall dictating laws to what was once Venice." When the motion was put to the vote the ballots for and against were found to be equal, and a casting vote decided the fate of Venice. It was known afterwards as the vote of Providence.

CHAPTER V

Peace and War—The Holy Inquisition—Conflict with the Genoese—Loss of Constantinople

"Who hath taken this counsel against ... the crowning city, whose merchants are princes, whose traffickers are the honourable of the earth."—Isaiah.

THE Easter of 1214, falling in a year of general peace and prosperity in Italy, was celebrated by many great festivals. The Trevisans had sent invitations to the whole surrounding country, especially to the Venetians, and never was so magnificent a spectacle. The procession of the Trade Guilds was witnessed by a great multitude, among whom were 2600 noble gentlemen and 3600 gentlewomen with a numerous train of squires and pages and ladies-in-waiting. The principal feature was a Castle of Love erected in the Piazza, with portcullis and turrets complete, decorated inside and out with precious tapestry and other sumptuous ornaments, wherein were placed the fairest and most graceful dames and damsels richly clothed with silk and resplendent with jewels.

It was ordained that they should be striven for *per amore* by three companies of noble youths. On the one part the Trevisans essayed to effect a surrender to them by calling, *"Madama Beatrice, Madama Fiordelice! ora pro nobis!"* On the other part the Paduans exhorted the ladies to yield to them, and shot into the Castle sweets, pasties, tarts and roast chicken that they might eat and be well-disposed. But, if we may believe Sanudo, the Venetians, with a profounder insight into feminine psychology, cast in, with nutmegs, ginger, cinnamon and sweet-smelling spices, *some ducats and other coins.* The fair garrison, seeing the *gentilezza* of the Venetian youths at once capitulated. Whereupon was great rejoicing and the standard of St Mark was run up on the Castle ramparts. This proved too much for the Paduans; they waxed wroth and tore down the Venetian standard and broke it to pieces. An undignified scuffle ensued and the celebration of peace ended in open war. The Paduans aided by the Trevisans, wasted Venetian territory, advancing near to Chioggia and threatening the fortress of Bebbe, but by the prompt action of the Podestà of Chioggia, who called out the militia without waiting for orders, the garrison was relieved and the Paduans routed. Four hundred prisoners were made, among whom were two hundred nobles, and taken to Venice. The Paduan prisoners were humiliated—it is said by offering ten of them to any Venetian who brought a white hen—and afterwards released without ransom through the mediation of the Patriarch of Aquileia. The Chioggians were relieved of a tribute of twenty couples of hens due to the Doge, and their Podestà was richly rewarded.

For twenty-five years save one, Ziani presided over the destinies of the Republic. Her commercial influence was extended. Valuable treaties were concluded with Germany, Hungary, Aleppo, Egypt and Barbary.

"In this reign," says Sanudo, "were two most saintly men, Francis of Assisi and Domenic of Spain. Now St Francis returning[21] from beyond the seas came to Venice where he found that many birds were come to sing on the boughs of the trees in the marshes. He having gone thither with his companion, stood in the midst of the birds reciting the offices and commanded them to be silent; whereupon they kept silence, nor did they depart until he had given them leave. And he stayed in a certain oratory where at present are a church and monastery of the friars called San Francesco del Deserto." The traveller to-day on his way to Torcello will see in the distance on his right hand the island and monastery, with its picturesque setting of pine and cypress. It is still inhabited by a few brothers and recalls the sweetest, gentlest human soul that ever breathed since Him of Galilee.

The choice of Ziani's successor gave rise to a novel incident. The votes of the College were equally divided between Marino Dandolo and Giacomo Tiepolo. For five days they were scrutinised in the vain hope of finding a casting vote. The Senate then authorised an appeal to chance. Lots were cast, and fortune declared in favour of Giacomo Tiepolo on the 6th of March 1229. During the interregnum between the resignation of Ziani and the election of his successor opportunity was taken to strengthen still further the power of the aristocracy and to weaken that of the Doge. A Board of Correctors of the Ducal *Promissione* or Coronation oath, and another of Inquisitors of the dead Doge were formed. The former was composed of five men of great wisdom and experience, whose duty it was to examine and reform the *Promissione* at the death of each Doge. On the latter board three sat who were charged to listen to the complaints of those who felt aggrieved at any action of the late Doge; to examine his papers for any unpaid debts, and award praise or blame of his conduct whether as citizen or as head of the state. As a result, the *Promissione Ducale* exacted from Dandolo and Ziani was made still more stringent in the case of Tiepolo. He was forbidden to communicate with foreign princes or to interfere in ecclesiastical matters: he was made to pay taxes. The *Promissione* sworn by Tiepolo is given in full by Romanin, and covers nine closely-printed large octavo pages. The details are curious: the number of his cooks was fixed; he swore to receive no gifts nor presents of any kind from any person save and except rosewater, flowers, sweet-smelling herbs and balsam, "which it shall be lawful for us and our agents to receive."

ISLE OF S. FRANCESCO DEL DESERTO.

A great work was done in the codification and reform of the statute laws. The navigation laws were made a model of humane legislation.

Meanwhile anxious eyes were again turned to the East. As the Latin kingdom waned the Republic had increased her power at Constantinople, and in return for naval services the arsenal was ceded to her. On the death of Robert Courtenay the crown descended to his brother, Baldwin II., a lad of ten. But in stirring times a child emperor was impossible, and John of Brienne, titular king of Jerusalem, a heroic old crusader, was during his minority chosen as Emperor.

John of Brienne had filled his thankless office but two years when the capital was menaced by the allied forces of the Emperor of Nicea and the King of Bulgaria. It was a critical moment. The Latin army was much reduced by desertion, and it is said Brienne had less than two hundred knights and four hundred footmen to oppose an army of many tens of thousands. But the brave old Emperor—he was eighty years of age—put himself at the head of his little band and sallied forth to meet the host. An impetuous charge scattered them like chaff. The Venetians, too, were not slack. An urgent message had been sent for help, and a fleet of twenty galleys was hastily sent to Constantinople, which swooped down on the Greek fleet at the entrance to the Dardanelles. The whole *Armata* and transports were destroyed or taken, and the Venetian admirals made triumphant entry into Constantinople to receive the felicitations of the Emperor. Two years later the Greeks were again foiled by the irresistible onslaught of the Venetian and Latin fleets.

At the death of John of Brienne financial ruin was impending and a strange expedient was adopted to raise a loan. Of the sanctuary spoils at the taking of Constantinople, the crown of thorns had been appointed to the emperor. It was now brought forth with the lance of the passion and mortgaged to the Venetian Bailo of Constantinople, Alberto Morosini, for the loan of 14,000 *perperi* subscribed by the leading merchants. The bill fell due: the money was not forthcoming and the security was legally forfeited. But a third party was found in the person of a rich Venetian banker, who, towards the end of the year 1237, advanced the sum for a month to give breathing time. If the payment was again deferred the lender might remove the relic to Venice for a period of four months, which being expired the mortgagee was empowered to foreclose. Meanwhile the saintly king, Louis IX. of France, had heard of the transaction and was much scandalised. He sent two Dominicans to Constantinople to redeem the pledge and secure the precious relic for Paris. It was, however, already on its way to Venice when the two black friars reached the capital of the Empire. The good ship that was freighted with the thorns arrived at Venice on the 4th of September 1238. Hastily the envoys retraced their steps and sought an audience of Tiepolo, who straightway led them to St Mark's and showed them the sacred treasure. They then went to the banker and offered the money to redeem the pledge. It was handed to the friars who returned joyfully to Paris. King Louis, barefoot and in his shirt, took part in the solemn procession that accompanied the relic through the streets of Paris and the Sainte Chapelle, the richest gem of Gothic architecture in North Europe, was built to receive it.

Commercial expansion continued through Tiepolo's reign. Trieste renewed her fealty and treaties were concluded with Ravenna, Padua and Ragusa. The Sultans of Aleppo and of Egypt confirmed and extended privileges granted to the Venetians, and owing to the skill of their ambassadors Barbary and Armenia were generous in concessions. To the tale of saintly relics were added the bodies of St Marina and of St Paul the first hermit, minus the head.

"In Tiepolo's time," says Sanudo, "so I have read, our citizens went as magistrates to all the cities of Italy, for they were righteous men." They were usually chosen by the free communes of Lombardy, where their capacity and incorruptibility made them eagerly sought for. The Doge's son, Pietro, ruled at Treviso; a Zeno at Bologna; a Morosini at Faenza; a Dandolo at Conegliano; a Badoer at Padua. The cities of the Lombard League deposited their funds with Venetian bankers. The papacy which had consistently taken the side of the free cities of Italy against the western emperors now found herself sorely pressed in her fierce struggle with Frederic II. Pope Gregory IX. turned with longing eyes to the one Italian state that could decide the contest. Desire for vengeance and state policy made it easy for Venice to join the league—at a price. Eccelino da Romano, at Frederic's instigation, had devastated Venetian territory up to Mestre and Murano to punish the Republic for her moral support to the league. It was agreed that the Venetians should fit out a punitive expedition to Sicily, of which half the cost was to be met by the Pope, who promised moreover to cede Bari and Salpi to them and to grant in feud all the territory they might conquer in Apulia and Sicily.

Ferrara, formerly held from the Holy See by Azzo of Este, had become a Ghibelline stronghold and Azzo had been banished. To Venice happily Guelph and Ghibelline were but names. No factions destroyed her domestic peace; no feudal tyrants spoiled her citizens, or fury of popular jealousy flung itself against her nobles. But in Ferrara valuable trading rights granted by the Countess Matilda and maintained by the Guelphs were ignored by the Ghibellines. The restoration of these rights was made the price of her alliance with the Papal forces in an attack on Ferrara. The siege was a long one. The city was defended by the Imperialists under the most famous soldier of the day, Taurelli Salinguerra. At a critical moment the Papal legate appealed for help to the Doge, who, impelled by memories of his great predecessor, determined to take command of the forces in person. His son was left to rule in his absence, and after mass in the Church of Santo Spirito the expedition sailed forth, the Bucintoro, with the Doge on board, leading. Ferrara was subdued and the Doge was careful before leaving to exact from the restored Azzo the reinstatement of the Venetians in their former advantageous position as traders. Meanwhile the naval expedition had reached Apulia and after devastating many cities, returned to Venice with a rich booty.

Tiepolo is said to have possessed a prodigious memory. "This note I have found," says Sanudo, "*solum* in one chronicle, yet it was the truth. This Doge was very wise and had great fame through all parts of the world. When any ambassadors came to deliver their suits he held his eyes shut: after he had heard he recited chapter by chapter and answered everything which they had expounded in such manner that all marvelled greatly at so profound a memory, for he was a most wise Doge." On the 20th of May, 1249, Tiepolo, weary of his burden of the state, laid it down to retire to his house in S. Agostino.

The foundation in 1234 of the Dominican Monastery and Church of Santi Giovanni e Paolo (S. Zanipolo) was due, the chroniclers relate, to the piety of the Doge, who saw in a vision the oratory and neighbouring Piazza of San Danieli filled with flowers and white doves bearing on their heads crowns of gold, and two angels came down from heaven and perfumed the place with golden censers. Then a voice was heard saying: "This is the spot I have chosen for my preachers." Thereupon the Doge made over certain marshy lands near Santa Maria Formosa to Brother Alberico of the Dominicans, and aided by papal favour and the piety of individuals the building was so far advanced by 1293 that it was ready to accommodate the general chapter of the order. The facade was finished in 1351, and after the lapse of a century the mortal remains of the founder were laid there. His simple tomb wrought with figures of doves and angels, recalling the visions, still exists on the left of the entrance. The great church and monastery of the rival order of friars, S. Maria Gloriosa dei Frari, was also begun in Tiepolo's reign. Until that time the friars of St Francis, says Sanudo, had no monastery in this city and dwelt near S. Lorenzo, where they worked with their hands and lived by their labour and by alms.

At Tiepolo's death the electoral college increased to forty-one, chose Marin Morosini, an experienced magistrate and civil servant, as his successor. Meantime the Inquisitors had met and decided that the late Doge had been too zealous in the advancement of his sons. A new clause was therefore added to the coronation oath forbidding the Doge to ask or cause to be asked any office for any person, or to accept any charge outside Venetian jurisdiction or in Istria.

The short reign of Morosini was marked by one important innovation. The Republic by tradition and policy was eminently tolerant. It was essential to a great commercial metropolis that men of all nations and of all creeds should freely assemble and carry on their business without fear of ecclesiastical penalties. Venice therefore had consistently refused to admit the tribunal of the Holy Inquisition within her boundaries. In the *Promissione Ducale* of Morosini, however, an article was inserted by virtue of which the Doge was ordered to name in agreement with his Council certain religious men of integrity and wisdom who were to search out heretics, and commit to the flames those who were declared to be such by the Patriarch of Grado or any of the bishops of the Dogado. But before condemnation the consent of the Doge and his Council had first to be obtained. The Republic thus asserted her authority and defended her subjects from arbitrary and ecclesiastical domination. This, however, was far from satisfying the papal authorities. The Venetians were repeatedly exhorted to admit the jurisdiction of the Holy Office itself, but nothing further was effected until 1289 when it was decided to accept the Inquisition, but under stringent limitations. Two of the three Inquisitors appointed by the Pope were made subject to the veto of the Doge. Three lay representatives, *the Savii all'Eresia*,[22] over whom the Vatican should have no power to assert direct or indirect power, were to be present at every session of the tribunal with the object of preventing abuses, false accusations, or any exercise of arbitrary power. They had the right to suspend proceedings or stay execution of sentences, and were charged to keep the Government informed of all that transpired at the sessions of the Holy Office. Generally they were to maintain the purity of the faith while safeguarding the rights of the State. No extradition was allowed. The property of condemned heretics[23] was to descend to their heirs. The funds of the

Holy Office were to be under the charge of a Venetian treasurer who was to render his account and be responsible to the civil authorities alone.

Morosini's reign was a peaceful and happy one. "So long as he was Doge," says Da Canale, "the Venetians were doubly blest, and with joy and gladness their hearts were filled. Every man, rich or poor, increased his substance, for Messer Marino Morosini was right gracious and none durst assail him in war. His ships went beyond the seas to all places without guard of galleys: he had peace with all: the sea in his time was void of robbers."

The advent of Renier Zeno in 1253 to the Ducal throne was marked by a further suppression of popular rights. It was decreed that, before publication of the new Doge's name by the electoral college of the forty-one, the people should swear to accept their choice. The blow was accompanied by an application of Napoleon's favourite device—Amuse the people with toys. A magnificent tournament and gorgeous processions celebrated the new Doge's election and enthronement. Zeno was a tried administrator and soldier; he had commanded as *podestà* the Bolognese forces at the siege of Ferrara. Nor did his military genius rust for lack of use. In his troublous reign of sixteen years began the long and exhausting struggle with Genoa for naval supremacy and commercial monopoly.

At St Jean d'Acre was a church dedicated to St Sabbas, and there the Genoese and Venetians were wont to worship in common—each, however, claiming exclusive ownership in the building. A dispute as to an alleged Venetian corsair captured by the Genoese ended in a riot. The Genoese raided the Venetian ships, sacked their quarter of the city, and burnt the church.

After vain and perhaps insincere attempts at pacification Venice determined to wreak vengeance on her rival, and in 1286 Lorenzo Tiepolo was despatched with a fleet to Acre. He spoiled and burned the Genoese vessels in harbour, landed and destroyed part of their settlement, and after some fighting captured their stronghold, the castle of Mongioia. They sued for a truce, which was granted for two months. As trophies and palpable sign of his success, Tiepolo sent to Venice the short column of porphyry which now stands at the south-west angle of St Mark's known as the *Pietra di Bando*, (proclamation stone), because there were promulgated the laws of the Republic; and the two beautifully decorated, square, marble columns that stand side by side facing the Piazzetta, over against the south side of the church.

The truce was a hollow one. Each side was eager to try its strength again, and fleets were hastily collected. A desperate battle was fought between Acre and Tyre. The Genoese were defeated and their admiral was taken prisoner. Meanwhile a second Venetian squadron raided the Genoese settlements all over the Levant. Domestic troubles at Genoa prevented for a time further action, but in 1258 a new fleet was fitted out and set sail under Rosso della Turca to retrieve her fortunes. The Venetians, too, had reinforced their admiral, and the hostile squadrons met on Midsummer Day near the scene of Tiepolo's former victory. A day was spent in vain attempts by the Genoese admiral to outmanœuvre his enemy. On the morrow he was forced to give battle. Before the action Tiepolo delivered a stirring oration to his men, exhorting them to brave deeds. He bade them remember that the honour of Venice, the command and security of the seas, were at stake. A great shout of *Viva San Marco protettore del Veneto dominio* was raised, and the attack began. It was a long, bloody and stubborn fight. In the end the Venetians were again victorious. Twenty-five galleys and 2600 men were captured and sent to Venice, the prisoners being lodged in St Mark's granaries. The remainder of the fleet was scattered and Tiepolo's damaged vessels returned to Acre to refit, where the Venetians in the heat of victory stained their country's reputation by a wanton attack on the Genoese quarter, which they sacked and burned.

It was a heartrending spectacle to Christian Europe: another act in that pitiful and suicidal struggle between the two most powerful maritime states which in the end reduced one to impotence, and left the other too exhausted to resist the advancing tide of Turkish conquest. The Papacy, generally solicitous to compose the differences of Christian states, intervened, and an honourable but temporary peace was made.

S. MARCO, FROM COLONNADE OF PALAZZO DUCALE.

Three years passed and a fresh storm burst in the East. Under the feeble rule of Baldwin II. the Latin Empire was tottering to its fall. Self-indulgence and corruption had destroyed the character of the Frankish knights, death, desertion and private interest had reduced their numbers. The Emperor, poor futile creature, had employed most of his reign in wandering about Europe from court to court, whining for outside help. The Crown of Thorns had already been pledged, the rich jewels and precious objects *alla greca*, the beautiful icons of gold and silver, known in Sanudo's time as the jewels of St Mark, had followed, and the emperor's son was now left at Venice, a princely pawn, for a loan advanced by the Cappellos. Meanwhile by the energy of her princes the Greek empire of Nicea was being welded into a powerful military state. In 1260, Michael Paleologus, guardian of the heir to the throne, had bid for and won the imperial office. To make his hold secure he aimed at nothing less than the restoration of the Greek Empire at Constantinople. By prudent and virile measures he had collected an army of 25,000 men near the city under the command of his favourite general, Alexios. One of the gates was treacherously opened by night. The city was entered; the Greek inhabitants, weary of alien domination, welcomed the invaders, and the imperial city that cost the apostasy of a Christian army, two sieges and the flower of Frankish chivalry, was lost in a night. Venice truly had long foreseen the danger, and had kept a great armament in the Bosphorus to watch events. Was she playing for a higher stake and hoping ultimately to pick up the falling Frankish sceptre? *Chi sa?* What did happen to the amazement and disgust of the Home Government was that the fleet, when the critical moment came, was away on a punitive expedition in Thrace, and returned only in time to receive the fugitive Baldwin and the Venetian governor. The crestfallen admirals gazed impotently at the reddening sky, on a multitude of their fellow-countrymen and their allies on the shore stretching forth their hands to implore protection, and heard the cries of the victims, and the exultant shouts of the conquerors in the city. On the 26th of July 1261, Michael Paleologus made a triumphant entry into Constantinople, once more the capital of the Greek Empire, and the pillage was stayed. It was a bitter humiliation to Venice. She knew the Genoese had secretly allied themselves with the new Emperor, and soon learned the price of the alliance. The island of Chios, a Venetian possession, was made over to them for a trading station. The very palace of the Venetian governor was surrendered to them, and later was razed, the more precious of its marble decorations being sent as spoil to Genoa.

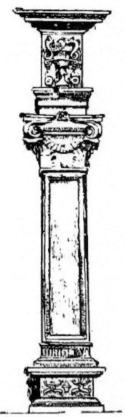

DETAIL: PALAZZO ZICHY-ESTERHAZY

Negropont, a Venetian fief, was with Michael's approval seized and the Venetians expelled. All the results of more than fifty years' effort and sacrifice were lost in a few hours, and the proud masters of the masters of the Latin Empire found themselves degraded to the level of Pisa in the city they perhaps regarded as their ultimate prize.

CHAPTER VI

The Duel with Genoa—The Closing of the Great Council

"The dire aspect
Of civil wounds ploughed up with neighbours' swords."
—*Shakespeare.*

BUT Venice was yet in the full vigour and buoyancy of lusty manhood, and nerved herself to regain her lost position. Alone among the Italian states she was able to evoke a fervent, whole-hearted patriotism. Rich and poor, patrician and plebeian were stirred. To the amazement of her enemies, fleet after fleet was expedited against the Genoese. Some minor engagements were fought with varying success, and at length the two powers met off Trapani in 1264 for a final battle. The Genoese were superior in numbers, and had the wind in their favour. The Venetians, having intoned the gospel for the day and called for help on Christ and Monsignor S. Marco, began the attack. A fierce struggle ensued on the interlocked vessels, which formed a vast battlefield. The carnage was terrible. At length Venetian courage and Venetian skill inflicted a crushing defeat on the Genoese, who lost the whole of their fleet.

The affection of the Greek Emperor for the Genoese was now chilled; he sued for terms, and after much debate, in which the forward party in Venice vainly pushed their policy of founding a new empire, with its centre at Constantinople, a treaty was signed in 1268, by which Venice recovered her commercial standing in the capital, though she chafed under the necessity of tolerating the presence of her rivals.

S. MARCO—FAÇADE AND CAMPANILE

In 1265 the banner of the Cross was again raised in Venice, this time against an Italian prince, Eccelino da Romano, the black-browed monster of Padua, who for his infamous cruelty was immersed by Dante up to his eyes among the tyrants in the river of boiling blood. A platform was erected in the Piazza, from which the papal legate, the Archbishop of Ravenna, inveighed against the atrocities committed by the *serverissimo tiranno* whom the Pope had excommunicated, declaring that if he were permitted to live longer it would be to the shame of Christendom. The Doge made an oration in support of the crusade, and Venice joined the league against the tyrant. Eventually Padua was stormed and captured, Eccelino's victims released, himself in a later engagement mortally wounded by a bowshot. He fell, asking the name of the place where he was struck. "Sire," replied his attendant, "it is called Cassano." An astrologer had foretold that he should die at Bassano. "Bassano, Cassano," the dying lord was heard to mutter, "small difference is there between Bassano and Cassano." He plucked the arrow from the wound, thrust aside a friar who sought to confess him and died impenitent. Never was such joy in Italy, says Da Canale, as when the news came that the tyrant, more cruel than Pharaoh or Herod, was slain. The bells were rung all over Venice in praise of God, even as they do on saints' days. In the evening all the towers were illuminated with candles and torches so that it was a great marvel to see. The same annalist, writing of Venice with all the enthusiasm of an Elizabethan singing the praises of England, gives a vivid picture of his native city as it appeared towards the end of the thirteenth century. "In the year of the Incarnation of our Lord 1267, I, Martin da Canale, toiled and travailed so that I found the ancient story of the Venetians and how they made the fairest, noblest and pleasantest city in the world, filled with all beauty and excellency. And I have set me to translate this story for the honour of that city men call Vinegia from Latin into French, for that language hath course throughout the whole world and is more delightful to read and to hear than any other. For I would have all men to know, who may travel thither, how the noble city is built; how filled with all good things and how mighty is the lord of the Venetians, the most noble Doge; how powerful are her nobles; how full of prowess her people and how all are perfect in the faith of Jesus and to Holy Church obedient, for within that noble Venice neither heretic, nor usurer, nor murderer, nor thief, nor robber dares dwell. And I pray Jesus Christ and His sweet mother, St Mary, and Monsignor St Mark, the Evangelist (in whom after Jesus Christ we have put our trust), that they may grant health and long life to Monsignor the Doge and to the Venetians. From all places come merchants and merchandise, and goods run through that city even as waters do from fountains. Provisions in abundance men find there, and bread and wine and land-fowl and water-fowl, meat, fresh and salt, and great fish from the sea and from the rivers. You shall find within that fair city a multitude of old men and youths, who, for their nobleness, are much praised; merchants, and bankers, and craftsmen, and sailors of all kinds, and ships to carry to all places, and great galleys to the hurt of her enemies. There, too, are fair ladies, youths and maidens adorned most richly." The chronicler describes the Piazza much as we see it in Gentile Bellini's picture (p. 262). "St Mark's is the most beautiful square in the world. Towards the east is the fairest church in the whole world, the Church of Monsignor St Mark, and next is the palace of Monsignor the Doge, great and most marvellously beautiful. Towards the south is the end of the Piazza over the sea, and on the side of that Piazza (the Piazzetta) is the palace of Monsignor the Doge, and on the other side are palaces to house the commoners, and these hold as far as the Campanile of St Mark, which is so great and high that the like could not be found. And there, next the Campanile, is a hospital which Madonna the Dogaressa has built to receive the sick, and men call it the Hospital of St Mark. Next are the palaces of the treasurers, whom the Venetians call the procurators of St Mark, and next to their mansions are the palaces to lodge nobles, and these houses go far along the Piazza up to a church (S. Geminiano). On the other side (N.) are noble buildings for high barons and gentlemen, and these reach as far as the church of St Mark."

The firm hand kept by the aristocracy on civil government was felt during Zeno's reign. The Genoese were too high-spirited to submit to terms while under the shame of defeat and a new naval war was imminent. To meet the cost the corn tax was increased and a bread riot took place on the Piazza. The Doge tried in vain to reason with the mob, and at last was driven to resort to force. Troops were levied; the sedition was crushed; the ringleaders were beheaded between the red columns. But when order was restored the obnoxious tax was quietly withdrawn. The Government was severe to aristocratic brawlers. Two of the Dandolo family sided with the people, and Lorenzo Tiepolo, son of Doge Giacomo, headed the Government party. The rival leaders met in the streets and Tiepolo was assaulted. The Dandoli were at once heavily fined and a law was passed forbidding the people to have the escutcheons of any nobles painted on their houses or to wear any of their emblems. The Doge died in 1268 and was honoured with a sumptuous State funeral in S. Zanipolo.

Before the election of a successor the most complicated machinery ever devised by the wit of man for the election of a chief magistrate was elaborated by the Venetian aristocracy.

The youngest of the Privy Councillors having invoked the divine blessing in St Mark's, issued forth and laid hands on the first boy he met on the Piazza. Meantime the Great Council met and having excluded all members who were under thirty years of age, those that remained were counted. Ballots equal in number to the purged Council were then prepared, into thirty of which was inserted a piece of parchment inscribed with the word "*lector.*" The ballots[24] were placed in a hat; the captured boy was introduced and bidden to draw out the ballots and hand one to each Councillor. The ballots were then opened and the thirty who held the parchment stayed in the chamber; the others left. The thirty reduced themselves to nine by the same process; which nine sat in close conclave until they had chosen forty, each by a majority of at least seven votes. These forty were reduced by lot to twelve. The twelve elected twenty-five, each by a majority of at least nine votes. The twenty-five were again reduced to nine, who chose forty-five, each by at least seven votes. The forty-five reduced themselves to eleven who made the final choice of forty-one by at least nine votes each. The electoral college of forty-one thus formed, having heard the Mass of the Holy Ghost, met and chose three presidents and two secretaries. Each elector in turn placed the name of his candidate in an urn. The secretaries unfolded the papers and read out the names. The papers were again folded and placed in the urn and one was extracted. If the candidate thus selected were in the room, he was ordered to withdraw, and each elector invited to state his objections to him. The candidate was then called in to refute any charges made against him, and a last vote was taken for or against the candidate. If he obtained twenty-five ballots he was declared Doge. The election was proclaimed, and a deputation led the Doge-elect to the Ducal Palace, and then by the ducal staircase to St Mark's. He ascended the marble pulpit to the left of the choir and showed himself to the people. Having heard mass, he swore fealty to the State and to observe its laws. The Primicerio then solemnly invested him with the ducal mantle and handed him the standard of the Republic. He was then chaired and made the usual tour of the Piazza, distributing largess to the people. Afterwards he ascended the great staircase (after the Giants' Staircase was built he stood between the statues of Mars and Neptune), where the oldest Councillor placed the ducal cap on his head. A banquet given by the Doge to the electors completed the ceremony.

DOGE'S PALACE FROM ISOLA S. GIORGIO.

Such, with slight modifications, was the machinery by which the Doges were elected until the fall of the Republic. The ceremony over, public festivities followed. By Da Canale's vivid description of the rejoicings that attended the election of Lorenzo Tiepolo in 1268 we are able to gain some idea of what they were like. "On the day of S. Apollinare was such great joy in Venice that the mouth of man could not tell of it. For the Venetians had remembrance of Messer Jacopo Tiepolo, father of Lorenzo, how noble and debonnair, how famous for good deeds he was, and great were their hopes of Messer Lorenzo." Soon as the good news was known the bells rang a glad peal, and all the people, even the little children, ran to St Mark's shouting, "Messer Lorenzo Tiepolo is made Doge!" After mass and consecration he was given the gonfalon of St Mark all of gold. Having ascended the palace stairs he stood, gonfalon in hand, while the lauds[25] were sung, and again swore fealty to the people and spake wisely to them. Meanwhile his chaplains went to S. Agostino to fetch the Dogaressa, and to her also were praises sung. On the morrow, having made a public reconciliation with the Dandoli, a naval review was held on the Grand Canal in front of the Ducal Palace, led by Pietro Michiel, who with a great fleet of galleys was about to sail overseas. Choirs were aboard who sang the ducal lauds. The waters were alive with boats of all kinds, those of Torcello and Murano adorned with banners and shields distinguishing themselves by their splendour. A grand procession of Guilds next defiled before the Doge. First came the master smiths, two by two, each wearing a garland, accompanied by their trumpeters and other musicians and by their standard-bearers. As they came in front of the Doge they saluted him and wished him long life and victory. His serenity returned a gracious answer, and they then went their way shouting, "*Viva nostro Signor Messer Lorenzo Tiepolo,*" to S. Agostino, to salute the Dogaressa. Then followed the furriers, dressed in ermine, calimanco and taffeta; the tanners, richly clothed in rare furs and bearing silver cups and phials filled with wine; the weavers, clad in finest cloth; the tailors, magnificently arrayed in white garments, adorned with vermilion stars and trimmed with furs, "and the great joy they made must be truly told, for they set their gonfalon in front, with trumpets and instruments of music, and gave themselves up to great gladness, singing *canzoni* and folk-songs; and having in their turn saluted their new lord right well, went their way to Madame the Dogaressa rejoicing exceedingly." The wool-workers bore olive branches in their hands and garlands of olive on their heads—they, too, were filled with great joy. The silk-weavers, "they that make pellisses right richly," decked their bodies all anew with coats and mantles of fustian. The makers of quilts and doublets, to honour their lord, arrayed themselves newly with cloaks of white, trimmed with *fleur-de-lys*, and each cloak had a hood richly dight with pearls set in gold; little children marched in front of them. The makers of cloth of gold were apparelled in cloth of purple and of gold, with crowns of pearls set in gold; the shoemakers and mercers in fine silk and cloth of gold; the cheesemongers and pork butchers in cloth of scarlet and purple and divers colours, wearing garlands of pearls and gold; the fishmongers and poulterers followed, "and know, sirs, that right well should Messer Lorenzo Tiepolo have them that sold fish in remembrance as they passed, for many a fair trout and sturgeon and other great fish had he obtained from them." The glass-makers bore some of the finest of their wares in their group, and the comb-makers a cage full of birds of all kinds, and as they passed, opened the door and set the birds free to delight the Doge. And "there, sirs, you would have heard great laughter on all sides." But the barber surgeons were they that most distinguished themselves by their ingenuity. They had with them two men on horseback armed cap-à-pie, called knights-errant, who escorted four damsels, most gorgeously apparelled, two on fair steeds and two on foot. On reaching the Doge one of the horsemen dismounted and making obeisance, cried: "Sire, we be two knights-errant who rode to seek adventure, and enduring pains and travail have won these fair damsels. Now are we come to your Court, and if there be any knight who is minded to prove his body and win these strange damsels we are ready to defend them." "Sirs," answered the Doge, "ye are welcome, and may the Lord let you rejoice in your conquest, for I will that ye be honoured at my Court." The knight then remounted his steed and all cried, "Long live our lord, Messer Lorenzo Tiepolo," and went their way to repeat the play before the Dogaressa.

How many were the Guilds that took part in the procession we know not for Da Canale stays his narrative to tell of the Genoese wars, after describing the goldsmiths wearing on their caps and cloaks, pearls and gold and silver, sapphires, emeralds, jacinths, amethysts, jaspers and carbuncles and other precious stones. After the procession an exhibition was held in the palace, of all the arts of Venice, in honour of the Dogaressa.

Scarcely had the echoes of the music and shouting in the Piazza died away when the gaunt spectre of famine hovered over Venice. The wheat harvest had failed in Europe, the Crusaders had devastated Africa, and she appealed to her allies on the mainland for help. A strong state ever fighting for its own hand may win the respect born of fear, but sympathy, never. The entreaties of Venice fell on deaf ears. Strenuous efforts were made to collect cargoes of corn from Dalmatia, Greece and even Asia. In the nick of time a small consignment came in from Dalmatia and was immediately distributed with absolute impartiality among the people. When the pressure was relieved, a corn office, consisting of three *magistrati delle Biade*, was created to control the corn trade and take measures to prevent any future possibility of famine. The bas-relief in the Ducal Palace, now known as the Cobden Madonna (p. 253), commemorates the wise means adopted by these magistrates in a time of scarcity two centuries later.

The coronation oath sworn to by Tiepolo was made even more stringent on the accession of Jacopo Contarini in 1275. The Doge was fast becoming little more than the official mouthpiece of the aristocracy. A clause binding the Doge to keep himself informed of the number of prisoners in the cells at the Ducal Palace and to see that each and every prisoner should be brought to trial within a month of his incarceration, demonstrates how careful the aristocracy were to justify power by wise principles of government. Contarini was an old man of eighty when he accepted office, and after six years retired on an annuity of 1500 lire, the first pension ever granted to a Doge. The steady pursuance of commercial aggrandisement brought Venice in the previous reign into conflict with Bologna. Duties were levied on all ships trading in the ports between Ravenna and Fiume, and a captain of the Gulf of Adria appointed to exact them by force of arms. It was only too apparent that Venice aimed at making the whole Adriatic a Venetian sea, and in 1283 the territories of the Republic in Dalmatia were menaced by a formidable coalition of Aquileia, Ancona, and the Count of Goritz.

The Republic replied by laying siege to Trieste. During the armistice granted by Morosini, the Venetian commander, to enable the Patriarch of Aquileia to bury his nephew, fallen in battle, a certain Contestabile of Infantry, Gerard of the Long Lances, was found to have corresponded with the enemy by means of slips of paper attached to his arrows. He confessed under torture and was shot from a mangonel into the enemy's camp, a mangled mass of treachery. The siege was, however, a failure, and Morosini on his return was disgraced and imprisoned. The victorious allies marched on Caorle, captured the *podestà* and burned his palace: they even singed the very mane of the Lion of St Mark by a descent on Malamocco. The executive, endowed with unlimited powers, made a levy *en masse* on the whole able-bodied population, another armament was fitted out and at length Trieste fell. The Pope, anxious to buttress the tottering fabric of the Latin dominion in the East, effected a peace, and a huge bonfire in the Piazza made of the surrendered Triestine artillery satisfied Venetian pride, though her attempt to dominate the Adriatic was but partially successful.

The sleepless eyes of Venetian statesmen were now turned southwards. Constance of Swabia, unhappy Manfred's

"bella figlia, genitrice
dell' onor di Cicilia e d' Aragona,"[26]

by her marriage brought the strong arm of Peter of Aragon to enforce her claims to the throne of the Two Sicilies, which the Pope's darling, Charles of Anjou, had won by the defeat of Manfred and the destruction of the Ghibelline cause at Benevento.

The Republic, still smarting under the commercial condominium of the Genoese at Constantinople, and enticed by the prospect of regaining her former ascendency, was drawn into an offensive and defensive alliance with the Pope and Charles against the Greeks. But on Easter Eve, in 1282, an insult offered to a noble Sicilian damsel by a French soldier fired the rage of the Sicilians, and before the dawn of Easter Day the blood of eight thousand

French in Palermo alone had glutted their vengeance. The Sicilian Vespers wrecked Charles's fortunes, and the Republic turned to renew her former understanding with the Greek Emperor. Martin IV., enraged at the defection of his ally, laid Venice under the ban of the Church, but his opportune death soon made reconciliation possible.

DOGE'S PALACE—THE JUDGMENT OF SOLOMON CORNER

Visitors to Venice may have noticed a traditional motto written in brass nails on some of the gondolas that ply for hire which admirably sums up the old popular Venetian idea of government: *Pane in Piazza: Giustizia in Palazzo* (Bread in the market-place: Justice in the palace). This principle always inspired the rule of the aristocracy. In 1284, during Giovanni Dandolo's reign, a calamitous inundation had plunged the people into misery. To meet their urgent needs a loan was raised on Government security, and ten thousand bushels of wheat were distributed at a nominal cost among the people.

In October of the same year the mint issued the first gold ducat of Venice, which for centuries was famous for its purity, fineness and weight throughout the whole commercial world. Orders were given that it was to be similar to and even purer than the golden florin of Florence, which had been coined thirty-two years before. Sanudo remembers to have seen an inscription on marble in the mint, dated 1285, commemorating the first striking of the gold ducat of the Venetians in honour of the Blessed Mark the Evangelist and of all saints, in the reign of the renowned Doge of the Venetians, Giovanni Dandolo. This beautiful zecchino (sequin) was worth about nine shillings and sixpence in English money, and admirably illustrates the dress of the Doges during a period of five hundred and thirteen years. The evolution of the *corno* or horn on the ducal bonnet may be clearly traced on the coins issued between the reigns of Francesco Foscari and Leonardo Loredano.

The sepulchre had hardly received the body of Giovanni Dandolo in 1289 when a formidable demonstration in favour of Giacomo, son of Doge Lorenzo Tiepolo, put the new constitution to a severe test. Giacomo, son and grandson of Doges, was known to have popular leanings, and so threatening was the attitude of the crowd on the Piazza that the Privy Council personally urged him to disclaim any intention of accepting the proffered honour.

Tiepolo, preferring his country's peace to the gratification of his own ambition, exhorted the crowd to respect the law, and left for the mainland till the crisis should be past. But the delicate electoral machinery was never for a moment put out of gear. The provisional Government was appointed; through all the tumult the electors calmly rattled their ballots in the Ducal Palace, and to the sullen displeasure of the popular party a prominent aristocrat, Pietro Gradenigo, was proclaimed Doge twenty-three days after the death of his predecessor. For the first time the officer who recited the formula: *Quest'è il vostro doge si vi piacerà*, turned aside without staying to receive the approbation of the people.

The long reign of Gradenigo (1289-1311) is one of the most important in the annals of Venice. By the fall of Acre in 1291 the doom of the Christian power in the Holy Land was sealed, and Venice, whose interest in the Crusades and in the Latin dominion over Syria was frankly a commercial one, turned the new situation to her own advantage. Her policy was to frustrate her rivals, the Genoese. To the scandal of Christendom a treaty was concluded with the infidel in 1299, and ere long slaves and materials of war were openly sold by the Venetians in their ports. The Sultan declared in the charter his steadfast will that the Venetians should be protected and honoured beyond all people in the world, and entitled to the sole right of a Saracen escort for Christian pilgrims to Jerusalem. The Genoese found themselves squeezed out of the coast towns, and Venice in exclusive possession of the Syrian trade.

ON THE GRAND CANAL.

The Pope, anxiously revolving the sad vicissitudes of the Christians in the east, turned to Venice and Genoa, praying them for the love of Christ to combine and save the fair island of Cyprus, still unpolluted by the presence of the infidels. But the lion of St Mark was a fierce yoke-fellow. The more restricted the field of influence became between Venice and Genoa the more bitter grew their jealousy. Two fleets were, however, fitted out in response to the Papal appeal. Their prows had scarcely touched Cyprian waters when a fight took place between some of the allied ships, and to the edification of the Saracen the two greatest maritime powers of Christendom were soon engaged in mutual destruction. Unavailing efforts were made by the Church to heal the strife, for while the Dominican envoys were treating at Venice the feverish activity at the arsenal told too plainly that the time for the peacemaker was not yet come. Rumours soon reached Venice of an alliance between the Genoese and the Greeks and of the threatened closure of the Dardanelles to her ships. She delayed no longer to strike. All her seamen between sixteen and sixty were enrolled; her patrician houses were called to furnish their part of a new armament, and on October 7th, 1294, the fleet was under sail. The admiral, Marco Besegio, sighted the Genoese fleet under Nicolo Spinola off Ayas, in Asia Minor. The enemy was inferior in strength, and Besegio, too confident perhaps of victory, was out-manœuvred, defeated with heavy losses, and himself slain. The Genoese, to clinch their victory, despatched a mighty fleet of nigh two hundred sail manned by forty-five thousand men, among whom were the chiefs of their noble houses. Meanwhile Venice, shrewdly calculating that the heavy financial strain involved in the maintenance of so huge an armament would soon wear the enemy out, steadily equipped a new fleet, called out a fresh levy, and concentrated her force on the defence of the lagoons. Before a year was past the Genoese, after spoiling and slaughtering the hapless inhabitants of Canea in Crete, returned to port.

Early in 1295 news came to Venice which stung her to fury. A street row at Constantinople had developed into a general attack by the Genoese on the Venetians. The former were victorious, and after flinging the Venetian Governor out of the windows of the palace, dashing him to pieces, proceeded to an indiscriminate massacre of the inhabitants of the Venetian colony. The Greeks sent envoys to disclaim any responsibility in the outrage, but they were hectored by the Doge, who demanded an enormous indemnity, which served but to cement their alliance with the Genoese. Late in the spring the Venetian commander, Ruggieri Morosini, with a fleet of forty galleys, forced the Dardanelles, wasted the Genoese suburb of Galata and laid siege to Constantinople. Meanwhile another fleet, under Giov. Soranzo, entered the Black Sea and sacked the Genoese settlement of Caffa; but the elements amply avenged the Genoese. Soranzo returned to Venice bearing an unheroic story of vessels disabled and men frozen to death by the rigours of an Euxine winter. The year 1297 passed in petty expeditions, and towards the end of the autumn Boniface VIII. essayed to negotiate a peace. The magnanimous Pope (Dante's pet enemy) went so far as to offer, if the Genoese paid one-half, to pay himself the other half of the claims of the Venetians, but the latter rejected all compromise, and Boniface despairing of success inculpated the pride of Venice, and washed his hands of the whole business. Each power prepared for a final struggle.

Among the wealthy Venetians whose enthusiasm took the form of offering themselves and their ships to the common cause was a certain Marco Polo but recently returned from adventurous journies in the mysterious lands of the Grand Khan of Tartary; in Persia, China, Japan, and the Indies; and who from his wonderful stories of the million peopled cities and millions of jewels and treasure he had seen in his twenty-five years' wanderings was popularly known as Messer Marco Milione. In August 1298 all was ready and a fleet of ninety-five sail, under the command of Andrea Dandolo, set its course southwards and came upon the Genoese squadron of eighty-five vessels, under Lamba Doria off the island of Curzola. The fleets were about evenly matched, and on September 8th the action began. Doria, by superior seamanship, got the weather gauge and the Venetians, fighting too with the sun in their eyes, were routed. Twelve galleys, whose captains, panic-stricken, had abandoned the fight, alone escaped. With abject mien they told the extent of the disaster. The fine fleet was sunken, captured or burned, the loss in killed appalling, and seven thousand of their countrymen were on their way to Genoese prisons.[27] Among the captives was Messer Marco Milione himself, who to relieve the tedium of his imprisonment, dictated in halting French to his prison comrade Rustichello the story of his wanderings and adventures. A small court, in which Marco Polo's house stood on a site now covered by the Malibran Theatre, is called to this day the Corte del Milione.

REMAINS OF MARCO POLO'S HOUSE

Venice, conscious that her staying power was greater than her rival's, without a moment of panic set about equipping another fleet of a hundred galleys.

But Genoa, exhausted by her costly victory, was willing to treat, and in 1299 the Imperial Vicar of Milan effected a peace between the Republics on honourable terms.

During the Genoese war the aristocracy had quietly matured plans for fencing off their preserves from any intrusion of the democracy. Two abortive attempts had been made in 1286 and 1296 to restrict membership of the Great Council to members of the aristocracy. Gradenigo, who was a leader of iron will and indomitable purpose, succeeded the next year in achieving the revolution in the Constitution known as the shutting of the Great Council (Serrata del Gran Consiglio). The Quarantia[28] were charged (1) to put to the ballot one by one all who for the past four years had sat in the Great Council. Those who received not less than twelve votes were to be members up to Michaelmas, when, after being subjected to a new ballot, they were to serve for a further period of one year. (2) Three electors were to be appointed who should submit further names of non-members of the Great Council for election under the same system of ballot. (3) The three were to sit in the Council until Michaelmas, when they were to be superseded by other three, who should sit for a year. (4) The law could not be repealed save with the consent of five of the six privy councillors, twenty-five of the Quarantia, and two-thirds of the Great Council. Such were the chief provisions of the measure which transformed the aristocracy into an oligarchy and created the Maggior Consiglio.

DOGE'S PALACE—SALA DEL MAGGIOR CONSIGLIO

It will be seen that by the second clause an avenue was left open by which a Venetian, not a member of the favoured class, might enter the aristocratic close, but it was rendered inoperative by the principle which the three laid down for their guidance, that only those whose paternal ancestors had been members of the Great Council between 1172 and 1297 should be eligible for ballot. The effect of the change was to increase the number of the Council. In 1296 it consisted of two hundred and ten members. In 1311 they had risen to ten hundred and seventeen; in 1340 to twelve hundred and twelve; in 1490 to fifteen hundred and seventy; and in 1510 to sixteen hundred and seventy-one.

In 1315 it was enacted that a book be kept for the inscription of the names of all persons above eighteen years of age who had the right to enter the Council. So keen was the ambition to be inscribed that in the year following a fine of thirty lire was imposed on all those whose names were unlawfully entered and who did not remove them within a month. In 1319 *Avvogadori*, a sort of heraldic officers, were appointed and charged to subject to the severest scrutiny the titles of applicants for inscription, and in order to frustrate any attempt to tamper with the electors it was ordained that as many ballots should be used as there were names inscribed, and that of these, a number equal to the candidates to be elected should be of gold. The names were read out in the order of their entry and a boy extracted a ballot as each man was called. Those to whom the gold ballots fell were declared elected. It was further ordained that after the lapse of two years all who had reached the age of twenty-five years and were in possession of the necessary qualifications should *ipso facto* be entitled to enter the Council. Thus the electors' functions ended, and any descendant of an aristocratic family who fulfilled the conditions required by the law became at that age a member of the Great Council. This was the actual and definite *Serrata* (Nov. 25th, 1319).

Every noble was bound to notify his marriage and the birth of his children at the Avvogaria to be entered in a book and stringent regulations were from time to time laid down to insure the purity of the family record. Owing to the association of the golden ballots with the right to enter the Council, this book was called the *Libro d'Oro*, the Golden book. The Council elected all officers of State, imposed taxes, decreed laws, made peace and war, concluded alliances, until owing to its unwieldy growth many of its powers were delegated to the Senate, the Council retaining as its chief function the election of the officers of the Republic. The Senate was definitely established in 1230 and consisted of sixty members, nominated by four electors of the Great Council, to whom later other sixty were added called the *Zonta* or addition. The *Consiglio Minore* (Privy Council) was still composed of six members chosen from the wards of the city. They, with the Doge, presided over the Senate, and with the three chiefs of the *Quarantia* formed the *Serenissima Signoria* (Signory). They could act in the absence of the Doge but the Doge could take no action without them. They opened dispatches, received petitions, prepared the agenda for the Great Council and the Senate, read the Coronation oath every year to the Doge and if need were admonished him. The *Quarantia* (Council of forty) was the judicial authority and controlled the Mint, heard complaints from the subject cities and provinces, and gave audience to ambassadors. In the fifteenth century the civil and criminal functions of the *Quarantia* were separated and two *Quarantie* established. The Doge, the living embodiment of the Republic, presided over all these assemblies. In 1308 a small *giunta* of seven *Savii* (wise men or experts) was formed to deal with Ferrarese affairs and did its work so well that it continued in office. It was subsequently enlarged and subdivided in 1442 into three bodies, one dealing with home affairs, one with mainland affairs, the third with the arsenal. The three united formed the *Collegio* (Cabinet). By the permanent appointment of the Council of Ten in 1335 was evolved the famous constitution of Venice which for its stability and efficiency became the admiration of every statesman in Europe, and filled with envy the Italian states of the mainland.

BOATS AT ANCHOR.

CHAPTER VII

The Oligarchy—Commercial supremacy—The Bajamonte Conspiracy—The Council of the Ten— The Prisons

"O thou that art situate at the entry of the sea which art a merchant of the people for many isles, ... thou hast said: I am of perfect beauty. Thy borders are in the midst of the seas, thy builders have perfected thy beauty.... Thy wise men were thy pilots.... All the ships of the sea were in thee to occupy thy merchandise.... Syria was thy merchant ... they occupied in thy fairs with emeralds, purple and broidered work, fine linen and coral and agate."— *Ezekiel.*

THE fourteenth century opens the era of the oligarchy. Venice had made peace with the only rival that could challenge her maritime supremacy. She had not yet entangled herself in an aggressive continental policy. The tramp of the advancing Turk was too far away to echo in the lagoons. The wealth of the Indies and of the far East flowed through her markets. Her merchants laid the known world under contribution. "By way of the Syrian ports and of Alexandria came the cloves, nutmegs, mace and ebony of the Moluccas; the sandal wood of Timor; the costly camphor of Borneo; the benzoin of Sumatra and Java; the aloes, wood of Cochin China; the perfumes, gums, spices, silks and innumerable curiosities of China, Japan and Siam; the rubies of Pegu; the fine fabrics of Coromandel; the richer stuffs of Bengal; the spikenard of Nepaul and Bhutan; the diamonds of Golconda; the Damascus steel of Nirmul; the pearls, sapphires, topazes and cinnamon of Ceylon; the pepper, ginger and satin wood of Malabar; the lac, agates and sumptuous brocades and jewelry of Cambay; the costus and graven vessels, wrought arms and broidered shawls of Cashmere; the bdellium of Scinde; the musk of Thibet; the galbanum of Khorossan; the assafœtida of Afghanistan; the sagapenum of Persia; the ambergris, civet and ivory from Zanzibar; the myrrh, balsam and frankincense of Zeila, Berbera and Shehr."[29] The bare recital of this catalogue has the effect of a poem and fills the imagination with visions of Oriental splendour. Every year six trading fleets averaging about five hundred vessels each sailed, one for the Black Sea, another for Greece and Constantinople; others for the Syrian ports; for Egypt, Barbary and North Africa; for Flanders and England. These ships were the property of the State, and in due time a public crier announced the number of galleasses ready for the annual voyages. They were farmed out to the highest bidders, who were required to prove their qualifications and the amount of their capital, and to provide on each galleasse accommodation, a suitable mess, and space for a small cargo, for eight young nobles, who thus were trained in naval science and gained experience of commerce. The vessels were constructed on fixed models and convertible at will into men-of-war. Every man aboard, passenger or seaman, bore arms, and was compelled to fight the ship in case of attack. Standardised fittings were obtainable at every Venetian maritime station to replace any that might be lost or damaged by storm or battle. The food and comfort of the seamen were carefully provided for. A cross painted or carved on the side served as a load-line, and Government inspectors checked any attempt to overload. Each ship carried a band of music.

The cargo of a Syrian or Egyptian galleasse was worth about two hundred thousand[30] ducats, and it has been estimated that the Republic in the fifteenth century could dispose of three thousand three hundred ships, thirty-six thousand seamen and sixteen thousand shipwrights. The consuls at every Venetian port were charged to inspect the weights and measures of the traders and to prevent adulteration or fraud. If the consul were found to be venal he was branded on the forehead. At home the same measures were taken to maintain the standard of quality. In 1550 English woollen goods from the Thames were exposed with the brand of the Senate upon them in St Mark's Palace as evidence of English dishonesty and the decay of English faith. In the fifteenth century, when Turkish pirates infested the seas, *navi armate* (war-ships) were built to convoy the merchant fleets, and a state navy was thus formed in which slaves or criminals were forced to work the oars.

In 1556, sixty out of a gang of Lutherans convicted of heresy, marching through Flanders on their way to the Venetian galleys, were rescued from slavery by the people of Maestricht and their guards stoned. In earlier times, before the navy was differentiated into merchant and war-ships, Sclavonians were employed for this exhausting labour, and those who manned the galleasses to Flanders and England possessed a burial vault in North Stoneham Church near Southampton.

In the event of a naval war a levy was made on all the male inhabitants. Those liable were divided into groups of twelve and lots were drawn to decide who should serve first. The unfit provided substitutes or were fined. Those on service were given free bread rations and were paid five lire a month by the Commune and one lira from each man of the twelve who was not chosen. Romanin estimates that the equipment of a galley in the early thirteenth century was equal to that of a frigate of seventy-four guns in his day (1850). The discipline was perfect. The seamen were said to obey their chiefs as sheep do their shepherd. Gambling or swearing was severely punished by flogging.

"When the hour of departure neared, the Commander came on board preceded by trumpeters and followed by his staff. Perfect silence reigned as he began his inspection. Every man was at his post, every oar in its place. All the arms, accoutrements and appointments were carefully examined, and when the trumpeters gave signal for departure the rowers simultaneously plied their oars, or if the wind were fair threw them up and sails[31] were set with marvellous alertness. A general holiday was observed with great pomp and magnificence. The ships were coloured white and vermilion, the sails bright with variegated stripes, the poop was richly gilt, the figure-head of the most beautiful design. The Doge and his Council with dazzling pageantry, senators in scarlet robes, the *élite* of Venetian ladies, famed for grace and beauty and arrayed in gorgeous dresses, and hundreds of citizens in gay gondolas witnessed the departure."[32] A stirring scene, surpassed alone by that when the clanging of bells from St Mark's tower called the people to view a victorious fleet sailing up the lagoons and the enemy's standards trailing on the waters.

In Gradenigo's reign we note the first indication of a policy of territorial aggrandisement on the Italian mainland. Little wars had already been waged: with the Paduans in 1142, to prevent the diversion of the course of the Brenta; and with Ferrara in 1240, to maintain trading privileges. In 1308 these were again endangered by a dispute between rival claimants for the lordship of Ferrara. Venice intervened and was brought into conflict with the Pope. His Holiness, as a temporal enemy, fought at a vantage, for to the material bolts of Mars he was able to add the spiritual thunders of the Church. When the Papal warning was received, the Doge addressed the Councillors, and stoutly defended his policy and told them that they were not children to be frightened by words. There was an angry scene in the council chamber, and for once the ominous cries, "Guelph and Ghibelline," were heard within the walls of the palace. The ducal party maintained their position and the ban was laid on Venice. The Doge, his Councillors and the citizens were excommunicated, their possessions in Ferrara confiscated, every treaty with them declared void, commercial relations forbidden, and all the clergy summoned to leave. The Pope's words, however, were winged with terror to the Venetians. News soon came of banks, factories and ships sacked in Italy, France and England, and even in far Asia. Their trade, except with the infidel, was paralysed; religious and civic life disintegrated. But the Republic never winced. On the very day that the papal interdict reached Venice instructions were sent to the Venetian *podestà* at Ferrara to fortify himself in *Castel Tebaldo* and manfully and potently to uphold the rights and honour of his country.

The Venetian garrison, however, weakened by disease, surrendered after a long struggle, and met the fate of the vanquished. The fleet was destroyed, and growing unrest in the State forced the Doge and his party to make terms with the Pope. Ferrara was acknowledged to be a papal fief, and an indemnity paid for the restoration of the trading privileges of the Republic.

In the year of the *Serrata* the corpses of Bocconi, a popular leader, and ten of his followers dangled between the red columns as a warning to the disaffected, but after the inglorious issue of the war the discontent of the people was intensified, and found a rallying-point in certain ambitious and disgraced nobles of the Quirini, Tiepolo and Badoer[33] families, who were united by a common hatred of the ducal party. Secret meetings were held in Casa Quirini near the Rialto, and Bajamonte, the people's darling, the *"Gran Cavaliere,"* son of Jacopo Tiepolo, was drawn into the conspiracy. It was determined to organise a revolution and assassinate the Doge and his chief supporters. The insurrection was fixed for Sunday, June 14th, 1310, the eve of St Vito's Day. Down the two main avenues of traffic that debouch from the north on the Piazza, the Calle dei Fabri and the Merceria, two divisions under the leadership of Marco Quirini, the chief conspirator, and of Bajamonte, were to march and simultaneously attack the palace, meanwhile Badoer was sent to collect sympathisers at Padua. All had been foreseen save the treachery of man and of the elements. In the early dawn, as the revolutionists rushed from Casa Quirini, shouting "Liberty" and "Death to Doge Gradenigo," their faces were lashed by a driving rain, their voices smothered by peals of thunder and the howling of the wind. The movements failed to synchronise, and the Quirini section encountered in the Piazza, not their allies from the Merceria, but a ducal force which scattered them and slew their leader and his son. Men who will betray the State will betray their fellows. The plot had been divulged by one Marco Donato, and the Doge had met the danger with his wonted courage and alertness. He increased his guards, summoned help from Chioggia, Murano and Torcello, called out the arsenal men, armed his Councillors and their servants. Having disposed of the Quirini, the Doge was able to deal with Bajamonte's division in the Merceria. During the fighting Bajamonte's standard-bearer met the fate of Abimelech.[34] A woman aimed a stone mortar from an upper window at him: it struck him on the head, and the bearer and the banner inscribed with the word, "Liberty," fell to the ground. Panic seized the rebels and they fled across the Rialto bridge. Meanwhile the remnant of Quirini's party rallied and made a stand on the Campo S. Lucia, only to be finally crushed by members of the Painters' Guild and of the Guild of Charity. A more serious task remained, to subdue Bajamonte and his followers, who had hewn down the bridge and fortified themselves in some houses yon side the Rialto. After many negotiations the rebels surrendered. Their lives were spared, but they agreed to banish themselves from Venetian territory. Ill-hap, too, had fallen on Badoer's reinforcements, which were defeated by the Chioggians. Badoer and his chief followers were captured and hanged between the red columns. To perpetuate the memory of this narrow escape from a great peril S. Vito's Day was made a day of public festival and thanksgiving for evermore. To Marco Donato and his descendants was granted membership of the Great

Council. The woman, Lucia Rosso, who had cast the fateful mortar, being asked to name her reward, begged permission to fly the standard of St Mark from her window on every feast day, and desired that the procurators of St Mark, to whom the house belonged, would not raise to her or to her successors the annual rental of fifteen ducats. The house, known as the *Casa e bottega della grazia del morter*, appears from an old painting in the Correr Museum to have stood on the site of the first house on the left-hand side of the Merceria entering from the Piazza. The mortar was cast from the third floor window. "The banner I have seen raised," says Sanudo, "but now that the new buildings are made it can no longer be seen from the Piazza. The under part of Marco Quirini's house in Rialto was made into shambles, and there they remain to this day" (about 1520).[35] Bajamonte's house in S. Agostino was razed, the site made over to the commune, and a column set up in the Campo S. Agostino with an inscription stating that the "land once Bajamonte's had been confiscated for his wicked treachery and to inspire others, with terror."[36] Certain of the marbles of the house were assigned by the Republic in 1316 for the restoration of the church of S. Vito. For eighteen years Bajamonte lived in exile and never ceased to plot his revenge until he was secretly disposed of by an emissary of the Ten.

THE CLOCK TOWER AND ENTRANCE TO THE MERCERIA.

The Consiglio de' Dieci shares with the *Comité du Salut publique* a sinister notoriety in history. Let us see how far the earlier and more enduring body deserves its reputation. The great plot had showed the urgent need of an executive able to act with rapidity and secrecy. The Council of Ten was appointed to deal with further developments of the plot, but proved so admirable and effective an instrument that it was more than once renewed and finally made permanent in 1335. The Ten were charged "to preserve the liberty and peace of the subjects of the Republic and protect them from the abuses of personal power." They were elected by the Great Council with careful deliberation among the most reputable of the citizens, and no more than one member of any family could serve. A member sat for one year, he was not eligible for re-election, he received no pay, he was obliged to retire if any of his relations were among the accused; it was a capital offence to receive a gift of any nature. His term of service ended, the dread decemvir passed again into private life. The Ten elected from themselves three chiefs (*Capi*) who served for one month, during which period they were forbidden to go about the city, to frequent shops or other public places where the nobility were wont to gather. Among other duties, on the first day of their month the *Capi* were required to send to the Signory a list of the prisoners detained by order of the Ten with suggestions for any reform or improvement in the prisons, and to take measures to expedite the trial of the accused. They were to report to the Council all the arrests made by the previous *Capi* and to remind the Council of all cases *sub judice* in the preceding month. The Doge and his six Privy Councillors were present at the sittings, and a legal officer without a vote watched the proceedings to check any abuse of power. Secret denunciations placed in the *Bocche del leone*, especially if unsigned, were subject to most elaborate procedure before they were acted upon. The accused were usually interrogated in darkness, but if five-sixths of the tribunal agreed, the interrogation might take place in the light. They could call witnesses. If the minutes of the trial exceeded a hundred and fifty sheets they were read a second time on another day, that the members might refresh their strained powers of attention. The defence was read entire. If the condemnation, after five ballotings, did not command more than half the votes of the Council, the accused was set at liberty or the case was retried. When the condemnation had gained an absolute majority it was subject to four re-ballots before being made final and irrevocable. The Ten dealt with—criminal charges against nobles; treachery and conspiracy in the State; espionage; unnatural crimes; secret information likely to be of advantage to the Republic; the regulations of the Greater *Scuole* or Guilds; the use of secret service money; disobedient State officials; false coiners and debasers of the precious metals used in jewellery; forests and mines; the glass industry at Murano; acts of violence on the water; the use of arms; theatres; masked balls and public morals generally; and, after 1692, the censorship of the printing press.

The tribunal could inflict pecuniary fines; corporal punishment; banishment, with power to compass his death if the proscribed one were found outside bounds; imprisonment for any period, and for life; the galleys; mutilation; death, secretly or publicly. The death sentence was generally carried out by decapitation or hanging from the columns of the palace or between the red columns in the Piazzetta. For the more heinous crimes the guilty were conducted in infamous guise along the Grand Canal, flogged and broken upon the wheel. Secret executions were rarely resorted to, and generally with the object of saving the prestige of the nobility by withdrawing from the public gaze the disgrace of an honoured name.

In 1539 the ever-present dread of Spanish plots fed by the gold of the New World led to the permanent establishment of *Il Supremo Terribile Tribunale* of the Three State Inquisitors. For among the large body of State officials and members of councils were many patricians who, impoverished by the decline of commerce, were peculiarly open to corruption, and the need was felt of a smaller and more expeditious body than the Ten. Of the *Tre Inquisitori di Stato* two were appointed by the Ten, one by the Doge's Privy Council. The latter sat in the middle clothed in red and was called the *rosso*; the former sat one on either side clothed in black, and were known as the *negri*. They served for a year and were eligible for re-election. Service was compulsory under a fine of 500 ducats. Their powers were delegated to them, as emergencies demanded, by the Ten, who reserved the right of revising their judgments, which were also published in the Great Council. If the Three were not unanimous they must refer the case to the Ten. Carefully indicted rules guarded against the abuse of secret denunciations, and against the venality or the errors of spies. Suspects were arrested at night and examined in secret, torture being used in accordance with the usual legal procedure of the day. Witnesses were also examined in secret by the Secretary or a ducal notary. The triumvirs acted with appalling swiftness[37] and secrecy, and stout of heart was he who did not quail when the officer of the Three touched him on the shoulder with the usual formula, "Their Excellencies would like to see you." During the sixteenth century the Ten and its Committee grew to be the dominant body in the State, until in 1582 the right of calling the *Zonta* was abolished, and having no longer the power of associating with them members of any and every council and of spending money they reverted to their former position.

The tribunals occasionally abused their powers, committed some crimes, and made errors. The murder of the Carraras was a national sin; the execution of Foscarini a grievous blunder. But they were a popular body, and withstood every attack upon them. They were a bulwark against treachery: they protected the people from the insolence and arbitrariness of nobles: they maintained equality, and were stern censors of morals. Their best defence is the fact that they endured to the fall of the Republic.

PONTE DI PAGLIA

Much undeserved obloquy has been cast upon the Ten even by historians of repute when treating of the famous prisons under their charge, the so-called *Pozzi* and *Piombi* (wells and leads). Lurid pictures have been drawn of victims tortured in cells hot as furnaces under the leads, and in dungeons beneath the canal, where neither *light* nor warmth ever penetrated, and where the prisoner *saw* the instruments of his torture on the wall before him. But in truth the *Pozzi* were as little underground as the *Piombi* were (immediately) under the leads. The Ducal Palace had been furnished with prisons from its construction by Angelo Participazio and its restoration by Seb. Ziani until the new prison over the Bridge of Sighs, and beyond the *rio del Palazzo*, was completed in 1606. Except the *Torreselle* (prisons in the towers), one of which, at the angle of the palace overlooking the Ponte della Paglia, was demolished in 1532 by order of the Ten, the old prisons were situated on the east wing of the palace between the inner court and the *rio del Palazzo*, and later extended to the other side towards the Molo on the south. They were on the ground floor, which was sub-divided into two storeys of cells. Some of the windows looked on the public courtyard, and at one period the prisoners could talk with passers-by. They were not known as *Pozzi* before the seventeenth century. After the erection of the new jail on the opposite side of the Rio the so-called *Pozzi* were used for the more dangerous prisoners, and on the fall of the Republic in 1797 four only were found therein, scoundrels who richly deserved their fate. The Republic bore a unique reputation for its humane treatment of prisoners. Zanotto,[38] from whose admirable monograph we mainly draw, quotes the testimony of Friar Felice Fabri, who, visiting Venice in the middle of the fifteenth century, was struck by the merciful treatment of the prisoners of the Republic. In 1443 the Great Council appointed an advocate to defend the cause of the poor detained prisoners, and in 1553 a second advocate was chosen. In common with the whole of Christian Europe Venice used torture to extract confessions, but she honourably distinguished herself by appointing a surgeon to examine the prisoners and to report if they were able to bear the infliction. In 1564 the Ten ordered an infirmary to be prepared for sick prisoners. The disinfection and cleanliness of the cells and the quality and quantity of the food and wine supplied to the incarcerated were carefully inspected.

In 1591 the Senate permitted the Ten to make use of a floor above the Sala de' Capi in order that the detained might be in more comfortable, lighter and better-ventilated cells than those allotted to the condemned. The rooms were known as the *Piombi*, since they were on the floor next below the roof, which was covered with lead. According to Zanotto, between the ceilings, which were made of a double layer of larch planks, and the roof, was a space of several yards, varying with the slope of the roof. The rooms were small; roughly, about twelve by fourteen feet, and from six feet to eight feet high, and were wainscoted with larch. They were lighted from a corridor, and ventilators were fixed in the doors. The detained dressed as they pleased, were allowed to see visitors, and to walk in the corridor.

S. GIORGIO AND S. MARIA DELLA SALUTE.

Gradenigo died before the papal ban had been removed, and found quiet sepulture at Murano. A distinguished senator, Stefano Giustiniani, was chosen his successor, but renounced the office and retired to the monastery at S. Giorgio. The annalists relate that while the electors sat anxiously pondering the situation thus created, a saintly old man was seen passing the palace on his daily round of charity, followed by his servant carrying a load of bread. It was deemed a happy omen, for the need of an understanding with the Pope was urgent, and *Zorzi il Santo* would be an excellent mediator.

Being entreated, he accepted the charge and filled the ducal chair for ten months, during which period he was able to obtain a relaxation of the interdict, which was finally removed in the next reign.

Giorgio the Sainted left a troublesome legacy to his successor, Giov. Soranza. Zara, aided by Hungarians and Croats, was again recalcitrant, and only subdued after a heavy expenditure of men and treasure. But Soranza's sixteen and a half years of office coincided with a time of great prosperity, and the strain was lightly borne. Venetian trade, aided by diplomacy and enterprise, expanded eastward and westward. The arts of life were developed. Refugees from Lucca founded a silk industry, which became a source of great profit to the Republic. They were governed by their own magistrates, the *Provisores Sirici*, who were located in the Corte della Seda, near Marco Polo's house. The city was further embellished, and Soranza enjoyed the popularity that comes to a prince ruling in times of plenty. It was in Soranza's reign, August 1321, that Dante came to Venice, an ambassador from Guido Novello da Polenta of Ravenna, to negotiate a peace with the Signory, and returned to die a few days after his arrival at Ravenna of a fever caught on the journey.

CHAPTER VIII

Conquests on the Mainland—Execution of Marin Faliero—The Fall of Genoa

"Ill-fated chief——
Him, only him, the shield of Jove defends
Whose means are fair and spotless as his ends."
—*Wordsworth*.

WHEN the Great Council met in 1328 after Soranza's death the oldest member rose, and after uttering praises of the late Doge and lamentations at his death, exhorted all around to be of good heart and to pray God for the election of a wise prince to succeed him.

And never had Venice greater need of wisdom in her rulers. Unhappy Italy, "reeling like a pilotless vessel in a mighty tempest," had seen the last vain attempt of the Emperors to execute their ideal function. The heroic spirit of Henry VII. of Luxemburg, *l'alto Arrigo*, had already ascended to fill the vacant and crowned seat, which Dante saw awaiting him among the ranks of the blest, and the poet's hopes of a Cæsar firmly seated in the saddle and curbing the wanton and savage beast of faction in Italy were shattered. From the political chaos three great families of despots emerged in North Italy, the Scalas of Verona, the Viscontis of Milan and the Carraras of Padua. In 1329 the lords of Verona under Mastino della Scala held sway over Vicenza, Padua and Treviso. Mastino, an ambitious prince subtly urged by the deposed Marsilio da Carrara of Padua, determined to tap the wealth of the Republic by levying duties on all Venetian goods passing through his territories. Venice retaliated by cutting off the supply of salt and a tariff war began. But her food supplies soon ran short and an appeal to arms impended. It was a tremendous choice, for the strength of Venice lay in her naval not in her military power. To fight the mainland despots she must employ mercenaries and successful *condottieri* were bad servants. Her infallible bulwark, the sea, would be gone, squandered for a vulnerable land frontier and the financial drain of a continental policy.

Such were the considerations that appealed to the mind of the new Doge Francesco Dandolo. But the time was past when a Doge could dictate the policy of the State. The oligarchy felt that inaction meant national suicide. If the passage for Venetian goods to North and West Europe was blocked, it meant ruin to her trade, and war was declared in the chivalrous fashion of the times. To the confines of Padua, envoys were sent, who delivered a protest and in token of defiance, three times cast a stone into the enemy's territory. A levy was made on all males between twenty and sixty years of age, and alliances concluded with Florence, Milan, Ferrara and Mantua. Mastino, alarmed at the coalition against him, sent Marsilio da Carrara to treat with the Signory. Marsilio was invited, so the story runs, to sit next the Doge at dinner. The "wily old fox" made a sign to the Doge that he wished to speak with him. The Doge let fall his knife. Marsilio bent down to pick it up and as the Doge bent down too, whispered: "What would you give him who gave you Padua?" "We would make him lord of Padua," replied the Doge. Mastino was unable to stand before so powerful a combination. Padua by collusion with the Carraras fell to Venetian arms, and Alberto della Scala, Mastino's brother, was led captive to Venice. Marsilio became once more lord of Padua. The provinces of Treviso and Bassano were made over to Venice, who thus came into possession of one of the passes into North Europe and a rich corn land in North Italy. The glorious initiation of this new and vaster policy was celebrated with great rejoicings at Venice and the prophets of evil were silenced. The Republic proved herself a wise and tolerant mistress. Her new subjects were ruled with a paternal regard for their welfare, while local feeling and characteristics were tenderly treated. The device which still remains from Venetian times over the town-hall of Verona, *Pro summa fide summus amor*, admirably expresses the attitude of the Republic towards her mainland provinces. The citizens of many a State scourged with the scorpions of Italian despots hailed with delight the advent of Venetian rule. Sanudo in his diary describes the entry into Faenza of the Venetian governor on its occupation in 1495. The streets were decorated with tapestry and cloth. For many days the painters had been doing nought but paint *San Marco* on the doors of the houses. The whole city with great demonstration of joy came forth to receive the new governor, shouting "Marco! Marco!" A quarter of a century later the Venetian ambassador was able to tell Cardinal Wolsey that although the Duke of Milan and the Marquis of Mantua were candidates for the governorship of Verona, the Venetian army as it defiled through the mountains was received by the Veronese with joyful cries of "Marco! Marco!" and the Venetian commissioner installed in the seat of government. St Mark's lion on his column standing in the market-place of an Italian city was the symbol of a firm, just, enlightened rule.

While Bart. Gradenigo was Doge, Venice was visited by an awful tempest. For three days the angry waves surged against the city. On the third night, February 25, 1340, so runs the legend, as the storm increased in violence a poor old fisherman was making fast his boat at the Molo when he was accosted by a stranger who craved to be ferried over to the island of S. Giorgio Maggiore. The fisherman, terrified by the awful storm, would not venture, but being urged and reassured by the stranger, he loosed his boat and they set forth and reached the island. Here a mysterious knight embarked and commanded that they should be rowed to S. Nicolo on the Lido, and on the boatman protesting the danger of going with one oar he was again comforted and promised good pay. Arrived at S. Nicolo, a third stranger, a venerable old man, joined them and demanded to be taken out to sea. Scarcely had they reached the open Adriatic when they beheld a ship filled with devils pressing swiftly forward to wreak destruction on Venice. Soon as the three strangers sighted the vessel they made the sign of the cross and ship and devils vanished. The sea grew calm: Venice was saved. The three strangers were then rowed back whence they departed and revealed themselves as St Mark, St George and St Nicholas. As St Mark stepped ashore he was stayed by the boatman, who demurred to accepting the honour of taking part in the miracle as adequate payment. "Thou art right," answered the saint, "go to the Doge and tell what thou hast seen and ask thy reward. And say this has happened because of the master of a scuola at S. Felice, who had sold his soul to the devil and at last hanged himself." The old man protested: "Even though I tell this, the Doge will not believe me." St Mark then drew a ring from his finger the worth of which was about five ducats, gave it to the fisherman, saying, "Show this to the Doge and bid him keep it in my sanctuary." The saint's bidding was done and the fisherman well rewarded.

In 1343 Andrea Dandolo was raised to the Dogeship. The first patrician who had taken a doctor's degree at Padua, he had already served on the Ten, and filled the office of Procurator of St Mark, when at thirty-six years of age he was elected Doge. Plague, earthquake and war scourged the Venetians during the scholar Doge's reign. Zara, tempted by the Hungarians, tried another fall with her Venetian masters for independence. Marin Faliero, a member of one of the most ancient and illustrious families of Venice, who had served as *podestà* of Padua and of Treviso, was placed in command of a land force: forty galleys set forth under Pietro da Canale to attack by sea. Faliero met the Hungarians forty thousand strong about eight miles from Zara, and won a decisive victory. Meanwhile Canale had forced the harbour, and in a few months the tough old fortress again surrendered. The walls were dismantled, and this time a strong Venetian garrison was left to overawe the Zarantines.

For a century Genoese and Venetians had been rivals in the Crimea for the control of the fur trade with Tartary. In 1346 Marin Faliero was sent to Genoa to complain of certain piratical acts by the Genoese. The latter retorted by accusing the Signory of bad faith in dealing with the Tartars. But the ravages of the Black Death in 1348, when two-fifths of the people of Venice are said to have perished, and fifty noble families to have become extinct, absorbed for a time the attention of the Republic. In 1349 friction with the Genoese led to a definite breach, and another act in the tragedy of Christendom was begun. Two years of naval warfare passed with little advantage to either power. In 1353, in alliance with Peter of Aragon and the

Emperor of Constantinople, the Venetians sailed up the Bosphorus and came upon the enemy under Paganino Doria, off Pera. Two hours before sunset the engagement began and a long and bloody struggle raged through the night, illumined only by the lurid glare of burning ships. The Venetians were defeated, and Nicolo Pisani, their commander, retired to Crete to recruit and await reinforcements. In February 1353 he was able to join the Aragonese fleet in Sardinian waters and attack the Genoese under Ant. Grimaldi off Lojera. The enemy were outmanoeuvred, their armament utterly destroyed, and Grimaldi, with a few shattered galleys, reached Genoa crushed and humiliated. Panic seized the city. In the despair engendered by defeat a momentous step was taken. The cowed Genoese surrendered their independence and implored the protection of Giov. Visconti, Lord Bishop of Milan. Time for recuperation was, however, needed, and Visconti sought peace for his new vassal by sending Petrarch to Venice as his envoy. The poet had already, by an epistle to Dandolo, which reads like an echo of his pathetic canzone *All'Italia*, besought the rivals to exchange the kiss of peace and not persist in a war which must end in one of the eyes of Italy being quenched, the other dimmed. As well appeal to two eagles fighting for their quarry. After some weeks at Venice, honoured as a poet but unheeded as a messenger of peace, he returned sorrowing to Milan. A year passed, and a new fleet left Genoa under Doria, who cleverly slipped by Pisani, sailed up the Adriatic, devastated Lesena, Curzola and Parenza, and anchored within striking distance of the lagoons. It was now the turn of Venice to feel alarm. The channels were fortified, a new fleet was equipped, a war tax levied. The Doge, prostrated by the news, never recovered, and died of a broken heart on September 7th, 1354. He lies in the Baptistery that he did so much to beautify, and under his noble and simple monument there still remains the Latin epitaph composed for him by Petrarch, his friend. Andrea Dandolo is remembered as a Venetian historian and an accomplished legist, a lover of the arts, and a great humanist.

On October the 4th the Bucintoro was sent to Chioggia to meet Marin Faliero, recalled from the Roman legation to assume the ducal cap. The great State barge set forth, but so dense a fog enveloped Venice that it was deemed prudent to land in small boats. The gondola bearing Faliero failed to make the usual stage by the Ponte della Paglia, and, sinister augury, landed the Doge between the red columns of the Piazzetta.

Faliero, however, began his term of office happily by signing a truce with the Genoese. The breathing time was used in concentrating the fleet, and scarcely was the term ended when Nicolo Pisani, with his son Vettore, sailed for the Ionian Isles in search of Doria. But the Genoese refused to be drawn, and Pisani went into winter quarters at Portolungo in the Morea behind the island of Sapienza. Doria saw an opportunity to trap his enemy. By a brilliant manœuvre he got part of his fleet between the Venetians and the shore, and attacking front and rear routed them with terrible loss, no less than six thousand being made prisoners. Pisani and his lieutenant, Quirini, escaped with the remnant of the armament to be impeached and degraded in Venice. Under the shadow of this disaster Venice displayed her wonted fortitude. With admirable self-control the Signory exhorted all their *podestà*, consuls and agents to be of good courage, and called for men and ships in defence of the fatherland. Eight thousand ducats were despatched to Genoa to soften the lot of the captives. Before, however, the spring made further operations possible, a truce was effected by the mediation of the Emperor; and while negotiations were pending for a definite peace, Europe was shocked by the news of the trial and execution of a Doge of Venice. The chroniclers give very circumstantial details of the drama, but to Petrarch, who was on terms of closest intimacy with the Doge, and to other contemporaries the whole business was shrouded in mystery. No record of the trial exists.

Faliero was of a proud and fiery temper. While *podestà* at Treviso he is said to have boxed the bishop's ears for having kept him waiting at a religious procession. After the usual bull-fight and festivities in the Piazza on Carnival Thursday the Doge gave a sumptuous banquet and dance in the palace. Among the guests was a young noble, Michel Steno, who, heated with wine, misconducted himself and was by the Doge's orders expelled from the hall. Steno, furious with rage, pencilled on the ducal chair, as he passed through the Doge's apartment, an insulting reflection on the Doge's honour: *Marin Falier della bella mujer tu la mantien e altri la galde*. Steno was accused before the Quarantia and let off with a punishment which the Doge regarded as derisory. On the morrow it befell that a choleric noble, Marco Barbaro, went to demand certain things of the Arsenal authorities, and being refused struck the Admiral Ghisello with his clenched fist. He was wearing a ring and an ugly wound was left. The Admiral, with bloody face went straightway to the Doge and prayed to be avenged. "What would you?" said the Doge; "Look at the shameful words written of me and the way that ribald Steno has been treated." "*Messer lo dose*," answered Ghisello, "if you will make yourself lord of Venice and get all those cuckold nobles cut in pieces I am prepared to help you." The tempter spoke to willing ears. A vast conspiracy was formed to make Faliero despot of Venice. Secret meetings were held in the palace, and it was arranged that sixteen leaders should each prepare an armed force of forty men, who, however, were not to be told for what purpose they were wanted. On Wednesday, April 15th, a rumour was to be spread that the Genoese were in the lagoons, and the alarm-bell of St Mark's to be rung. The leaders with their men were to converge on the Piazza and cut down the nobles and influential citizens who would hasten to answer the call. Faliero was then to be acclaimed lord of Venice. To incite the people to hatred of the nobles, hired roysterers were sent by night about the city doing violence to and insulting the women of the people, calling each other by well-known names of nobles as they mockingly rioted through the streets. "But the Lord God who hath ever watched over this most glorious city," says Sanudo, "inspired Beltrame Bergamasco, one of the leaders, to go secretly to a beloved patron, Nicolo Lioni, and warn him as he valued his life not to leave his house on the 15th." Lioni's suspicions were aroused; he questioned Beltrame and finally locked him in a room while he went to seek Giov. Gradenigo, dubbed Nasone (big nose) and Marco Cornaro in order to take counsel together. They returned to Lioni's house and after again questioning Beltrame decided to send messengers with an urgent summons to the Ten and the chief Councillors and officers of the State to a meeting in the sacristy of S. Salvatore. Blanched with terror they hurried together. Up to that time the complicity of the Doge was not known, but the immediate arrest of two other conspirators discovered the full danger of the situation. The Ten were equal to the emergency. The chief police officials and heads of the wards were sent for and asked to take good men and true, and arrest the leading conspirators. Armed forces were summoned from Chioggia. All means of egress from the palace were guarded; the bell-ringer forbidden to stir. On the dawn of the 16th the Ten summoned a *Zonta* of twenty of the wisest, best and most ancient of the nobles of Venice to join them in trying the Doge. He made no attempt to defend himself and was sentenced to death. On the 17th, the biretta removed, stripped of his ducal robes and clothed in a black gown, he was led to the spot on the landing of the staircase[39] in the courtyard where seven months before he had sworn to defend the Constitution. At one stroke his head was severed from his body. A *capo* of the Ten then went to the arcade of the palace over the Piazza and showed the executioner's bloody sword to the assembled people, crying: "The great judgment has been done on the traitor." The gates were opened and the people rushed in to see the body. At night all that remained of Marin Faliero was placed in a boat with eight lighted torches and carried to burial at S. Zanipolo. No record of the sentence is found in the acts of the Ten. On the unfilled space where the minutes should be entered are the words Ñ. *Scbatur*, "Let it not be written." A year later his portrait was blotted out and the place covered with a black veil with the inscription: *Hic est locus Marini Faletro decapitati pro criminibus.* Meanwhile the leaders of the plot as they were captured were hanged in a row, with iron gags in their mouths, from the columns of the palace. St Isidore's Day, April 16th, was made a public festival and as late as 1520 Sanudo saw carried in procession the white damask cloth bespattered with blood which was used at the execution.

THE PALAZZI GIUSTINIANI AND FOSCARI

On the 21st the vacant chair was filled by the election of Gradenigo *il nasone*, who had been largely instrumental in frustrating the plot. The Genoese negotiations dragged on, and not until the June following was the treaty of peace signed at Milan. Venetian statesmen had short rest from foreign complications. The defeat of Sapienza and the supposed laming of the executive by the miserable end of Doge Faliero, tempted the Hungarians, who were rapidly increasing in population and civilisation, to achieve their purpose of acquiring possession of a sea-board. War was declared and Francesco Carrara, who held Padua under Venetian tutelage, was called to aid his suzerain. But the Carraras aimed at founding a dynasty and gave secret assistance to King Louis of Hungary, who was besieging Treviso. The defence of Treviso and of Dalmatia was beyond the power of the Republic. After a two years' struggle and bitter hours of humiliation, Dalmatia, bought with so much blood of Doges, patricians and people, was surrendered by the peace of Zara, in February 1358, to the King of Hungary in exchange for the retention of Treviso. Meantime Gradenigo had died (in 1356) and left to Giov. Delfino the signing of the great renunciation. Delfino was stoutly defending Treviso when elected, and being refused a permit to pass the Hungarian lines broke through by night and met the Senate at Mestre. Broken-hearted, his sight failing, he died of the plague in 1361. Under Delfino's successor Lorenzo Celsi, Crete, never wholly subjugated, burst into revolt and terror reigned in the island. At this time Petrarch, seeking peace and security, had settled in Venice, the "only nest of liberty and sole refuge of the good." He lived simply, at the sign of the Two Towers on the Riva degli Schiavoni, where it was his delight to stand at his window watching the huge galleys, big as the house he lived in, and with masts taller than towers, passing and repassing. The poet, honoured and cherished, was on intimate terms with the Signory and advised the employment of the famous Veronese *condottiero* Lucchino del Verme to subdue the island. On the 4th of June about the sixth hour the poet was at his window chatting with the Archbishop of Patras when the friends saw a galley gliding swiftly up the lagoons, her masts wreathed with flowers; her deck crowded with men waving flags; hostile banners trailed in the waters behind her. She brought the news that Lucchino, falling upon the insurgents, weakened by divided counsels, had defeated them and punished the leaders. A thanksgiving festival was ordered which lasted three days. "The Doge," writes Petrarch, "with a numerous train took his place to watch the sports over the vestibule of St Mark's, where stand the four bronze horses (a work of ancient and excellent art) that seem to challenge comparison with the living and raise their hoofs to tread the ground. An awning of tapestry in many colours kept off the heat of the sun and I myself was invited to sit by the right hand of the Doge." The great Piazza, the church, the Campanile, the roofs, the arcades, the windows, were a mass of people. A magnificent pavilion next the church was filled with more than four hundred gaily dressed ladies.

English knights took part in the jousts. The poet, bored by the length of the festivities, pleaded pressure of business on the second day and came no more. But the rejoicings were premature, the revolt soon flamed forth again, and a costly campaign of twelve months was needed to quench it. Petrarch, to show his gratitude to the Venetian State, offered to make over his great collection of books to found a public library if the Republic would house them. The procurators of St Mark accepted the charge, but the ultimate fate of this priceless gift is unknown. During the short and peaceful reign of Marco Corner, Guariento of Verona was employed to paint on the walls of the Hall of the Great Council the story of Alexander III. and Barbarossa, for which

Petrarch composed inscriptions. In 1368 a deputation from the Great Council headed by Vettor Pisani went in search of the procurator, Andrea Contarini, who had been chosen Doge, and found him grafting fruit trees on his farm by the Brenta. Contarini had been warned against accepting the Dogeship by a Syrian sooth-sayer, and threats of confiscation were necessary to force him from his retreat.

At the peace of Zara, Louis of Hungary had shielded Carrara from Venetian vengeance, but the erection of two forts on the Brenta now gave the Venetians a pretext for paying off old scores. Louis again stood by his ally until the lucky capture of the King's nephew by the Venetians enabled them to exact the abandonment of the war as the price of his ransom, and Carrara was made to pay heavily for disloyalty. Petrarch accompanied the Paduan peace envoys—a grateful task to the poet of peace and concord.[40] It was his last mission to Venice.

The final act in the struggle with Genoa now draws nigh. A quarrel for precedence took place at the Coronation of the King of Cyprus between the Venetian and Genoese envoys, Malipiero and Paganino Doria, in which the latter, "being full of anger and venom," made use of coarse and unseemly words towards the Venetians. The quarrel was renewed at the banquet that followed, and loaves of bread and other meats were used as missiles. The Cypriotes sided with the Venetians, and many of the Genoese present were flung out of the window and dashed to pieces. But it was a dispute for the possession of the classic Tenedos *notissima famæ insula* which made war inevitable. The Signory offered the Greek Emperor for the cession of the island (which by its position south of the Dardanelles was of great strategical importance) the sum of three thousand ducats and the return of the Imperial jewels which were held in pledge at Venice. The offer was made a demand by a threat to treat with the Turks if the Emperor refused the bargain. Paleologus had emptied his treasury to meet the cost of the Ottoman wars, and accepted the offer. The Genoese retaliated by taking in hand Andronicus, the Emperor's rebellious and renegade son, who in return for their support promised to make them masters of the island. The islanders confronted by the rival claims, came forth bearing crosses in their hands to welcome the Venetians, and the Governor declared for St Mark. A Venetian garrison was accepted and an attempted landing by the Genoese was defeated with great slaughter. Each of the powers prepared for the struggle: Genoa by allying herself with the King of Hungary and the Carraras of Padua; Venice with Barnabo Visconti, lord of Milan, for the Milanese patronate of Genoa was of brief duration. Carlo Zeno, whose varied career and charmed life form one of the romances of history, was sent to harass the Genoese in the Mediterranean, and Vettor Pisani given command of the home fleet. After some minor successes Pisani was ordered by the Senate to go into winter quarters at Pola. While resting his exhausted crews and refitting his ships, the enemy appeared in the offing. Pisani, whose better judgment was overruled by the civil Commissioners, was compelled to give battle. Stung by a reflection on his courage he grasped a banner and led the onslaught, crying, "Who loves Messer S. Marco, let him follow me." Luciano Doria the Genoese admiral was slain, and victory inclined at first to the Venetians, but a clever feint broke their formation. The Genoese turned and the whole Venetian fleet, save six galleys that escaped to Parenzo, was annihilated. Pisani on his arrival at Venice was accused of defective scouting, impeached, and punished by degradation and imprisonment. Venice reeled under the blow. Zeno was far away. The enemy was reinforced by Pietro Doria's command, and for the first time during many centuries a hostile fleet swept down on the lagoons. But Venice never lost faith in herself or in her destiny. With grim determination she set her teeth and tightened her armour. The approved measures were taken to fortify the city and block the channels. Messengers were dispatched to recall Carlo Zeno. A Franciscan friar was sent to learn the price of the King of Hungary's neutrality. But the Genoese and Paduan envoys at Buda were already singing the dirge of Venetian independence. A garrison was to be planted at St Mark's and a castle built at Cannareggio. Her inviolable bulwark the sea was to be breached and indomitable Venice chained by a causeway to the mainland. The attempt to detach the King from his ally failed. The miserable remnant of the fine fleet was entrusted to Taddeo Giustiniani, who to hearten the men decided to attack some Genoese galleys that were hovering off Lido. As he sailed forth, a prisoner leapt from one of the enemy's ships and swam towards the Venetian fleet. A Genoese bowman took aim and shot him in the head, but he pressed on, and when picked up warned his compatriots that the whole Genoese fleet under Pietro Doria was following. Giustiniani turned back, and his little armament was saved.

Doria had sailed into the gulph, burning Umago, Grado and Caorle. He turned towards the *lidi*, devastated Pelestrina, captured and utterly destroyed Chioggia *minore*, and prepared to attack Chioggia *maggiore*. On the mainland, the Hungarians had occupied important Venetian possessions; Treviso was besieged; Carrara, by strenuous engineering, had joined hands with his ally, and given Genoa a base on the mainland. On the 16th of August a general assault was made on Chioggia. The garrison fought bravely: Emo, their commander, with a handful of men resisted to the last. But he, too, was at length overpowered, and the banners of Genoa, Hungary and Padua floated over Chioggia. It was about midnight when the calamitous news reached St Mark's. The great bell was tolled, and under the gloom of the disaster it was decided to open negotiations with the enemy. But the offer of the Signory was haughtily rejected. "Ye shall have no peace," answered Doria, "until I have bridled S. Mark's horses." Venice prepared for a death-grapple with her adversary. The common peril evoked a noble enthusiasm. Patrician offered to share the last crust with plebeian and fight shoulder to shoulder in defence of the fatherland. After an unsuccessful attempt to secure the services of Sir John Hawkwood, prince of *condottieri*, as Captain-General, the post was given to Taddeo Giustiniani. But the people, with finer insight, shouted for Vettor Pisani, under him alone would they fight. The Senate gave way. A great multitude welcomed his release from prison, and bore him in triumph to St Mark's, crying, "*Viva Messer Vettor Pisani.*" But their hero rebuked them, and bade them keep silence or shout, "*Viva Messer S. Marco.*" They only cried the more loudly, "Long live Vettor Pisani *and* St Mark! Long live Vettor Pisani our father." As he was borne along, his veteran pilot, Corbaro, shouted, "Now is the time to avenge thee, make thyself dictator." The answer was a blow from Pisani's clenched fist. From St Mark's to his house in S. Fantino, so great was the press of people that there was no place on the ground for a grain of millet seed. He reached home to find that his brother was dead, that his father, too, had gone to an obscure grave. On the morrow he went to the basilica to pray for divine aid, and after his devotions stood by the high altar, and made a *bellisima sermone* in the vulgar tongue to the people. With cries of "Galleys! galleys! arms! arms!" they streamed out to the Piazza. So great, however, was the disappointment when it became known that Pisani was to share the command with Giustiniani that the seamen refused to serve, and the Senate again gave way. The people's leader being assured them, enthusiasm knew no bounds. Everyone able to bear arms enrolled himself. A forced loan produced the magnificent sum of more than six and a quarter millions of lire. Gold and silver, jewels and precious stones were cast into the treasury; citizens stripped themselves even of the clasps of their garments. The Signory decreed the ennoblement after the peace of thirty families who should have contributed most in men and treasure to the State. Foreigners were offered citizenship. The Doge himself, seventy-two years and all, reared his gonfalon of gold in the Piazza and decided to lead the armament. A new fleet was equipped: the fortifications strengthened. Meanwhile Doria planned to winter in Chioggia, and Pisani with daring and masterly resource determined to take the offensive and imprison the Genoese in the harbour. On the night of December the 21st, the Venetian fleet left its moorings, towing behind it great hulks filled with stones. Before dawn it had reached the channel of Chioggia. Five thousand men were disembarked on the tongue of land at Brondolo. They were soon attacked and forced by the Genoese to regain their ships. But the diversion had enabled Pisani to sink two of his hulks across the passage, and soon an insuperable barrier blocked the issue. Swiftly he turned under the very jaws of the Genoese cannon and succeeded in holding the enemy while his sappers dammed the channel of Brondolo. With equal skill and bravery the canal of Lombardy was choked, and Carrara cut off from his ally. In a few days every issue from Chioggia was barred, and

Pisani hastened out to sea by the Porto di Lido to deal with any reinforcements that might be sent to raise the blockade. Slowly the dark, cold December days dragged on: the strenuous fighting, privation and hunger broke down the spirits of the Venetians. Some there were who murmured, saying, "rather than die here let us abandon Venice and migrate to Crete." But the Doge met them, drew his sword and swore that though on the verge of eighty he would die sooner than return defeated to St Mark's. The end of the year was at hand, a mutiny threatened, the Doge again appealed to them, and promised that if on January 1st Zeno had not been sighted, the blockade of Chioggia should be raised. On the morning of New Year's day anxious eyes scanned the seas. At length a watcher on St Mark's tower raised a cry. Fifteen sail were on the horizon. Was it invincible Zeno bringing salvation to Venice, or Genoese reinforcements bearing her doom? Some light, swift vessels were sent to reconnoitre. As they neared the squadron St Mark's banner was run up on the foremost galley. The darkest hour had passed.

SUNSET—MODERN VENICE.

For six months after Zeno's arrival the Genoese held out, but there was never any doubt as to the ultimate result, and on June the 24th the Lion of St Mark again waved from the Tower of Chioggia.

Two Genoese fleets were, however, still at large. Pisani was sent to run them down and died of fever and wounds at Manfredonia.[41] Zeno took up the chase, but the Genoese successfully eluded their pursuers. It was the end of Genoa as a great maritime power. Even as Spain did in her struggle with

England two centuries later, Genoa had entered on a contest which tried the nation beyond its powers. Hostilities on the mainland continued till, by the mediation of the House of Savoy, a congress met at Turin and a general treaty of peace was signed in August 1381. For three years no merchant ship had left Venice, yet she emerged from the contest stronger than ever, the acknowledged mistress of the seas.

In September 1381 the Great Council met to elect the thirty contributors to the success of the war, who were to be ennobled. The balloting lasted all day and great part of the night, and on the morrow the names were cried at the edict stones of the Rialto and St Mark's. Those thus honoured went each bearing a lighted taper in solemn procession to St Mark's, and the ceremony ended in popular rejoicings.

CHAPTER IX

Aggression on the Mainland—Arrest and Execution of Carmagnola—The Two Foscari

"Are these thy boasts—
To mix with kings in the low lust of sway,
Yell in the hunt and share the murderous prey."
—*Coleridge.*

IN June of the next year the venerable and faithful Doge Andrea Contarini was laid to rest in the cloister of S. Stefano, and Michele Morosini was elected in his stead. Morosini was one who in the gloomiest time of the Chioggian war had given an inestimable pledge of his faith in the Republic by buying some house property belonging to the commune for 25,000 ducats, and when rallied by his friends for his folly, replied,[42] "If ill befall the land, I have no desire for fortune."

Plague carried off Morosini in less than a year, and in October 1382 Antonio Venier became Doge. Peace was a brief sojourner in Italy. A long period of war and diplomacy with the despots of North Italy opens, in which Venice is now the ally and now the foe of Carrara or Visconti. Bribery, treachery and violence were among the weapons used on either side. More than once the Senate and the Ten connived at attempts to poison their country's enemies. It was the time of the great Condottieri. Patriotism was an affair of the highest bidder. Martial courage and science were sold for a price. No gold, no army. Turk or Christian, English or German, Italian or French, all were welcome who would sell a strong arm and professional skill. English soldiers were much in demand. "Let us have as many English as possible and as few Germans and Italians." "It would be well for the Paduan contingent to be furnished with the English company, for a thousand lances of theirs are worth more than 500,000 of others." Such were the instructions of the Signory to their commanders.

In 1387, by a secret treaty, Galeozzo Visconti of Milan and the Carraras of Padua agreed to partition the Scala dominions between them. Visconti was to have Verona: the Carraras, Vicenza. The feeble descendant of Can Grande, Dante's "magnifico atque victorioso domino" became a Venetian pensioner until poison did Visconti's work in Friuli, and the widowed and orphaned family of the lord of Verona was reduced to beggary.[43] Before, however, the Carraras had realised what had happened, Visconti had stealthily seized Vicenza. They weakly appealed to Venice for support. But the wounds left by the Chioggian war were not yet healed, and the Signory lent a more willing ear to Visconti, who offered the bitter-sweet morsel of revenge and a tempting prize. Treviso became Venetian once more and territory commanding two passes into North Europe was ceded to the Republic. She averted her eyes while Visconti grabbed Padua. Lord of a wide domain, he now turned his lustful regard on Florence. Venice, alarmed at the monster she had fostered, swung round and helped the Carraras to regain Padua. But in 1402, when the aim of his life seemed near achievement, death struck Visconti down and his dominions became a prey to his generals and his enemies. The Carraras joined in the scramble and attacked Vicenza. Visconti's widow appealed to Venice for help. The deal was a hard one: Verona and Vicenza were the price of a Venetian alliance. The Carraras, summoned to raise the siege of Vicenza, stood defiant. When their herald reached the edict stone at St Mark's to deliver the formal challenge, he would have been stoned to death on the Piazza by the boys and populace, if some nobles who happened to be passing had not shielded him; for a story had reached Venice that when the trumpeter of the Republic arrived at the Paduan camp before Vicenza he was seized by order of Jacopo Carrara, his ears and nose cut off, and himself dismissed with the brutal jibe: "Now I have made thee a S. Marco."

The war was a triumph for Venice. In 1404 she occupied Vicenza, in 1405 Verona. Three months later Padua fell to her arms. The Carraras, father and son, were captured and sent to join Jacopo (who had been taken at Verona), in a Venetian prison. So bitter was the feeling at Venice, that as they passed the people cried—"Crucify them! crucify them!" The Signory treated them leniently at first, but the seizure of the Carraras' papers at Padua revealed a great conspiracy against the Republic in which some of her own most exalted officers were implicated. The Ten assisted by a *Zonta* sat day and night to try the accused. On a January evening in 1406 it was bruited about the Piazza that old Carrara had been strangled in his cell. On the morrow, his two sons, it was rumoured, had met the same fate. "Dead men wage no wars" was the grim comment of the people. Another day passed and to the stupefaction of Venice Carlo Zeno, now venerable and honoured, was summoned by the Ten and ordered to be put to the question.[44] The stern decemvirs were no respecters of persons. Zeno was convicted of having corresponded with his country's enemies, stripped of his honours and imprisoned.

During the early fifteenth century, Venice was riding on the full tide of territorial expansion. On the north she touched the Alps, on the west and south the Adige. Dalmatia, bought back for 200,000 florins, was retained by force of arms, and for the eighth time St Mark's banner was run up over Zara. Several feudal lords dying without heirs left their domains to the Republic. After a war with the Emperor and his allies she gained the province of Friuli, and reached the Carnac Alps in the east. In 1422 she had acquired Corfù,

Argos, Nauplia and Corinth. A Venetian sat on St Peter's chair and two of her bishops were elevated to the Sacred College. Over this vast empire she ruled, a mother city of less than 200,000 inhabitants,[45] mistress of provinces and of the seas. Her wealth was prodigious.[46] The pomp and circumstance of public and private life grew more and more sumptuous. Four frocks prepared for the trousseau of Jacopo Foscari's bride cost 2000 ducats. In 1400 the famous *Compagnia della Calza* (Guild of the Hose) was founded to give honourable and princely entertainment among its members and to the guests of the Republic, and to contribute to the magnificence of State festivals. Brilliant suppers, serenades, jousts and regattas were organised by the members, who were drawn from the richest families. They were divided into various companies bearing fanciful names—the *Sempiterni*, the *Cortesi*, the *Immortali*. They wore embroidered on their hose, lengthwise or crosswise, some quaint pattern in many colours—arabesques, stars, or figures of birds or quadrupeds. On solemn occasions the designs were formed of gold, pearls and precious stones. The doublet was of velvet or cloth of gold with slashed sleeves laced with silk ribbons. The mantle of cloth of gold or damask or crimson *tabi* cloth was fitted with a pointed hood, which, falling on the shoulders, displayed inside the richly embroidered device of the Company. The head was covered with a jewelled red or black cap. Pointed shoes adorned with jewels completed the costume. Ladies were admitted to membership and wore the *Calza* device embroidered on the sleeves of their dress. The *Compagnia* was subject to the control of the Ten.

RIO AND PONTE DI SANTA MARIA MAGGIORE.

The festivities which celebrated the elevation of Michel Steno in 1400, now an experienced and upright officer of the State, are said to have lasted nearly a year. A significant change, however, had been made by the correctors of the Coronation Oath—the Doge was no longer to be addressed as *domine mi*, but plain *Messer lo Doge*.

On a midsummer day in 1405 a great platform was erected outside St Mark's, where the Doge sat supported by his chief officers of State to receive the homage of Verona. The twenty-one Veronese ambassadors rode, clothed in white, on chargers caparisoned with white taffeta. They alighted in front of the Doge and bowed three times. High mass was then sung, after which the chief orator presented his credentials, and read an address beginning— "Glory to God in the highest." He then handed to the Doge the official seals and surrendered the keys of the Porta S. Giorgio, the Porta Vescovo and the Porta Calzoni, the first representing the knights and doctors, the second the merchants and citizens, the third the common people. Two banners, one with a white cross on a red field, another with gold cross on a blue field were then presented to the Doge, and a white wand, emblematic of purity and perpetual dominion. The Doge rose and made a speech beginning, "The people that walked in darkness have seen a great light," and applied the text to the good fortune of the Veronese in coming under the dominion of Venice. The orator began his reply with, "My soul doth magnify the Lord," at the end of which the Doge gave him the golden banner of St Mark, and all cried, "Viva Messer S. Marco." The two banners of Verona were then placed on either side the high altar at St Mark's. The same ceremony was used at the homage of Padua.

Tomaso Mocenigo, "one of the noblest and wisest of her children," came to the throne at a critical epoch of Venetian history. Visconti's son, Filippo, inherited the fierce passions and regal ambition of his father. Having assassinated his elder brother, Giovanni, he secured the services of the greatest *condottiero* of the time, Francesco Bussone da Carmagnola. Brescia and Genoa were quickly recovered, and assuring himself of Venetian neutrality, he seized Forlì and became a menace to Florence, who prayed for a Venetian alliance in the face of a common danger. The procurator, Francesco Foscari, his sails filled with successful acquisitions in Friuli, beckoned to a forward policy and favoured the Florentine alliance: Visconti was a danger to the State: when Florence had been bludgeoned he would turn on Venice and rend her. Foscari was answered in the Senate by Tomaso Mocenigo, in whose mouth Sanudo places a long oration. The venerable Doge after reviewing the story of the Milanese troubles, ranged through the whole of sacred and profane history to enforce his plea for peace. He prayed the fathers to be content with defending their present frontiers if attacked: "Let the young procurator beware of the fate of Pisa that waxed rich and great by peace and good government but fell by war." He summarised the national balance-sheet and the incidence of her trade. "Let the *procurator giovane* remember that commerce was the basis of Venetian prosperity, peace her greatest interest. Let them trade with Milan, not fight her. They were everywhere welcomed as the purveyors of the world; their islands were a city of refuge from oppression." He then lifted his hearers to the higher spheres of religion and ethics, and warned them that God would wreak vengeance on an aggressive and unrighteous nation. Foscari was intriguing for the reversion of the Dogeship. He had been chief of the Quarantia; three times a *capo* of the Ten. His influence was great among the patricians, by reason of his lavish distribution of money, when procurator, to decayed gentlemen whose daughters he dowered from the public charities. A few days after his speech in the Senate, Mocenigo lay on his sick bed; some senators stood around him, and the Doge feeling his end draw nigh again took up his parable and solemnly entreated them as they loved their fatherland not to elect Foscari as his successor; to preserve the priceless inheritance he was about to leave them; and to keep their hands from their neighbours, for God would destroy Venice if she waged an unjust war. Let them live in peace, fear nought and mistrust the Florentines. But in truth Mocenigo's warning came a century too late. The Nemesis of Empire was already upon Venice. She was impelled to grasp more and more in order to retain what she had already won. The time had passed when so great was the fame of the incorruptible justice[47] of the Fathers that sixty envoys of princes might be found waiting in her halls to ask the judgment of the Senate on important matters of State.

Foscari was elected after a close contest. At his proclamation the last feeble echo of the popular voice was drowned. The Grand Chancellor, reviewing the old formula, asked of the *Quarant' uno*, "What if the choice is not pleasing to the people?" and himself answered, "Let us simply say we have elected such a one." Foscari was presented to the people in St Mark's with the maimed formula, "*Quest' è il vostro doge.*" "*Se vi piacerà*" was no longer heard. But the coronation festivities were more gorgeous than ever and lasted a whole year. The responsibility of power and the strained relations with the Emperor, for a time sobered the impetuous Foscari. Once and again the Florentine envoys were dismissed unsatisfied. After suffering a severe defeat at Zagognara, the Florentines for the third time appealed to Venice, and in an impassioned oration threatened that if the Venetians permitted Filippo Visconti to make himself King of North Italy, they would help him to become Emperor. Meanwhile Carmagnola, who had risen from a Piedmontese hind to be an arbiter of States, had roused Visconti's suspicions and fled to Venice, where 30,000 ducats of his fortune were safely invested in the funds. The Signory paid him a handsome retaining fee and sent him to Treviso. Foscari's opportunity was now come. Carmagnola had been made a senator, and in supporting the Doge's war policy laid bare the weak parts in Visconti's position. It was to be an easy and glorious campaign. The terms of the alliance with Florence were drawn up. On February 19th, 1426,

Carmagnola was appointed Captain-General, and on March 3rd laid siege to Brescia.

Carmagnola proved a careful, not to say leisurely tactician, and professed much reliance on divine aid. April came, and the Captain-General asked permission to take the waters at Abano for his health's sake. The Senate consulted physicians and suggested that his presence at the siege was essential, and that an aperient might meet the case. The Captain-General did not take the hint, and spent a pleasant time at the baths. Again in November the delicate state of his health necessitated another journey to Abano. At length Brescia surrendered. Visconti offered to negotiate, and on the last day of the year a treaty signed at S. Giorgio Maggiore gave the whole province of Brescia and a large sub-Alpine territory to the Republic.

CLOISTER OF S. GREGORIO

In February of the next year Carmagnola took the field with the finest army ever seen in Italy, for Visconti had recommenced hostilities in the Bresciano. It was a fair country. The gentle Italian spring gave way to lusty summer. A battle had been fought in which the Republic suffered a heavy loss in *horses*; in another some unfortunate cavaliers, including the Captain-General himself, were dangerously hurt by falling from their chargers during a surprise attack. The Senate protested, and urged greater energy and decision. In October Carmagnola's professional pride was stung. He bestirred himself, won a brilliant victory at Macolò and captured 8000 cavalry. History is silent as to the dead and wounded. He was lavishly rewarded, made a Count, and given a house in Venice and an estate in the country. The Senate now advised him to follow up his advantage, strike at Milan and end the war. But Carmagnola's aim was to live, not to perish by the sword. The Republic was an excellent paymaster, and it were sorry economy to bring so profitable a business to a premature conclusion. Moreover, his adversary of to-day might be his patron of to-morrow, and his delicate constitution again required the stimulus of the baths. Visconti, too, was anxious for breathing time, and began intriguing with his former general. In 1428 another instrument of peace gave the province of Bergamo to Venice. Carmagnola received princely honours but soon gave in his resignation. The Republic offered him a salary of one thousand ducats a month in peace or war, and all ransoms and prize-money when on active service. The promise of the dukedom of Milan was held before him, but when the third Milanese war began the General's strategy was more exasperating than ever. He had no plan of campaign, and was known to be in correspondence with Visconti. The patient Senate resolved at last to act. Their members were bound to secrecy, and the Ten with a *Zonta* of twenty Senators were ordered to deal with the case warily but vigorously. Carmagnola's arrest was voted. Giovanni de' Imperi, secretary of the Ten, a pallid-faced notary, left for the camp with instructions to invite the General to Venice for a conference with the Doge. If he failed to take the bait, the secretary bore letters-patent addressed to the staff of the army, commanding them to concert measures for the arrest and detention of their chief. It was a perilous mission, for the mighty Captain-General held the State in the hollow of his hands. But Giovanni of the pale face and nerves of steel successfully achieved his purpose, and Carmagnola left for Venice. On his arrival he was met by eight nobles whose business it was to divert him from his home and lead him to meet the Doge. When he reached the palace the secretary of the Ten disappeared, and Leonardo Mocenigo, procurator of the *Collegio*, informed the General's suite that their master was honoured by an invitation to dine with the Doge and that they might retire. As the guest passed through the apartments he noticed with some concern that the doors were closed behind him. On asking for the Doge he was answered that his Serenity was confined to his room with kidney disease, and would see him to-morrow. At the *Sala delle quattro porte* Carmagnola turned to go home: the officer touched his shoulder and pointed to a corridor that led to the prisons, saying, "This way, my lord." "But that is not the way!" exclaimed the great captain. "Yes, yes; quite right," repeated the officer. A signal was given. Guards surrounded him and he was hustled down the stairs, crying, "I am a dead man." The eagle was snared. At the trial Carmagnola was put to the question. As the executioner prepared the cord, Carmagnola pointed to the arm that had been broken in the service of the Republic. A brazier was applied to his feet instead. On May 5th, 1432, the unhappy soldier was led with a gag in his mouth to his doom between the red columns. After three blows his head fell from his shoulders.

The awful tragedy had been planned and executed with consummate skill and resolution. Two hundred officials were cognisant of the process. Not one opened his mouth to betray the secret. From the time the victim left Vicenza he was practically under arrest, though this he never suspected. The remains were buried in the Frari and afterwards removed to Milan. His widow was pensioned and his daughters were dowered. Four years later another enemy of the Republic lost his head between the red columns. The only surviving son of old Carrara had been convicted by the Ten of an attempt to plot an insurrection in Padua.

STATUE OF BARTOLOMEO COLLEONI

During the long remaining years of Foscari's reign the resources of Venice were drained by a succession of costly campaigns in defence of her conquests. The most famous condottieri, Gonzaga of Mantua, Gattamelata, Francesco Sforza, and Bartolomeo Colleoni were employed, at enormous expense. At length, in 1454, weary and exhausted by the financial, if not by the mortal drain of thirty years' war, and sobered by the appalling news of the capture of Constantinople by the Turks, the three chief belligerents—Venice, Florence, and Milan—laid down their arms and signed a defensive alliance against any power that should disturb the peace of Italy. The Venetians had held, and even added to, their conquests. Ravenna was occupied in 1440 and the last of the Polentas, father and son died in exile in Crete. Although St Mark's Lion never looked down from his pillar on a Milanese Piazza, Venice had won the primacy of North Italy. In fifty years she had annexed eleven provinces—Treviso, Vicenza and the *Sette Comuni*, Verona, Padua, the Friuli, Brescia, Bergamo, Feltre, Belluno, Crema, Ravenna. Her yoke was easy. The subject peoples had small reason to regret the change of masters. The Brescians endured the horrors of a three years' siege rather than revert to Milanese dominion. The Signory "that could not sleep till Brescia were relieved" organised the transport of a fleet of thirty vessels across the mountains, a distance of two hundred miles in mid-winter, lowered them down the precipitous flank of Monte Baldo and launched them on Lake Carda, a stupendous feat of engineering skill and energy.

Venice never denied her enlightened and paternal rule, which embraced even the cut of ladies' dresses and the duties of wet nurses. But St Mark's "insatiable greed" had aroused the jealousies of the transalpine monarchies. The League of Cambrai, which broke down for ever the power of Venice on the mainland, was a direct outcome of Foscari's policy.

While men's minds were pre-occupied with the Milanese war and the news of the occupation of part of the Morea by the Turks, a grave domestic scandal weighed upon the Fathers. Charges of corruption were openly made against the Foscari, and in February 1445 the Doge's only surviving son, Jacopo, was denounced to the Ten for having accepted bribes to use his influence with his father in the allocation of State appointments. The young Foscari was a cultured, but pleasure-loving noble, whose magnificent marriage festivities in 1441 had aroused even the critical Venetians to enthusiasm. He was charged with "having regard neither to God nor man, and accepting gifts of money and jewels against the law," and cited to appear on the 18th before the Tribunal of the Ten, who were assisted by a *Zonta* of ten nobles. The arrest of his valet, Gaspero, on the previous day had, however, aroused Jacopo's suspicions; and when the officer of the Ten tried to serve the warrant, it was discovered that Foscari had fled to Trieste with all the money he could lay hands on. The tribunal having excluded the Doge and all his relations, proceeded to try the accused in default. The members were declared inviolable and permitted to wear arms. Jacopo was found guilty, and banished for life to Nauplia. The Dogaressa was refused permission to visit him at Trieste, and Marco Trevisano with a galley sent to deport him. Messer Jacopo, however, treated the warrant with contempt, and refused to embark.

The price of contumacy was outlawry, and decapitation between the two columns. The Ten did not enforce the extreme penalty, and entreated the Doge to persuade his son to obey the law. But efforts were of no avail, and on April 7th the sentence was confirmed, and Jacopo's property confiscated.

For more than a year the outlaw had been living defiantly at Trieste, when fresh revelations led to the appointment of another *Zonta* to deal further with the scandal. Five months passed. Marco Trevisano died, and Jacopo fell sick at Trieste. The Ten thereupon resolved to accept, in the name of Jesus Christ, the excuses of the invalid for not proceeding to Nauplia, and to substitute his own country house near Treviso for the place of exile.

We hear nothing more of the case until April 1447, when a chest containing 2040 ducats and some silver plate was discovered, and proven to have been received by Jacopo from the Duke of Milan. The contents of the chest were confiscated, but no further action was taken. In September, the Doge presented a piteous petition for his son's pardon. The Ten resolved that, since the present critical state of public affairs demanded a prince with a clear and untroubled mind, Jacopo should be restored to his family, as an act of piety to our lord the Doge. Three years elapsed. On a November evening, as Ermolao Donato, one of the *Capi* who had tried Jacopo, was leaving the palace after attending a meeting of the Senate, he was fatally stabbed. The Ten and a *Zonta* met to investigate, but failed to penetrate the mystery. On January 2nd, 1451, a signed denunciation was found in the *Bocca del leone*. Jacopo Foscari was arrested, and put to the question. Incoherent muttering, which the Ten thought to be an incantation, was all that could be forced from his lips. The trial dragged on until March 26th, when Jacopo was declared, on purely circumstantial evidence, guilty of the murder, and banished to Canea, in Crete, where he was to report himself daily to the Podestà. The Doge was exhorted to patience, and on the 29th the condemned Jacopo was put on a galley that was sailing for Crete. In the June of 1456 important despatches in cypher from Canea came before the Ten. The home-sick and intolerant Foscari had written a letter to the Duke of Milan, asking him to intercede with the Signory, and another to the Turkish Sultan, begging that a vessel might be sent to Crete to abduct him from the island. Jacopo and all his household were cited to Venice. Before the Ten he frankly confessed all, and the sentence was then debated. A *Capo*, Jacopo Loredano, proposed the death penalty. The motion was lost, and his relegation to Canea and a year's imprisonment were voted. His family were permitted to see him and Jacopo, bearing marks of the torture, was led into the room, where his father awaited him. The poor old Doge fell upon his son's neck, while Jacopo cried, "Father, father, I beseech you procure for me permission to return to my home." "Jacopo," answered the Doge, "thou[48] must obey the will of the land, and strive no more." As the door closed on his son for ever, the miserable father flung himself upon a chair, uttering lamentations and moaning, "O! the great pity of it!" In six months came news from Canea: Jacopo Foscari was dead. The Doge never recovered from the blow. He secluded himself in his room, and sank into hopeless, sullen grief. The most urgent affairs of State could not divert him from his sorrow. The very Government was paralysed, and the Ten were called to devise a way out of the dead-lock. Having excluded the Doge's relations, after long debate they decided to invite the Doge in his great charity to take pity on the land and freely resign. They offered a pension of fifteen hundred ducats, and gave him a day to consider his answer. On the morrow, he would say neither yea nor nay, and complained of the unconstitutional suggestion. A second deputation was no more successful. It was then intimated to the Doge that he must resign, and leave the palace within a week, or suffer the confiscation of his property.

A FRUIT STALL.

On Sunday the 23rd of October, in the presence of the Ten and the chief officers of State, he silently drew the ducal ring from his finger. A *Capo* broke it in pieces and removed the ducal cap from his head. The discrowned Foscari was bid to retire to his home in S. Pantaleone. As the Councillors were leaving the room he noticed that one of the Quarantia lingered awhile and gazed pityingly upon him. He called him, took his hand and asked: "Whose son art thou?" "I am the son of Marin Memo," was the reply. "He is my dear comrade," said the Doge. "Prithee bid him come to see me, for it will be a precious solace to me: we will visit the monasteries together." Early on the morrow Francesco Foscari left his apartments leaning on a crutched stick accompanied by his brother Marco, his only suite a few sobbing kinsmen and servants. As they neared the principal staircase Marco said: "It is well, your Serenity, that we go to the landing-stage by the other stairway which is covered." "Nay," answered Foscari, "I will descend by the same stairs up which I mounted to the Dogeship." Stripped of his honours, forsaken by his Councillors, bent beneath the weight of his eighty-four years and the long tenure of a great office, the humiliated Foscari tottered down those steps in silence, which more than the third of a century before he had climbed, erect, exultant, full of hope, amid the acclamation of a whole city.

NERIDYCIN

BUST OF FRANCESCO FOSCARI

The Great Council met the same day: the electoral machinery was set in motion and on the morrow, the 30th October, Pasquale Malipiero was chosen and proclaimed Doge two hours before sunset. Two days after, on All Saints' Day, the new Doge, and his Council were at mass at St Mark's when a messenger came in hot haste with the news that Francesco Foscari was dead. The Councillors gazed mutely at each other. The Ten were convoked and, pricked perhaps by remorse at their severity, voted a magnificent and honourable funeral, the widow protesting against the mockery and declaring that she would sell her dowry to give her lord worthy burial. Wrapped in a mantle of cloth of gold; crowned with the ducal cap;

sword by side and spurred with gold, all that remained of the great Doge Foscari lay in state in the hall of the Senate, guarded by four and twenty nobles in scarlet robes to indicate that if the Doge were dead the Signory yet lived. The bier was borne by a picked body of sailors. Pasquale Malipiero, clothed as a simple senator; the officers of State; the clergy; the guilds followed. With solemn pomp the pageant went its way lighted by innumerable tapers along the Merceria and across the Rialto bridge to the Church of the Frari. The sumptuous monument, erected in the choir to his memory, by Ant. Riccio, still testifies to his fame. Those who would gaze on the striking, sensuous features of unhappy Doge Foscari will find his bust in the corridor that leads to the private apartments of the ducal palace, a faithful portrait carved by Bart. Buon. It was rescued when the original group over the Porta della Carta was destroyed in 1797.

Tomaso Mocenigo left Venice at peace with a flourishing exchequer: under Foscari it became bankrupt. In ten years the Milanese war had cost seven million sequins. The funds which stood at 60 when it began, sank to 18½ before its close. Her hands tied by the war, Venice had been compelled to look on while Constantinople fell to the Turks. Increased taxes, forced loans, national default and commercial crises: non-payment of salaries, depreciation of real estate, depression of industry and reduction of population—this was the cost of military glory; the dark background to the brilliant and memorable reign of Francesco Foscari.

CHAPTER X

*The Turkish Terror—Acquisition of Cyprus—Discovery of the Cape Route to India—
The French Invasions—The League of Cambrai—Decline of Venice*

"The gods have done it as to all they do
Destine destruction, that from thence may rise
A poem to instruct posterities."
—*Chapman's Homer*

IN the eyes of Italian and European statesmen, Venice at the death of Doge
Foscari seemed mightier than ever, but in truth she had already passed the
meridian of her strength and was on the descending arc of her destiny. For a
century her consuls had warned the Signory of danger in the East. Pope after
pope had summoned his children to cease their fratricidal strife and unite to
meet the Turkish peril. During the pauses in the fierce clash of Christian
passions and ambitions, could be heard, like the beat of muffled drums, the
tread of the advancing infidel hosts sounding the doom of an empire. But no
state in Europe, least of all Venice, grasped the full significance of the
portent.

In 1416 a fleet had been sent to chastise the Sultan for permitting a violation
of treaty rights, and although in the words of the commander, the Turks
fought like dragons, yet by the grace of God and the help of the evangelist S.
Marco they were utterly routed and the greater part cut in pieces: he was
confident on the testimony of a captured Emir that the Turks would never
again venture to oppose the Venetians on the seas. In 1438 the Greek
Emperor himself came to Venice to implore her aid and that of Europe
against the enemy of Christendom. Twice in 1452 the appeal was repeated,
but the Christian princes were too busy with their own quarrels to listen, and
before a year passed the scimitar of the Turk was red with the blood of the
Christians at Constantinople. Had not Venice herself proven that the strong
city was not impregnable? When it fell the Republic adopted her usual policy.
She accepted the situation and secured her trading privileges by treaty with
the Sultan. But when news came in 1463 of the conquest of the Morea and
Epirus and that the crescent was flying over the Castle of Argos almost in
sight of the Adriatic, Venice no longer stopped her ears to the Papal voice.
Friar Michael of Milan was permitted to preach the crusade in the Piazza and
a big, iron box was placed in St Mark's for offerings of money. Cristoforo
Moro, the new Doge, addressed the Great Council and in an access of zeal
volunteered to lead the crusade. By 1607 ballots against 11 the Great Council
approved. Moro[49] was a devout but not very robust creature, and pleading
age and infirmity asked permission to withdraw. He was bluntly told by

Vettor Cappello to think less of his skin and more of the honour and welfare of the land.

Pius II. came to Ancona with the Sacred College to organise the crusade. A league was made with Hungary. The Duke of Burgundy offered to join in person. Envoys were sent to other Christian princes. On July 30th, 1464, three hours before sunset—a time selected by the astrologers as the best— the Venetian fleet weighed anchor, the Doge leading in a new galley named after him. Scarcely had he disembarked at Ancona when the Pope died and all came to naught. The Doge returned to the ducal palace. The Venetians single-handed fought on sea and land with their usual intrepidity, but the State was already weakened by the Milanese wars. In 1470 she lost the whole island of Negropont. Dazed by the calamity the members of the Collegio slowly walked with leaden feet and downcast looks across the Piazza and, if spoken to, answered not a word. Were they listening to the rustle of the wings of the sable-robed avenging sisters? In the following year a crowd of panic-stricken refugees from Istria and Friuli streamed into Venice and camped on the Piazza and under the arcades of the ducal palace. An army of 20,000 Turks had ravaged the provinces even up to Udine. The Republic was now at the end of her resources. An attempted diversion from Persia had failed. A big loan from her mainland provinces had been swallowed up. The Pope sent her envoys away empty. Not one Italian state stirred to help her. The good Tomaso Mocenigo's warnings were verified. National wrong meant national sorrow. Venice was harvesting the acrid fruit of the Genoese wars and her fifty years of territorial aggression. At the Congress[50] of Carisano in 1466 Galeazzo Sforza, Duke of Milan, had warned the Secretary of the Republic that she was hated not only in Italy but beyond the Alps. "You do a grievous wrong," he vehemently exclaimed; "you possess the fairest State in Italy, yet are not satisfied. You disturb the peace and covet the states of others. If you knew the ill-will universally felt towards you, the very hair of your head would stand on end. Do you think the states of Italy are leagued against you out of love to each other? No; necessity has driven them. They have bound themselves together for the fear they have of you and of your power. They will not rest till they have clipped your wings."

Negotiations were twice begun with a view to peace, but the Sultan's demands were intolerable and the unequal contest continued. In 1476 Friuli was again devastated and the flames of burning cities could be seen from St Mark's tower. Sailors were clamouring for their arrears of pay on the very steps of the ducal palace. Scutari (in Albania), after heroically resisting two sieges, was nearing the end. A loan from the mainland provinces and 100,000 ducats from the sum left to the Republic by their condottiero Colleoni were swallowed up. In January 1479 Venice yielded. She ceded Scutari, Stalimene and other territory in the Morea occupied by the Turks during the war, in exchange for which the Sultan restored all that had been taken from her beyond her old boundaries. She maintained consular jurisdiction in Constantinople, but agreed to pay an indemnity of 200,000 ducats and a tribute of 10,000 ducats a year for her trading privileges. It was in Moro's reign that the last vestige of popular government was effaced. The title of "Communitas Venetiarum," long disused in actual practice, was formally changed to the "Signoria." During the wearing anxieties of the Turkish wars from the death of Moro in 1471 to the signature of the peace under Doge Giov. Mocenigo in 1479 four Doges, Nicolo Tron, Nicolo Marcello, Pietro Mocenigo, and Andrea Vendramin followed in rapid succession, the last a descendant of a family ennobled after the Chioggian war. The delimitation of the new frontiers had been barely concluded in the East when a dispute concerning salterns and custom dues on the Po and the arrest of a priest for debt by the Venetian Consul at Ferrara led to another war in the peninsula. In 1482 the whole of Italy was aflame, and states that had watched unmoved the agony of the sixteen years' Turkish wars now turned on Venice and accused her of sinister motives in concluding the peace. The Republic was now allied with Genoa and the Papacy against the Duke of Ferrara, supported by the King of Naples, by Florence and some minor Italian states. The early operations were in her favour, but in a few months the Pope, alarmed by an attack on Rome by the Neapolitans, joined the league against Venice, and as feudal lord of Ferrara, summoned her, under pain of excommunication, to abandon operations against that city. When the interdict reached the Venetian Embassy at Rome, their ambassador was absent and his agent refused to transmit the document to Venice. It was then fixed on the doors of St Peter's and afterwards forwarded to the Patriarch at Venice, who was ordered under pain of excommunication to serve it on the Signory.[51] The Patriarch fell diplomatically sick and secretly informed the Doge. The Ten were convoked. The Patriarch was warned to keep silence, and that the services of the Church must proceed as usual. The Pope was a long way off; the Ten were near; he obeyed them. A formal appeal was then made to a future Council of the Church and a copy nailed by a secret agent on the door of S. Celso at Rome.

The new combination was too powerful for the crippled resources of Venice. Driven into a corner she adopted the impious expedient of inviting the King of France to make good his claim to Naples and the Duke of Orleans to vindicate his rights over the duchy of Milan. The weight of the great French monarchy fell with decisive effect on the league. Peace was made and the treaty of Bagnolo (1484) added Rovigo and the Polesine to the Venetian dominions. Three days' bell-ringing, illumination and rejoicing celebrated the immediate results of the new diplomacy. But the successors of Louis XI. were now factors in Italian politics. The league of Cambrai was one stage nearer.

For a few years all went well. By a clever exploitation of dynastic trouble the Signory was able to acquire the long coveted island of Cyprus. On the death of King John II., Carlotta, the rightful heiress and wife of Louis of Savoy, banished her father's bastard son James and seated herself on the throne. By the help of the Sultan of Egypt James was able before a year was past to lead a revolt, expel the Queen and her consort from the island and seize the crown. He made friends with the Venetians and to ensure their goodwill desired the Signory to bestow on him the hand of a Venetian maiden of noble birth. Caterina, daughter of Marco Cornaro, who with two other patrician houses held the greater part of the island in mortgage, was chosen and given a dowry valued at 100,000 ducats. The espousals were quickly celebrated with great pomp, the Doge himself presenting a consecrated ring to James' proxy, the Cypriote ambassador, who placed it on Caterina's finger in the name of the King of Cyprus. The little maid was but fourteen years of age and went from the splendour of the ducal palace to her usual life at home, while James was affirming his authority in the island.

During the same year (1468) the Senate learnt that Ferdinand of Naples was intriguing to draw James into an alliance with his own family. Stern words were used to the King and at length in October 1469 Venice was able to proclaim that she had taken the King and the island of Cyprus under her protection. In the summer of 1472, escorted by a fleet of four galleys, Caterina sailed to make a royal entry into Cyprus, but in a few months her joy was changed to mourning. James died, leaving her with child. The Senate aware that Carlotta was busy with the Italian powers and the Sultan, despatched their Captain-General, Pietro Mocenigo, to protect Caterina and to fortify and garrison the chief stations on the island. Before he arrived, the partizans of Carlotta burst into the palace, slew Caterina's physician before her eyes and cut in pieces her uncle Andrea and her cousin Bembo who were hasting to her aid. Mocenigo on his arrival quelled the insurrection and hanged the ringleaders. Two Venetian Councillors and a Civil Commissioner were sent to watch events. A prince was born but died in a few months. Fearing a reversion of power to the former dynasty, James' mother, sister and bastard sons were deported to Venice and Marco Cornaro was despatched with instructions to comfort his daughter, to maintain the allegiance of the Cypriotes and to declare the absolute will of the Republic that no change should take place in the order of things. An emissary of Ferdinand, Rizzo di Mario, was caught plotting at Alexandria, sent to Venice and condemned to death by the Ten. The Sultan, who had known him as the ambassador of Naples, threatened the Republic with his displeasure if the sentence were carried out. The Ten had Rizzo strangled in prison and informed the Sultan that he had poisoned himself. The Signory now determined to force Caterina's hand. Subtly but firmly the two Councillors and the Commissioner usurped more and more power, and poor Caterina's position was made intolerable. She wrote pitiful letters to the Doge complaining of the insults and petty persecutions suffered by herself and her father; scuffles took place on the very stairs of the palace. In October 1488 her brother Giorgio was sent by the Ten to persuade her to abdicate, while Captain-General Diedo was instructed to haste to Cyprus and "by wise, circumspect, cautious and secure means to get the Queen on board a galley and bring her here to us at Venice." To persuasions and threats Caterina at last yielded. The banner of St Mark floated over Cyprus and an envoy assured the Sultan of Egypt of the sympathy of the new government which was the "consequence of the full and free determination of our most serene and most beloved daughter Caterina Cornaro." The deposed Queen received a pompous welcome at Venice; made a solemn renunciation and a formal donation of Cyprus to the Republic in St Mark's; and went to live in petty state at the little township of Asolo which was given to her by the Republic. There, the centre of a literary circle, she passed many years of her life in works of charity, until the storm of the league of Cambrai drove her for shelter to Venice where she died, universally mourned, in 1509. To the end she signed herself Queen of Cyprus, Jerusalem and Armenia, and Signora of Asolo.

THE FISH MARKET.

During the closing years of the fifteenth century the mercantile supremacy of Venice, already threatened by the Ottoman conquests, was doomed by two momentous geographical discoveries. The voyages of Columbus and of Diaz were to change the face of Europe from the Mediterranean to the Atlantic, and to shift the commercial centre of the world from Venice to the

Spanish peninsula and ultimately to England. The former event excited curiosity in Venice, but not alarm. The Secretary of the Venetian Embassy in Spain, with the alertness of his class, won the confidence of Columbus, and finding him short of money, was able to secure a chart of his discoveries and a copy of a long treatise on the voyage which he caused to be translated and sent to the Signory. Far otherwise was the effect of the latter event, by which the ancient trade routes to the East were to be superseded by the ocean route to India. Priuli gives a graphic story of the consternation which seized the citizens, when, in the early sixteenth century, the report was verified that Vasco da Gama with a Portuguese fleet had reached Calcutta by rounding the Cape of Good Hope, and had returned to Lisbon with a cargo of spices. The wiser heads at once saw the gravity of the news. Owing to the heavy dues exacted by the sultans and princes the cost of a parcel of spices was increased from one ducat to sixty or a hundred by the time it reached Venice. The Portuguese, carrying by sea, would escape the levies and undersell the Venetian merchants in the markets of Europe. Their large and profitable trade from the East would be captured. Leonardo da Ca' Masser disguised as a merchant was sent to Lisbon to get information. An attempt was made to throttle the nascent commerce by working on the fears of the Sultan of Egypt. Envoys were sent to warn him of the danger to his revenue if the Portuguese were allowed to succeed, and to urge him to ally himself with the Indian princes, and give military aid if necessary, to destroy their trade. But the efforts of Venice availed nothing, for they were directed against the very course of the world's evolution.

The flourishing Eastern trade began to wither, but events seemed to offer opportunity of compensation by permitting a forward policy on the mainland. Venice had opened the gates of Italy to the French king, and it was not long before Charles VIII. marched in with an army such as had never before been seen in the peninsula to achieve his designs on the kingdom of Naples. From his camp at Asti came to Venice Philippe de Comines as an envoy seeking alliance with the Republic. The French diplomatist in his memoirs has left us a charming description of Venice as it appeared in 1494.

PALAZZO DARIO

As he approached the city he marvelled at the innumerable towers and monasteries, the fair churches, the great mansions and fine gardens all founded in the sea. Twenty-five nobles, well and richly clad in fine silk and scarlet cloth, bade him welcome and conducted him to a boat, large enough to seat forty persons, covered with satin cramoisy and richly carpeted. He was prayed to take his seat between the ambassadors of Milan and Ferrara. "I was taken," he writes, "along the *grande rue*, which they call the Grand Canal, and it is very broad. Galleys cross it, and I have seen great ships of four hundred tons and more near the houses, and it is the fairest street I believe that may be in the whole world, and fitted with the best houses, and it goes the whole length of the said city. The mansions are very large and high and of good stone; the ancient ones all painted. Others, made a hundred years ago, are faced with white marble, and yet have many a great piece of porphyry and serpentine on the front. Inside they have chambers with gilded ceilings and rich chimney-pieces of carved marble, gilded bedsteads of wood, and are well furnished. It is the most triumphant city I have ever seen and that doeth most honour to ambassadors and to strangers, and that most wisely doth govern itself, and where the service of God is most solemnly done: and though they may have many faults I believe that God hath them in remembrance for the reverence they bear to the service of His Church." De Comines found the Doge (Agostino Barbarigo) an amiable, wise and gentle prince, experienced in Italian politics, and after a stay of eight months, left with his mission unfulfilled. The Most Christian King, if we may believe the Venetian ambassador Contarini, lacked many inches of regal majesty. He was short in stature, ill-formed, had an ugly face, prominent white eyes, a big, coarse, aquiline nose, thick lips always open, and a nervous twitching of the hands very unpleasant to see. He was slow in expressing himself and dull-witted. Nor was Anne of Brittany, the Queen, portrayed less rudely. She, says the ungallant diplomatist, was short, bony and lame, with a rather pretty face. She was only seventeen, but most astute for her age, inordinately jealous of the King's majesty, and always succeeded in getting her way by the use of smiles or tears. The *Cristianissimo* marched triumphantly through the length of Italy to realise his dream of winning Naples, and then overthrowing the Mussulman power in the East. Florence, Rome, Naples were successively occupied; the balance of Italian politics was disastrously overthrown, and the unhappy land soon became a cockpit where the rival ambitions of France and Spain were fought out. Milan and Venice had each thought to use the Transalpine Powers for her own ends; they both became their prey. Charles had himself crowned King of Naples, Emperor of the East, and King of Jerusalem, but soon discovered that to conquer was easier than to hold. The rival powers began to league themselves against him, and in the bewildering moves on the political chess-board Venice and Milan came into line. In March 1495 the Signory assured De Comines that his master should have a free passage for the return of his army through Italy; in July of the same year she concerted with Milan, and fell upon the French at Fornovo di Taro, as they were toiling down the Cisa Pass to Parma. The French were severely punished, and in the fighting the King himself narrowly escaped capture. How the news was received at Venice, a letter dated July 9, 1495, and transcribed by Malipiero, gives a vivid picture. "I arose early and went my usual way to St Mark's," says Nicolo Lippomano, "when I saw a great fury of people running to the Piazza, crying—'Marco! Marco!' I asked the cause and was told the French camp had been routed. I arrived at the corner of St Mark's, where the elders are wont to meet, and found them all glad and many shed tears for joy. I went to Rialto and found everybody talking of the victory, and one kissed the other for very gladness. In a trice all the banks and shops were closed. Boys with flags began to run about the streets shouting of the victory and sacking the fruit-sellers' shops on the way. On the Rialto they met eight Savoyards whom they pelted with eggs, lemon peel and turnips, and otherwise ill-treated. All the people shouted—'To Ferrara! to Ferrara!' All my days I never saw the city in greater uproar. To God be the praise."

The spot is still shown where, in 1498, Charles broke his foolish head against a beam in a dark passage of the castle at Amboise. His successor, Louis XII., to the ill-hap of Italy, united in his person the claims both of the Orleans princes to Milan and of the French kings to Naples. Ludovico Sforza, fearing for his duchy, approached the Signory, but, to his disgust, learned that Venice had already secretly agreed to aid Louis in his designs on Milan, in return for Cremona and other cities and lands on the east of the Adda. Sforza, to revenge himself on Venice invited the Turks to attack her. In twenty days Louis had won the Milanese, and Venice was paid the price of her shame.

In November 1499, despatches from Constantinople warned the Signory that the Sultan was preparing to attack. Strenuous efforts were made to raise money. Antonio Grimani was sent with a large fleet to the East, and came upon the enemy off Sapienza, a name of ill-omen in Venetian naval history. The Turks had made amazing progress in naval construction; one of their ships is said to have been manned by one thousand Janissaries and sailors. The first encounter, after four hours' fighting, ended on August 12, 1499, in a Turkish success. On August 20, a small French fleet joined the Venetians, and on the 25th the final engagement was fought. The Venetians suffered a disastrous defeat. Malipiero, who was present as civil commissioner, roundly accused Grimani of want of patriotism and faint-heartedness, and declared if he had done his duty, the whole Turkish fleet would have fallen into their hands surely as God was God, and that, owing to want of discipline among the Venetian sailors, the French had retired disgusted from the operations. "We have lost eight hundred men, and the reputation of Venice." Grimani was sent home in irons. As he landed, his son, Cardinal Domenico, fought his way through the crowd, and lifted his father's chains to lighten his burden as he was led to prison. At the trial Grimani defended himself eloquently, and was banished to Dalmatia. The operations on land were not less humiliating. Such was the paralysing terror inspired by the Turk, that the native militia in Friuli refused to take the field, and the commander of the Stradiote mercenaries struck not a blow. Venice sued for peace. She weakly tried to inculpate Sforza for the outbreak of hostilities, but was told that the Duke of Milan had no power to move the Sultan; the depredations of her own subjects were the cause of her chastisement. On trying to soften the hard conditions exacted, her envoy was advised to bid the Signory hasten to accept the Sultan's terms: "Tell your Doge," said the Pacha, "that up to the present he has wedded the sea; it will be our turn in future, for we own more of the sea than he does." The Signory rejected the terms offered by the Porte. Allies were sought, and a league was made with the King of Hungary and the Pope. The King of Portugal promised help; Spain sent a fleet; France a small contingent of men. Some small successes failed to compensate for the loss of Lepanto, Modone, Corone and Navarino. Practically Venice was left, as usual, to fight single-handed, and ultimately peace was made with the Sultan, at the price of further territory in the Morea. Before the treaty was concluded, Agostino Barbarigo, who had succeeded his brother Marco in 1486, died. In October 1501, Leonardo Loredano, whose shrewd, clear-cut and ascetic features in Giovanni Bellini's portrait, are so familiar to visitors to the National Gallery of London, was preferred to the Dogeship. Owing to poor health, says Sanudo, he lived abstemiously. He was kindly, though of uneven temper, wise in counsel, very skilful in the conduct of public business, and his opinion generally prevailed with the Council.

In August 1503 the death of Pope Alexander VI. had foiled the plans of his bastard son, Cesare Borgia, to recover Romagna for the Papacy. Venice had been closely watching events, and on the advent of the feeble Pius III., determined to slice up the Papal States. Instructions were sent to the *podestà* of Ravenna, informing him of certain negotiations between the Signory and some cities of Romagna. He was to confer with the military commanders, in order to bring the negotiations quickly to a successful issue; but he was to act cautiously and secretly. The chief cities, by promise of remission of taxation, placed themselves under Venetian protection. The Duke of Urbino followed their lead, and was promised an annual subsidy.

CURIOSITY SHOP NEAR PIAZZA.

During the short twenty-six days of Pius III.'s reign, and the interval between his death and the election of a successor, Venice had occupied Bertinoro, Fano and Montefiore, and was hastening to seize Rimini and Imola. Julius II., at first favourably inclined to Venice, was in a few weeks made her enemy by the occupation of Rimini and the capture of Faenza. To Julius' angry protests and his threat of winning back Romagna, cost what it might, Venice urged her devotion to holy Church and the benevolence of her motives in trying to free Italy of the tyranny of Cesare Borgia. "*Signor Oratore*," cried the Pope, "your words are good, but your Signory's deeds are evil. We have neither men nor money to make war, but we will complain to the Christian princes, and invoke divine aid."[52] To Julius' demand for restitution, the Signory answered, "We will never restore the territory, even though we have to sell the very foundations of our houses."

"I tell you," wrote De Comines, after his return from Venice in 1495, "that I have found Venetian statesmen so wise and so bent upon increasing their Signory that if it be not soon provided against, all their neighbours will curse the hour." The provisions made by the most Christian princes were characteristic. "By an unprincipled treaty of spoliation," says Rawdon Brown, "the Great Powers of the Continent bound themselves together to fall upon Venice by surprise in a time of profound peace, and, in despite of the most solemn obligations, to despoil her of her territories." After much treating and protocolling there met on a November day in 1508 in a secret chamber at Cambrai, the Cardinal d'Amboise acting for the King of France, and Margaret of Austria for the Holy Roman Emperor. The papal nuncio and the King of Spain's envoy were near, but their views were known, and for greater safety they were not allowed to enter. After many difficulties, says Romanin, and such altercations that they wellnigh tore out each other's hair (*s'acciuffassero pei capegli*) the plenipotentiaries decided "that it was not only useful and honourable but necessary to call upon all the Powers of Europe to take a just vengeance, and quench, as they would a general conflagration, the insatiable greed of the Venetians and their thirst of dominion." The modest reward which the Powers proposed to themselves for "making an end of the rapine and injury wrought by the Venetians and their tyrannical usurpation of the possessions of others," was as follows. His Holiness the Pope was to have Ravenna, Cervia, Faenza, Rimini and all the territory held by the Venetians in Romagna; the Emperor, Padua, Vicenza, Verona, Roveredo, the Trevisano, the Friuli and Istria; the King of France, Brescia, Bergamo, Crema, Cremona, the Ghiaradadda and all the dependencies of the Duke of Milan; the King of Spain and of Naples, Trani, Brindisi, Otranto, Gallipoli and other cities held in pledge by Venice for an unpaid loan to his cousin whom he had deprived of the kingdom of Naples. The King of Hungary, if he joined, was to have Dalmatia; the Duke of Savoy, Cyprus. Some offal was reserved for the jackals of the minor states, if they ran at the heels of the royal beasts of prey. Florence later on informed the Sultan of Turkey and invited him to seize the oriental possessions of Venice when she was down. The Pope was to reinforce the temporal weapons of the confederates by the use of the spiritual arm.

But the Lion of St Mark, though his claws were a little blunted and his joints stiffened, had not lost his cunning. Moreover, he was forewarned. A dramatic story of the premature disclosure of the plot is told in the Venetian State papers. Spinola, an emissary of Gonsalvo of Cordova, came secretly to Cornaro, the Venetian ambassador, at Valladolid, in February 1509, and asked him to meet the great captain at mass in an unfrequented church at the far end of the town. He went and the secret was revealed to him. He refused to believe it, but later Spinola showed him a copy of a letter from Gonsalvo's wife at Genoa in which the details of the proposed partition were given, and offered his master's services to the Signory. Cornaro informed the Ten. They, too, hesitated to believe in any cause for attack, advised caution, and asked for further proof. Secret information from England soon brought confirmation and the Ten sat day and night to prepare for the coming storm. The weakness of the league lay in the fact that each spoiler was to seize his own share of the prey. Self-interest was its motive power. Self-interest would lead individual members to abandon the hunt if their portion were thrown to them. This the Ten quickly saw and acted upon with consummate art and patience while pushing on with all speed defensive military operations. The aged and infirm Doge Loredano, so overwrought by emotion that it was piteous to see, addressed the Great Council begging them to turn to righteousness and offer their lives and substance in defence of the fatherland. Himself would give an example by sending his silver plate to the mint. On April 27, 1509, Julius flung a bull of excommunication couched in almost savage terms against the Republic. The Ten forbade its publication and sent officers to take down any copies posted on churches or on the walls. They consulted learned canonists; drew up an appeal to a future council of the Church and sent emissaries to Rome who nailed a copy on the doors of St Peter's. The secular arm swiftly followed. Sanudo tells us that while he and two other Senators were examining a map of Italy painted on the walls of the Senate hall, a courier arrived with the news that the French had crossed the Adda, fallen on the fine army of the Republic at Agnadello and utterly routed it with a loss of four thousand in killed alone. Faces gathered gloom and despair. "Give me my cloak, wife," said Paolo Barbo, one of the most experienced of the fathers, "that I may go to the Senate, speak a couple of words and die." One disaster trod on the heels of another. Bergamo and Brescia fell and before the month was ended nearly the whole of Lombardy was lost. Preparations were even made to defend and victual Venice. Envoys were sent to treat with the Kings of France and Spain. The Pope was tempted by an offer of partial restitution and help towards a crusade against the Turks. Meanwhile the Imperial Eagle swooped down from Trent. The Signory, by ceding Verona and Vicenza, hoped to conciliate the Emperor and save Padua. In vain were the civil commissioners with the army entreated to make a stand, "lest the whole of our cities surrender in an hour." Padua fell and Treviso alone stood by the Republic. At bay she now turned to the Sultan of Turkey and begged for money and men, especially men. If his Highness would advance them one hundred thousand ducats and would agree to buy no more cloth of the Genoese and Florentines, who only used his money to help a League that sought his hurt, the Signory would send him fifty thousand ducats' worth of cloth, and jewels worth fifty thousand more, as security. The Venetian consul at Alexandria was instructed to incite the Sultan of Egypt to ruin Genoese and Florentine commerce in his dominions. The good offices of the Kings of England and Scotland were sought.

But the gloom was wearing away. One day in July two tall, mysterious, armed men were observed leaving Fusina in the gondola of the Ten. Arrived at Venice they remained closeted with the Ten and the Doge far into the night, then were rowed back whence they came. On the night of the 16th there was a hurrying to and fro of transports and armed vessels between the islands. The Doge's two sons and two hundred noble youths, fully armed, left for the mainland. The police boats of the Ten allowed no one to go out of Venice without permission. Next day Padua, disgusted by the insolence and exactions of the Imperialists, was won back for Venice before the laggard Emperor could reach the city. Sanudo remembered the 17th of July, for did he not buy a Hebrew Bible worth twenty ducats for a few pence as he was going home? Two attacks by the Emperor were successfully resisted, and the foiled Cæsar retired to Vicenza in October with anger in his heart against the French. In February 1510, after long and tough negotiations, the Pope was given his prey and detached from the league, but at the price of a bitter abasement of Venice. Time had avenged the Empire. It was now the Queen of the Adriatic who, in the person of her ambassadors, bowed the neck before the enthroned Pope in the atrium of St Peter's, surrendered her ecclesiastical privileges, admitted the justice of the excommunication, craved pardon for having provoked it, and was at length absolved and bidden to do the penance of the seven churches. The Ten, however, entered in their register a protest of nullity, declaring that the conditions had been extracted from the Republic by violence. The Pope who, as he told Venice, had no pleasure in seeing the ruin of her State to the aggrandisement of the barbarians, now became her ally. Soon other cities, sickened by the atrocities of the invaders, returned to their allegiance, and by skilful playing of King against Emperor, and Pope against both, Venice was able to regain the bulk of her territory.

CHAPTER XI

Loss of Cyprus—Lepanto—Paolo Sarpi—Attack on the Ten—Loss of Crete—
Temporary Reconquest of the Morea—Decadence—The End

"Alas, alas that great city, that was clothed in fine linen, and purple, and scarlet, and decked with gold, and precious stones, and pearls!... Alas, alas that great city, wherein were made rich all that had ships in the sea by reason of her costliness."—*The Revelation of St John the Divine.*

WE may not here attempt to tread the maze of chicanery and violence which ended in the peace of Cambrai.[53] We are permitted to see a fighting Pope exhorting his soldiers and directing siege operations against an Italian city, and climbing by a scaling-ladder through the breach to take possession. In 1514 the Spaniards desolated the land up to the lagoons and levelled their cannon at Venice. In 1515 the encampments of four armies were exhausting and polluting Lombardy. King, Popes, and Emperor died and their successors took up the unholy heritage of war and duplicity. Gaston de Foix, Bayard and other renowned chevaliers perished. In 1521 the Emperor Charles V. came upon the scene, and in alliance with the great Medicean Pope, Leo X., swept the French and their Venetian allies out of Lombardy. In July 1523, when the power of France was waning, the Venetians made terms with the Emperor. They were suffered to retain their territory up to the Adda in return for an annual tribute of 250,000 ducats. Venice excused herself to Francis I. by professing solicitude for the peace of Christendom in view of the threatening attitude of the Sultan. Before the year was ended King and Emperor were competing for Venetian help in a renewed struggle for mastery. While the Republic was temporising, the Imperialists had descended on Lombardy, routed the French before Pavia and captured their King. "Nothing is left to me," wrote Francis, "but honour, and life which is safe,"[54] and proceeded to send his ring secretly to the Sultan and to grovel before Charles. The victorious Emperor brushed aside the subtleties of the Venetian ambassadors. "If you were to send all your lawyers," he cried, "you would not convince me. You must pay 80,000 ducats for the troops you failed to send to Pavia. You are rich: my expenses are heavy: you must help me."

After perjuring himself at the peace of Madrid, January 1526, the *Cristianissimo* returned to France. In less than six weeks a "holy league" of France, Venice and the Papacy had been signed at Cognac for the "liberation" of Italy from the Imperialists. But Francis, whose moral fibre had been rotted by lechery, was no match for the virile genius of Charles, strong with the united resources of the Empire and of Spain in her greatness. The Emperor was soon again master of Italy. Rome was captured and sacked; Pope Clement VII. imprisoned. But the miserable condition of Italy and the news that the

Turks were threatening Vienna disposed Charles to treat, and in July 1529 Margaret of Austria was once more at Cambrai negotiating on behalf of the Emperor with Louise of Savoy, who represented Francis.[55] Two adjacent houses were chosen and the party-wall pierced that the ladies might confer with absolute secrecy. In two months, while the Venetians were finessing, the "*paix des dames*" was concluded and Venice left to make the best terms she might with the Emperor. Francis had given way all along the line. "The peace of Cambrai," says Michelet, "was the moral annihilation of France in Europe." During the coronation festivities at Bologna the Emperor and the Pope found time to deal with the Venetians, who agreed to pay the balance of the annual tribute of 250,000 ducats due on the treaty of 1523; to restore the cities of Naples and Apulia to the Emperor; and to the Papacy Ravenna and Cervia, which they had seized during the Pope's imprisonment at Rome. Thanks to the impassable lagoons Venice preserved her capital inviolate, but her prestige and her military power were gone.

After the League of Cambrai a change comes over the Venetian temper. Patricians, instead of using their talent in commerce and discovery, chose to live on their invested capital and on the revenues of their mainland estates. The power of initiative was gone. In 1522, before Sebastian Cabot sailed for the New World, he contrived to meet Contarini, an emissary of the Ten, secretly at Valladolid, and told him he had no joy in selling his knowledge to the foreigner; that he had refused tempting offers from Cardinal Wolsey and was prepared to absolve himself from the King of Spain's service and spend his genius in the advancement of his fatherland. But Contarini talked of things possible and impossible, and success is to those who will achieve the impossible. The supreme opportunity of retrieving her mercantile position was lost to Venice for ever. Sadder still, when Loredano had called on the Senate for volunteers and patriotic gifts for Padua and Treviso, not a man stirred. Venice had lost faith in herself.

In 1521 Leonardo Loredano died and was buried with more than usual pomp at S. Zanipolo. Antonio Grimani, the disgraced of Sapienza, who had redeemed himself by faithful service, reigned for two years and gave place to Andrea Gritti, a distinguished civil commissioner with the army during the wars. Between Gritti's death in 1539 and the election of Sebastian Venier, the hero of Lepanto, in 1577, there follows a line of Doges, Pietro Lando, Francesco Donato, Marc' Antonio Trevisano, Francesco Venier, Lorenzo and Girolamo Priuli, Pietro Loredano, Luigi Mocenigo, worthy magistrates all, but without distinction.

The wars had exhausted the State treasury. Her Indian trade was withered, and the wealth of Venice was no more commensurate to the demands of a long naval war. Her military pride had been chastened by the rod of the Emperor, and a dread of Spanish arms and Spanish gold hung like a pall over men's minds. An era of subtle diplomacy begins, and the Council of the Ten, with its new instrument of the Inquisitors of State, tightens its grip upon the executive. Wave after wave of Ottoman fury surges against her Eastern possessions; one by one they are engulfed. In 1535 she lost Egina, Paros and Syra; in 1540, Malvasia and Nauplia. In 1570 Cyprus was marked out for conquest and the usual appeal to the Christian Powers was made. Spain and the Pope promised help. Zane, the Venetian commander, wasted his force waiting at Zara, then learned that the allies were at Corfù. He reached the island only to find the Spanish admiral without orders. Meanwhile the season had worn along and operations were judged inopportune. The whole island by this time was occupied by the Turks, Nicosia and Famagosta alone holding out. While the futile admirals were squabbling about plans the magnificent heroism of the garrisons and of the inhabitants was spent in vain, and the cities fell to the horrors of a Turkish pillage, and Marc' Antonio Brigadin, the Venetian governor of Famagosta, was treacherously flayed alive in the Piazza after having surrendered on terms to the enemy. Zane was recalled to Venice, and Sebastian Venier given command. A new alliance of Spain, the Papacy and Venice being concluded, at length on October 7, 1571, the allied fleets came upon the Turkish armament off Lepanto in the Gulf of Corinth. The Spanish admiral, Don John of Austria, was in supreme command. Venier led the Venetians; Marc' Antonio Colonna the Papalists.

It was a calm sunny morning. The line of the allied fleets was four miles in extent, the two armaments were a mass of glittering steel as the rays of the sun smote on the helmets, breastplates and shields, bright as polished mirrors. The banners of gold and tall galley lamps were resplendent in many colours. A beautiful, yet an awful spectacle. The Venetian flagship was fiercely assailed. Venier, spite of his seventy-five years, was seen, sword in hand, pressing to the thick of the fight, heartening his men and with invincible courage striking down his enemies, so that he wrought deeds beyond the belief of man. We cannot here linger on the vicissitudes of the struggle. Scenes of comic relief were not absent from the tragedy. Some Turks, their arms of offence failing, seized upon a quantity of oranges and lemons and threw them at their enemies, who with mocking laughter cast them back. At length after five hours of savage fighting, the Turks were scoured off the seas. The allied and victorious admirals met, embraced each other speechless from emotion; and as the venerable Venier and the youthful Don John of Austria stood clasped in each other's arms shedding tears of joy, the eyes of even the most hardened of sea-dogs were moist with tears. Some 30,000 Turks are said to have perished; 3486 prisoners were divided among the victors as slaves; 94 ships were burned; 130 ships and 356 guns captured; 15,000 Christian slaves set at liberty. The allies lost heavily: 8000 men were slain including 25 Venetian nobles.[56] Among the Spanish was Cervantes, who lost an arm in the engagement.

A WINE SHOP.

As day broke on October 18th, a galley was seen sailing up to Lido trailing the Turkish colours at her stern, a pile of turbans on her deck. Amid the booming of the guns could be heard cries of "Victory! victory!" The reaction from the gloom of Cyprian news was tremendous. A frenzy of joy possessed the people. Shops were shut *per la morte de' Turchi*. The streets from the Rialto bridge to the Merceria were covered with a firmament of blue cloth spangled with stars of gold; a pyramid of Turkish spoils stood on the Piazza, which was gay with scarlet cloth, tapestry and pictures. Four days' rejoicings celebrated the triumph of the Cross. But to Venice the battle of Lepanto (or *alle Curzolari*) was a sterile victory. Dynastic jealousy in Spain and the old suspicion of Venice, which still clung to the allies, permitted the Turks to recover from the blow, and in March 1573 Venice agreed to purchase a separate peace at the cost of an indemnity of 300,000 ducats and a threefold increase of the tribute for Zante. The fair island of Cyprus was lost for ever. "Was it the Turks who were the victors at Lepanto?" asks Romanin.

On Doge Venier was conferred the consecrated golden rose, a supreme token of papal favour, but during the seventy years' peace from Lepanto to the outbreak of the fifth Turkish war, the indictment at Rome against the refractory children of the lagoons increased in gravity, and in the beginning of the seventeenth century the Papacy determined to force them to yield to discipline. The Venetians were a stubborn folk when their national dignity was threatened by Rome. "These *Signori* of the Senate," said Paul IV. to the Venetian ambassador, "are tough fellows and take a lot of cooking" (*non sono molto buoni da cuocer*). In 1527, when the Papacy was under the heel of Charles V., the Republic had reasserted her rights to nominate to ecclesiastical offices. Disputes as to the taxation of Church property, the right of the Pope to inspect the monasteries, the right of the Republic to try criminous clerics, exacerbated the situation until at length Gregory XIII. declared in 1581 that he would no longer consent to be Pope everywhere but in Venice, and sent his nuncio to make a visitation of the Venetian monasteries. The Republic refused permission, and the conflict called of the *Interdetto* began. But the fight between Italian Popes and Italian sovereigns, even in our own times, has generally been a comedy played for the mystification of Transalpine Powers and all ended in compromise. The Signory appointed the Bishop of Verona as the nuncio's colleague, and persuaded itself that the nuncio went with the Bishop; the Pope satisfied his dignity by claiming that the Bishop went with the nuncio. In 1605 the Spanish party, ever the evil genius of the Sacred College, re-opened the quarrel. The Republic had refused to send their nominee to the Patriarchate of Venice for examination to Rome, and had tried and convicted two clerics on the mainland for criminal offences. On Christmas Day a brief from Pope Paul V. was delivered to the Signory threatening excommunication if they did not submit in the matter of the taxation of ecclesiastical estates. The Republic engaged the learned Augustinian friar Paolo Sarpi as their adviser at a salary of two hundred ducats and prepared for the struggle. In February 1606, a second brief followed on the matter of the convicted clerics. The Republic expressed her devotion to the Catholic Faith, but firmly though respectfully declined to surrender her ancient rights and privileges. On April 16th, the Republic was given twenty-four days to submit under pain of interdict. Venice calmly waited. In due time the bull of excommunication[57] and interdict was delivered. The Signory forbade its publication and ordered the clergy to continue their functions as usual. Some of the regular clergy who disobeyed were expelled. Sarpi advised the Republic with excellent prudence and wisdom, and became in the eyes of Europe one of the greatest protagonists of national liberty against papal aggression. A Spanish army having been mobilised on the Milanese frontier, Sir Henry Wotton, the English ambassador, suggested an alliance of Venice with England, France, the Grisons, and the German Protestant princes, but the Republic was deaf on that side. She declared to the Pope that the Venetians were as good Catholics as he himself, but that as Church property enjoyed the protection of the State, it must share its burdens, and that criminals, whether lay or cleric, must be equally subject to the laws of the land. Time wore on. Spain, humbled by the defeat of her Armada and the revolt of the Netherlands, was afraid to strike; the obsolete ghostly artillery of Rome failed to act; and the secular clergy stood loyally by the Republic. The Papacy reverted to her habitual policy of compromise. The services of Henry IV. of France as mediator were accepted and a solemn comedy was played. The Republic agreed to surrender the incriminated clerics, without prejudice, to the French ambassador; the Pope agreed to withdraw *informally* the bull of excommunication and interdict. The Republic continued to nominate for Church offices and try clerical delinquents as before. But the Spanish fanatics at the Vatican never forgave the Venetian friar for his share in their discomfiture. On October 25, 1607, three ruffians fell upon him as he was crossing the S. Fosca Bridge,[58] stabbed him, then left him for dead, and escaped to Papal territory. Sarpi, however, recovered. The surgeon who was dressing his wounds remarked on their jagged, inartistic nature. "Ah!" replied the witty friar, "*agnosco stylum curiæ romanæ.*" On his recovery the Republic gave him a pension of six hundred ducats and a house near the Piazza, where the great patriot-scholar devoted the remainder of his life to literature and science.[59] Two further attempts were made to assassinate him, in 1609 and 1610. He spent his last breath in the service of the Republic, advising the Senate in three important questions in 1623 as he lay on his death-bed. His mind soon began to wander. "It is growing late," he murmured, "I must hasten to St Mark's for I have much to do." His last words were a prayer for his country. "*Esto perpetua.*"

The university of "Fair Padua, nursery of the Arts," became under Venetian auspices the most famous and most honoured centre of learning in Europe. Liberal salaries and an atmosphere of intellectual freedom drew an array of the most eminent teachers in Christendom. Fallopius, in physiology and medicine; Galileo, in astronomy and mathematics, were names that crowded its halls with eager students. As many as eighteen thousand of all nations were gathered there daily in the sixteenth century. During his professorship of twenty years, Galileo invented the thermometer and the telescope. Tasso studied, and our own Harvey (Italians claim) learned the secret of the circulation of the blood there. The Earl of Arundel sent his two sons in 1622 to drink of its springs. The Admirable Crichton having called on one of the Aldi in 1580, was introduced to the Signory, and improvised before the Senate a Latin oration of "most rare and singular power." The Fathers voted the impecunious youth one hundred crowns as a courteous recognition of his marvellous powers, and sent him to Padua with a warm introduction.

To Sebastian Venier succeeded Doge Nicolo da Ponte in 1577, a worthy scholar and student of theology, who had represented the Republic at the Council of Trent. At his death, in 1585, Pasquale Cigogna, descended from an apothecary ennobled after the war of Chioggia, was preferred to the ducal office. Cigogna saw the erection of the new stone Rialto bridge, and, after ten years' peaceful reign, was followed by a popular and lavish prince, Marino Grimani, whose consort was exceptionally honoured by a gorgeous coronation ceremony.

Grimani died on Christmas Day 1605, the very evening of the delivery of the first papal brief, and Leonardo Donato was chosen to open the document, and to preside over the conflict with the Spanish papalists at Rome. When he died in 1612, weird stories were whispered by fanatics of shrieks and cries heard from his chamber as the Evil One bore him away.

During the short reigns of Marc' Antonio Memmo, Giov. Bembo, Nicolo Donato, and Antonio Priuli, the Ten had been accumulating evidence of a vast conspiracy to seize the city, concerted by the Spanish Viceroy of Naples and the Marquis of Bedmar, the Spanish ambassador at Venice. On May 12, 1618, three Frenchmen in Venetian pay were arrested, strangled, and hung head downwards between the red columns, and orders were sent to the fleet to despatch three others. The plot had been divulged by two of the conspirators, and in all some three hundred persons of various nationalities, including many poor Venetian patricians, were implicated, and paid the penalty with their lives. The Spanish ambassador was for a time in danger, and under guard. He protested his innocence of the plot, as did his colleague of France. Both, however, soon sought a change of air. Two years were spent in tracing the ramifications of the plot, and in 1620 a senator, Giambattista Bragadin, was found to be in Spanish pay, and hanged between the columns.

In 1622 the atmosphere of dread and suspicion which encompassed the State, so dulled the perceptions of the Ten that a grave miscarriage of justice was laid to their charge. In 1618 Antonio Foscarini, a noble of high family and Venetian ambassador at London, was accused by Mascorno, a disaffected member of his staff, of licentiousness, blasphemy and treason. Foscarini was recalled, arrested by the Ten, and, after a long trial, acquitted, but kept under surveillance. In 1622, as he was leaving the Senate, a cloak was flung over him, and he was hurried off to prison. His accuser, who had been sentenced to two years' detention in a fortress, had, on his release, fabricated some documents which the tribunal deemed conclusive. Foscarini was declared guilty of corresponding secretly with Spain and the Emperor, strangled in prison, and his dead body hung by the leg between the red columns. As he had been an occasional visitor at Casa Mocenigo, where Lady Arundel resided, she was suspected also; but Sir Henry Wotton prompted her to clear herself by asking an audience of the Doge. This she did, and was allowed to make a statement in the Senate, the only woman who ever addressed that Assembly. She was exonerated, and a present of sweetmeats and wax offered to conciliate her. Four months later poor Foscarini's innocence was entirely proved, and two of his accusers were put to death. The family was restored to honour, and his remains were dug up and buried in the Frari with great splendour and pomp. His bust may still be seen in the church of S. Eustacchio (S. Stae) near the old Foscarini Palace.

Doge Priuli died shortly after the Foscarini tragedy. The brief reign of Francesco Contarini followed, and Giovanni Cornaro was chosen to fill the ducal office in 1624. The shock of Foscarini's judicial murder had given a rallying cry to the poorer nobles in the Great Council, jealous of the power of the Ten and the monopoly of office by the more influential patricians; and Renier Zeno, a patrician, fearless and incorruptible—himself an ex-*capo* of the Ten—led an attack on the tribunal. Banished for a year, he did but return with added popularity, and forced himself again on the Ten as one of the *Capi*. He used his power to accuse the Doge of nepotism, and his Serenity was forced to cancel certain family appointments. Zeno, driving his advantage further, came into conflict with his colleagues of the Ten, and, leaning on the majority of the Great Council, emerged triumphant. Shortly after, while standing at the Porta della Carta, he was attacked by five persons and stabbed. The Doge's son and certain alleged accomplices were denounced to the Ten, whose laggard justice, however, made flight easy. Again appointed one of the Ten, Zeno, on his recovery, renewed the struggle with increased vigour; and, after a stormy scene in the Great Council, during which he came to high words with the Doge, the stout reformer was ordered to keep his house, and report himself to the Ten within three days. Ignoring the summons, he was fined two thousand ducats and banished. The Great Council quashed the sentence, and ordered it to be blotted out of the records of the Ten. At length Zeno's party succeeded in carrying a motion for a committee of inquiry into the constitution of the Ten, but the four years' bitter conflict ended in a virtual triumph for the tribunal, whose powers of criminal jurisdiction over the nobles were reaffirmed, though it had to submit to a modified capitulary.

During the latter half of the seventeenth century the power of Venice was declining to its setting in an aureole of glory. In 1644, Crete, the oldest and last remaining of her great possessions in the East, was marked for conquest, and, like an old warrior who takes down his armour and girds himself to make a last stand against his hereditary foes, Venice prepared to resist the Turk to the uttermost. The old heroic times seem to return as we watch the quarter of a century's struggle, but our admiration is touched with pathos, for we know that the dice are loaded against Venice. A Turkish pilgrim fleet for Mecca had been pillaged by the Knights of Malta, and the pious buccaneers had landed at Crete for provisions. This was pretext enough for hostilities. In 1645 a huge armament left the Bosphorus, ostensibly for Malta, actually for the conquest of Crete. Canea quickly fell, and the Turks promised themselves an easy occupation. But twenty-four years of fierce and exhausting fighting ensued before the Crescent floated over the island.

Seven million ducats were quickly raised in Venice by the sale of patents of nobility. By a marvellous re-birth of naval energy and capacity, her fleet was reorganised and spread terror along the Dardanelles. The Venetian Captain-General, Lazzaro Mocenigo, determined to force the passage and attack Constantinople, but a well-aimed shell fired his ship, and he was killed. Francesco Morosini, appointed his successor, won the admiration of Europe by his twenty-two years' defence of Candia. Inspired by his heroism, companies of Flemish and French volunteers, eager and impetuous, joined him, but their enthusiasm was soon spent, and, impatient of the long vigils and toils of the war, they left the Venetians to fight alone. Morosini did not save Crete, but he extorted an honourable peace. No indemnity was paid, and the Venetian garrison marched proudly out of Candia unsubdued.[60] Four thousand Candiots who opted for Venice were settled in Istria, where traces of their language and customs are said still to survive. Suda and other fortresses remained in the hands of the Venetians. To the Pope the result seemed almost incredible.

In 1684 Venice was invited to join the Emperor and the King of Poland in a league against the Turks. The Cretan war had cost her one hundred and twenty-six million ducats, and she felt too exhausted to run with the horsemen again. But bolder counsels prevailed. Morosini was despatched with an army, and ably seconded by Koningsmark, the great Swedish mercenary, overran the Morea, captured Coron, Sparta and Athens, which last was won at the price of the ruin of the Parthenon, the Turkish powder magazine there having been exploded by a Venetian shell. Morosini returned in triumph, bringing the Greek lions, which still stand in front of the Arsenal. He was made Doge in 1688, the coronation being deferred that he might return to Greece. Vast designs of the recapture of Negropont, even of Crete, lured him on, but ill-health soon necessitated his return, only, however, to be again entreated to take up the command and retrieve the blunders of an incompetent Captain-General. The veteran Doge and captain for the last time sailed from Venice amid scenes that recalled the great crusading times of old. After some successes at Corinth he went to winter at Nauplia, where he died on January 9, 1694. He was the greatest of the modern Doges. A tomb in S. Stefano and a triumphal arch in the Sala dello Scrutinio still witness to his fame.

PONTE DI RIALTO.

But Venice was too poor and too feeble to retain her conquests. During a short campaign in 1715 she lost the whole of the Morea, and by the treaty of Passarovitch in 1717 all that was left of her vast empire in the East were a few fortresses in Dalmatia, Albania and Herzegovina. The treaty of 1717 bore her last signature as a European Power.

The procession of Doges that stretches from Giov. Cornaro, the opponent of Renier Zeno, to the fall of the Republic contains but one name of historic significance—Francesco Morosini. Marco Foscarini, elected in 1762, a descendant of the ill-fated Antonio Foscarini, is known to students as the author of a "History of Venetian Literature," and Ludovico Manin has the unhappy distinction of closing the line for ever. Through all the vicissitudes of foreign affairs, the decadence of trade, the fear corroding at her statesmen's hearts, the social and ceremonial life of Venice waxed rather than waned in pomp and splendour. The recurring ravages of plague periodically purged her pride and luxury. Of all the great cities of Europe, Venice bears the deepest traces of the passages of the destroying angel. In her annals no less than seventy visitations are recorded. Two great churches, the Redentore founded in 1575 and the Salute in 1630, are votive offerings to Heaven for salvation from the scourge. Her greatest *scuola* is dedicated to the chief plague saint, St Roch. Indeed in all her churches the figures of the plague saints, St Roch, St Job, St Sebastian, have a sad pre-eminence. But the danger past, the lesson faded from her memory, and the traditional magnificence shone forth. She became again—

"The pleasant place of all festivity;
The Revel of the earth; the Masque of Italy."

Sanudo gives a list of nineteen great annual pageants, and after his time others were added. Besides these official festivals great patrician weddings or the visits of foreign potentates were the occasions of stately pomp and joyous revels. At the anniversaries of the greater *scuole*, each guild vied with the other to excel in splendour. Never before nor since was such magnificence. The greatest artists of the day were commissioned to execute the decorations. The Bucintoro was carved by the best sculptors. Palladio, Titian and Tintoretto designed and decorated triumphal arches.

The loan of the Bucintoro and a subsidy of five hundred ducats were voted to the Calza to entertain the Duke of Milan in 1530. On this occasion a *bellissima colazion* (luncheon) was prepared, says Sanudo, but so ill-arranged that the Milanese nobles got nothing, while some Venetian Senators filled the sleeves of their robes with sweetmeats to the shame of those who saw it.

Venice surpassed herself in the reception given to Henry III. of France in 1574. The young king was met at Malghera—the modern traveller will pass a fort erected there as he nears the railway bridge—by sixty Senators in gondolas covered with velvet, oriental carpets and cloth of gold, and was ferried to Murano, where he passed the night in one of the rich palaces with delicious gardens for which the island was then noted. Sixty halberdiers clothed in silk of azure and gold were his bodyguard: forty noble youths of the Calza were his attendants. On the morrow amid salvos of artillery he embarked for Venice in a great galley manned by four hundred Sclavonians clothed in yellow and turquoise taffety, followed by an immense train of galleys and gondolas decorated with carpets and tapestry, with banners and flags waving in the breeze. The procession of the trade guilds, formed of a hundred and seventy boats resplendent with crimson and silver and gold, was a dazzling pageant. The glass-workers excelled in splendour and invention. A marine monster, in whose body could be seen a furnace, and craftsmen making most beautiful crystal vases, led their section, breathing flames from his mouth. Then followed a boat in the shape of a great dolphin bestridden by Neptune; on the poop stood two winged angels to waft it along. Four river gods personifying the Brenta, the Adige, the Po and the Piove plied the oars. At S. Nicolo del Lido, Palladio had constructed a triumphal arch adorned with statues of Victory, Peace, Faith and Justice, and with ten paintings by Titian and Tintoretto portraying events in the King's life. His Majesty lodged in the Palazzo Foscari from which an opening was made into the Palazzo

Giustiniani to accommodate his suite, the whole being furnished with oriental magnificence. At a State ball given in the hall of the Great Council, two hundred gorgeously attired ladies were present glittering with jewels and precious stones. The Sala dello Scrutinio was made into a supper-room where twelve hundred and sixty plates of sweetmeats in the forms of griffins, ships, nymphs, deities, etc., tempted the palates of the guests. Regattas, serenades and jousts made the whole visit seem a dream of enchantment to the King. As trade languished and the population diminished, public shows increased in splendour. The sum expended at the election and coronation of the last Doge—forty-seven thousand, two hundred and ninety-eight ducats, was beyond all precedent. Venice was still the temple of pleasure. All the arts subservient to the luxury and vices of the rich flourished in rankest exuberance despite the efforts of the Ten to cleanse public morals and to enforce sumptuary laws. The excessive importance too of the stage and of its tinselled heroes and tawdry queens, was an infallible symptom of a decadent nation. The time came in the eighteenth century when the State was torn by the petty jealousies and vanities of a playwright and an actress, and when public appointments were controlled by the subtle influence of the boudoir and the drawing-room, and an ambitious and beautiful society lady was the central figure of Venetian life. It was the time of the fatuous masquerades and futile pomposities portrayed for us by Longhi, when the card table, the coffee house and the play were the absorbing interest of Venetian minds. But before she sinks into the deep night of subjection to Austria to rise again as a province of a free and united Italy,[61] a faint hue of naval splendour lights up the horizon. Soon after Goethe's arrival in Venice in 1786 he ascended St Mark's tower and under the bright noon-day sun saw a fleet of galleys and frigates lying off Lido. They were reinforcements for Tunis, where the last of the great Venetians, Angelo Emo, was fighting the Algerian pirates. Emo humbled the Bey of Tunis, cleared the seas, and died at Malta in 1792. Five years later Napoleon marched his battalions towards the lagoons and before the mere breath of his coming the Republic of Venice crumbled into dust. On May 16, 1797, for the first time in a thousand years the Realtine islands were trodden by the foot of a conqueror, and the hundred and twentieth Doge of Venice, handing his biretta to an attendant, said: "Take it away, we shall not want it again."

CHAPTER XII

THE FINE ARTS AT VENICE

Masons—Painters—Glass-workers—Printers

Some prefer the pure design:
Give me my gorge of colour, glut of gold
In a glory round the Virgin made for me!
Titian's the man, not monk Angelico
Who traces you some timid chalky ghost
That turns the church into a charnel.
—*Browning.*

OWING to the absorption of her energies in commerce and the eastern trend of her interests and activities Venice lagged behind the Tuscan masters in the practice of the finer arts. Her earliest craftsmen were Byzantines, and St Mark's was modelled on the Church of the Holy Apostles at Constantinople and adorned by mosaicists from the same city. They were artists, rich in invention, and endowed with a perfect sense of beauty in design. The reliefs imbedded in the façades of St Mark's and in scores of houses about the city of Venice bear ample testimony to their greatness. In the thirteenth and fourteenth centuries Byzantine art had become degenerate, and traces of native Venetian sculpture as early as the twelfth century have been argued from the rude carvings on the pillars which support the tabernacle of the high altar of St Mark's. But it is not till we reach the masters of the characteristic Gothic, Transitional, and early Renaissance styles, that the important place due to Venice in the history of the mason's craft is made clear. It is doubtful whether any of the Pisani actually worked at Venice, though their influence is beyond dispute. But Nicolo Lamberti, a Tuscan sculptor, worked on the decorations of the main archivolt of St Mark's, Florentine artists carved some of the best figures and capitals in the façades of the Ducal Palace, and wrought one of the finest tombs in S. Zanipolo; Michelozzo is said to have built the Medici library at the monastery of St Giorgio Maggiore; and the design so often met with in monumental sculpture in Venice, two angels, one at either end of the tomb drawing aside a curtain to display the recumbent effigy of the dead was invented by a Florentine, Arnolfo di Cambio. Of the earliest Venetian masters it may be truly said that their works live after them, for little beyond their works is known of the Massegne and the Buoni who reached a comparatively higher stage of excellence in sculpture than their contemporaries did in painting. Jacobello and Piero delle Massegne (*dei Macigni*[62]), thus called because of their craft, were working in Venice towards the close of the fourteenth century. The statues of the apostles, the Virgin, and St Mark over the choir-screen, and others in the choir chapels of St Mark's, the main portal of S. Stefano, the beautiful lunette over the Friar's door at the Frari, and the tomb of Simone Dandolo in the same church are excellent examples of the style of these great artists. How much of the sculpture on the façades of the Ducal Palace was due to the Buoni it is difficult to say. The Buoni seem to have been Giovanni, the father, his son, Bartolomeo, and a certain Pantaleone Buon, once believed to be another son, but actually of no kinship with him. To Bartolomeo, sometimes known as Bartolomeo della Madonna dell'Orto, is ascribed the Porta della Carta of the Ducal Palace (1439) on the strength of an inscription *opera Bartholomei*. The reliefs of the Lion and of Doge Foscari are modern reproductions, but the original head of Foscari, preserved in the palace still, bears witness to the genius of this great craftsman.[63] He must not be confounded with another Bartolomeo Buon, known as Master Bartolomeo of Bergamo, also claimed as a native of Venice, who in 1493 superintended the painters in the Ducal Palace, and in 1500 presided over the works designed by Pietro Lombardo for the Procuratie Vecchie.

Certain craftsmen dubbed Riccio or Rizzo (Curly pate) now claim attention. Their identity is much canvassed by Italian authorities. Before the use of surnames became common it was the custom to refer to contemporaries by their Christian or nicknames to the confusion of biographers and critics. We meet with three Ricci who are stated to have worked at Venice, (1) Andrea Riccio of Padua living about 1400, who is said by Vasari to have executed the statues of Adam and Eve to be referred to presently. (2) Antonio Riccio or Rizzo, sometimes called Briosco, of Verona, who, according to Zanotto[64] was employed by the Republic to assist Antonio Loredan at the siege of Scutari.[65] He returned, after most effective service, covered with wounds, and the grateful Senate voted him and his sons in 1483 a pension for twenty years, and appointed him architect of the Ducal Palace after the fire in the same year, authorising him to draw for funds on the salt office. To him, and not to Andrea, are ascribed by Zanotto the masterly statues of Adam and Eve in the niches opposite the Scala dei Giganti, the Scala itself and the adjoining façade in the cortile and the rio façade. These on Francesco Sansovino's authority are more commonly attributed to Antonio Bregno (also called Il Riccio or Rizzo). He is said to have been a contemporary of Scarpagnino (Antonio Scarpagni), who, in 1514, submitted designs for the new stone Rialto Bridge, and succeeded Sante Lombardo in the erection of the Scuola di S. Rocco. Bregno, however, is a mysterious figure who, so Zanotto declares, either never existed or was none other than Riccio the Veronese. It is clear, however, from the annals of Malipiero that in 1498, one Antonio Riccio or Rizzo, architect of the Ducal Palace, after spending 80,000 ducats left the work not half done, that he had by forged vouchers defrauded the Salt Office to the extent of 12,000 ducats, and bolted to Foligno, where he soon died.[66] To the family of Venetian masters (or, according to some authorities, Lombard immigrants from Carona on Lake Lugano), known as the Lombardi, are due the most beautiful and original of the early renaissance architecture and sculpture in Venice. Pietro Lombardo, said to have been the son of a mason named Martino, was working in Venice in 1462. In 1481 his design for the Church of the Miracoli was chosen, and the building was erected under his superintendence. When Ant. Riccio fled from Venice, Pietro succeeded him at the Ducal Palace, with a salary of 120 ducats, and for twelve years was the official architect of the Republic. Among his works in Venice are the fine statues of St Anthony and three other saints in S. Stefano. The altars of St James and St Paul in St Mark's are also attributed to him. He is probably best known as the sculptor of the Dante Memorial at Ravenna. Antonio Lombardi, born before 1453, assisted his father at the Miracoli and on the tomb of Doge Pietro Mocenigo at S. Zanipolo. He collaborated with Aless. Leopardi on the bronze work in the Cappella Zen at St Mark's. The statue of St Thomas Aquinas in S. Zanipolo is attributed to him. Martino Lombardo, whose relationship is unknown, was architect of the Scuola di San Marco after 1485, and was believed by Temanza to have built S. Zaccaria.[67] Moro Lombardo, probably a son of Martino, assisted his father in the Scuola di S. Marco. In 1524-7, Giulio Lombardo, probably son of Pietro, was acting in an advisory capacity to Sante or Zante Lombardo, a son of Pietro, born 1504, in the works at the Scuola di S. Rocco. The Church of S. Giorgio dei Greci ascribed to Sansovino is now attributed to Sante and one named Chiona.

PONTE DI RIALTO, FROM THE MARKET.

Tullio Lombardi (1453-1537) was the son of Pietro, and the best sculptor of the family. Beside his work in the interior of the Miracoli, he executed the reliefs on the façade of the Scuola di S. Marco and the monument to Giov. Mocenigo in S. Zanipolo. He also collaborated with Leopardi on the Vendramin tomb in the same church. To the Lombardi school we owe the beautiful Cappella Giustiniano at S. Francesco della Vigna, and a fine relief in S. Giov. Grisostomo (Coronation of the Virgin and the Twelve Apostles).

Aless. Leopardi (1450-1521) raised Venetian sculpture to its highest plane of technical perfection. The Venetian artist was peculiarly privileged. Unlike the Pisani and other Tuscans who drew their inspiration from Roman antiques, he was able to draw from the fountain-head. The lands of Hellas were subject to the Republic, and, doubtless, many a young apprentice spent his *Wanderjahre* there. Enthusiasm gave insight, and both in technique and design we seem to trace in Tullio Lombardo and Aless. Leopardi the influence of Greek originals. To Leopardi are due the Vendramin tomb in S. Zanipolo, the finest of renaissance sepulchral monuments, and the completion of the Colleoni statue. He modelled the Six Virtues and the Madonna Della Scarpa in the Cappella Zen. The three magnificent bronze bases for the flagstaffs in front of St Mark's were wrought by him. But soon aversion from the study of nature, and the growing pomp of private and public life reacted on the renaissance artists; their work became mannered and feeble; they lost individuality and character. They found in Venice a rich field for exploitation. She was not only the wealthiest, she was the most tranquil of European states. Imperial in policy, oligarchical in government, she sought by the splendour of the arts and by magnificent pageantry to feed the pride of her nobles, and lay any spirit of political freedom that might have survived in her people.

A giant among the sixteenth century masters who were attracted to Venice was Jacopo Tatti (1477-1570) of Florence, the bosom friend and colleague of Andrea del Sarto, known as Sansovino, from his intimate association with his master, Andrea Contucci, of Monte Sansovino. Jacopo, while sketching from the antique at Rome, attracted the notice of Bramante, who was charmed by a wax model of the Laocoon executed by the young student, and judged by Raphael to be the best of four others. It was cast in bronze, and subsequently found its way to the Signory of Venice. In 1527, after the sack of Rome, he came to Venice, and was employed by Doge Gritti to strengthen the domes of St Mark's. He did his work so amazingly well (*fece stupire Venezia*, says Vasari) that he was appointed in 1529 chief architect, with a house and a salary of 80 ducats, afterwards increased to 180. In 1536 the Senate decreed the erection of a library to contain the books left to the Republic by Petrarch and Cardinal Bassarione. Sansovino was charged with the building, now known as the *Libreria Vecchia*, and esteemed by Palladio to be probably the richest and most ornate edifice erected since the time of the ancients. The Signory were royal pay-masters, but intolerant of bad work; and when, on December 18, 1545, part of the vaulting fell, Sansovino was imprisoned, fined a thousand crowns, and deprived of his office. He succeeded, however, in proving his innocence, and was released and compensated by a solatium of 900 crowns, and restored to his former position. Sansovino's work, however, ends at the sixteenth arch from the Campanile corner. Twelve years after his death it was finished by Scamozzi. He was a most lovable artist, ever ready with help and counsel to those who entreated him; the friend of every great man of his time; in youth a most winning personality; in age venerable and alert. At ninety-three, if we may trust Vasari, his eyes were undimmed, and he bore himself erect as ever. Among other works by him at Venice may be specified the beautiful loggia destroyed by the collapse of the Campanile, in July 1902, and the bronze doors leading to the sacristy, St Mark's, on which he is said to have worked during a period of twenty years; the six bronze reliefs in the choir of the same church; the colossal statues of Mars and Neptune at the top of the giants' staircase, and the Scala d'Oro in the Ducal Palace, and many mansions and churches, the choicest of which, S. Geminiano, no longer exists.

Of all his followers, Girolamo Campagna is the most talented. Good examples of his works are the bronze statues of St Mark and St Francis in the Redentore, the small statues of St Francis and St Clare in the Miracoli, and the reclining figure of Doge Cicogna (1595) in the Gesuiti. Aless. Vittoria of Trent (1525-1603) was a facile artist. Among his works are the statue of St Sebastian in S. Salvatore, the fine bust of Cardinal Gasparo in the Madonna dell' Orto, the ruined chapel of the Rosary in S. Zanipolo, and his own tomb in S. Zaccaria. Michele Sammichele (1484-1559), the great Veronese master and famous military engineer, was employed by the Republic between 1530 and 1550, and designed the great fortifications in the mainland provinces, on the Dalmatian coast, at Corfù, Cyprus and Romania, many of which remain to this day. On his return to Venice, he constructed the magnificent fortress of S. Andrea del Lido, a stupendous work, now threatened with ruin, owing to erosion by currents set up by the new dykes near the Lido. The Palazzo Grimani on the Grand Canal, the Ponte del Bucintoro at the Arsenal are by this master, whose architecture so dominates Verona. He was an earnest, God-fearing man, of grave, subdued, yet cheerful disposition, generous and tender-hearted.

The once famous, but now depreciated, Andrea Palladio of Vicenza (1518-80), came to Venice about 1550, where he designed, among other edifices, the noble cloister of the Carità; the refectory, cloister and church[68] of S. Giorgio Maggiore (1556-79); and the Redentore, the greatest of his ecclesiastical buildings (1578-80). The interiors of Palladio's churches, by their austere beauty, their symmetry and proportion, are among the greatest achievements of the later Renaissance. He had an extraordinary vogue in Venice, and designed many patrician villas on the mainland.

Vicenzo Scamozzi of Vicenza (1552-1616) was attracted to Venice by the fame of Sansovino and Palladio, under whom he studied; like his masters he spent much time at Rome. On returning to Venice he was employed to complete the Libreria Vecchia in 1582, and two years later carried on the Procuratie Nuove, spoiling Sansovino's beautiful design by adding a storey. The *porta dell' anticollegio* and other works on the Ducal Palace are by him. He, too, was in much demand as a designer of palaces in Venice and on the mainland.

Greatest of the seventeenth-century masters, and one who laid the most monstrous burdens of stone on the patient Venetian soil, was Baldassari Longhena (1600-82), a native of Venice and pupil of Scamozzi. He helped to complete the Procuratie Nuove in 1638, and in 1640 was appointed the official architect of the Republic. The foundation-stone of his most famous work, S. Maria della Salute, was laid in 1631. The church was still unfinished in 1660. The curious will find the design of this edifice to have been suggested by the section and ground-plan of a temple described by Poliphilus and illustrated in the Hypnerotomachia[69]—that treasure-house of design so often looted by Renaissance and modern artists. Two massive edifices on the Grand Canal, the Pesaro and Rezzonico Palaces (1650); the high altars of S. Francesca della Vigna and S. Pietro di Castello; the interior of the Scalzi, "that pandemonium of details surpassed only by the greater delirium of Pozzo's high altar," were all designed by this master, whose heavy hand may also be seen in the masonry erected to Doge Pesaro in the Frari.

IN THE PROCURATIE NUOVE.

More completely than her masons were Venetian painters dominated by rigid Byzantine formalism. It seems barely credible that Jacobello del Fiore, who for twenty-one years was head of the painters' guild in Venice, and Michele Giambono should have been the contemporaries of Masaccio and Fra Angelico. The emancipation of Venetian painting from the numbing tradition of the East did not begin until the employment of the Umbrian masters, Gentile da Fabriano and Vittore Pisano, to decorate the Ducal Palace in 1419, and the rise of the Vivarini in Murano in 1440-1500. The marked German character of the earliest work of the Vivarini is due to the association of Antonio Vivarini with Giovanni Alemano (John the German), who was trained in the Cologne school, and by some authorities is believed to be a Vivarini. Later, Antonio collaborated with his younger brother, Bartolomeo. Then the brothers separated, and each worked alone. Bartolomeo, by far the greater personality, was much influenced by Mantegna and the Paduan school, and under him Venetian painting takes a big step towards naturalism. The sacred altar-picture becomes less conventional, the figures are less cramped, the colours brighten, the decoration is richer. When Antonello da Messina, about 1473, brought the perfected Flemish method of painting in oils to Venice, Bartolomeo was not slow to adopt the new medium. Alvise Vivarini, his younger kinsman, made further use of Antonello's innovation, and touched, moreover, by the spirit of the Bellini, the young painter, whose works cover the period between 1464-1502, begins to foreshadow the future glories of Venetian painting. The earnest, severe, almost harsh features become softened, a strange grace and gentleness comes like a breath of springtime and promise over the whole field of Venetian art.

Besides several paintings by the Vivarini in the Accademia there are in Venice fine examples of Bartolomeo's work, the St Augustine, in S. Zanipolo; a Coronation of the Virgin by Giovanni Alemano and Antonio Vivarini, with marked German traits, in S. Pantaleone; three altar-pieces by the same two painters in S. Zaccaria; an early work (1473) in three compartments by Bartolomeo, the Meeting of Joachim and Anna, the Birth of the Virgin, and Mary as the Mater Misericordiæ in S. Maria Formosa; a Virgin between St Andrew and St John (1478), in S. Giovanni in Bragora, where are also two works by Alvise, one, the Resurrection, a masterpiece. In the Frari are two altar-pieces by Bartolomeo (1474 and 1478), and a fine example of Alvise's work, St Ambrose Enthroned, finished after his death in 1502 by his pupil Basaiti. The beautiful Virgin and Child with two angels in the Redentore, formerly attributed to Giovanni Bellini, is now generally given to Alvise. The striking and noble figure of St Clare (No. 393) in the Accademia is by this master, to whom modern criticism assigns a very high place[70] in the history of Venetian painting. Many portraits formerly ascribed to Antonello da Messina are now recognised as Alvise's work.

PALAZZO LAYARD—PORTRAIT OF SULTAN MAHOMET II
By Gentile Bellini

But it is to the paintings of Gentile, and Giovanni, sons of Jacopo Bellini, that the traveller will turn again and again with increasing admiration and reverence. In 1421 Jacopo, who had worked under the Umbrian masters in the Ducal Palace, went with Gentile da Fabriano to Florence, and there for several years was his pupil in the very centre of the renaissance of art. In 1430 he set up a workshop in Venice, and about 1450, having moved with his two sons to Padua, came under the powerful influence of Mantegna, who married his daughter Nicolosa. Venice possesses but two examples of his work, No. 582 in the Accademia and a Crucifixion in Room XV. of the Correr Museum.

Only from the master's sketches in the British Museum and in the Louvre can an adequate conception of his genius be obtained. Gentile, the elder of the sons, whose name was given him in memory of Jacopo's beloved master Gentile da Fabriano, was born in 1429, Giovanni about 1430. Vasari tells of the affectionate rivalry of the artist family; the father's joy as the growing excellence of his sons already eclipsed his own fame; the sons, after separating each to his own workshop, holding one another, and both, the father, in great reverence, each praising his brother's work and depreciating his own, seeking modestly to excel in kindness and courtesy as well as in the practice of his art. In 1464 Gentile painted the shutters of the organ in St Mark's with the figures of Saints Mark, Jerome, Theodore and Francis. They still exist, but almost ruined, in the Office of Works. No. 570 in the Accademia, a faded painting, the Apotheosis of the Patriarch S. Lorenzo, is an early work, refined and dignified. In 1479 the Doge, being asked by Sultan Mahomet II. to recommend a good painter of portraits from Venice, sent Gentile and two assistants to Constantinople and appointed Giovanni to continue his brother's work in the Ducal Palace. His remarkable portrait of the Sultan is now in the Layard Collection in Venice. Gentile returned, after a comparatively short stay, loaded with presents and honours, to rejoin his brother at the Ducal Palace. In 1487 Titian is said to have entered his workshop as an apprentice. Later, the master painted for the guild of St John the Evangelist the three scenes illustrating the miracles of the Holy Cross, now in the Accademia. Towards the end of his life he began the Preaching of St Mark, now in the Brera at Milan, and, falling sick, left his sketch-book to his brother on condition that he completed the picture. Gentile was a good draughtsman, a brilliant colourist, an alert observer, boldly making use of his Eastern experiences to add local colour to his subjects. His compositions, however, are rather crowded and wanting in central emphasis; his treatment is flat and hard. His death, February 23, 1507, is noted by Sanudo.

Giovanni, his more gifted brother, is the tenderest and noblest of Venetian painters. He gave more attention to individual figures than Gentile, uniting grace and firmness of outline with warmth and splendour of colouring; dignity and strength with variety and beauty of form. His creations, once seen, haunt us like memories of beloved friends. In early life Giovanni was much dominated by the personality of his brother-in-law Mantegna, to whom some of his works[71] have been attributed. A good example painted in *tempera* of his early Madonnas may be seen (No. 583) in the Accademia. An apocryphal story is told of the artist going to Antonello to have his portrait painted in order to learn the secret of painting in oils. But the new method must have been too well known to have made the trick necessary. Venice possesses several altar-pieces by Giovanni, besides the collection in the Accademia, now conveniently placed in Room XVIII. The altar-piece in the Frari and that in S. Zaccaria are the finest examples of the master's art in

Europe, painted in the maturity of his genius—1488 and 1505. They are held by Ruskin to be the two finest pictures in the world. In S. Pietro Martire at Murano is another of the same period. In 1474, says the annalist Malipiero, Zuano and Zentil Bellini, brothers, were employed at the Ducal Palace to restore the pictures of the meeting of Pope Alexander and the Emperor Barbarossa, which had fallen from the walls because of damp and old age. The brothers promised that their work should last two hundred years. They reckoned without the demon of fire, for a hundred years later it was devoured by the conflagration of 1577. An altar-piece in S. Giovanni Grisostomo, painted when Giovanni was eighty-seven years of age, proves that the old craftsman was ever a learner. Albert Dürer, when in Venice, was profoundly impressed by the veteran painter and wrote that although very old, he was still the best in his art. He died in 1516, full of years and rich in fame. Dürer was well treated at Venice. The Doge and the Patriarch came to see his paintings. Bellini praised him highly and offered to buy one of his works. His only complaint was that the Painters' Guild summoned him three times before the magistrates, who ordered him to pay four ducats to the guild for permission to practise his art.

S. ZACCARIA—MADONNA ENTHRONED AND FOUR SAINTS
By Giovanni Bellini

S. GIORGIO MAGGIORE—ST GEORGE AND THE DRAGON
By Carpaccio

Vittore Carpaccio is the chief of the newer generation of painters trained under the influence of the Bellini. His talent for telling a story with richness of detail and quaint simplicity has never been surpassed. The series painted for the Guild of S. Ursula (1490-95) are admirable examples of his power, and of capital importance for the study of contemporary Venetian costume and architecture. Smaller in scale but equally charming and naive are the St George and the Dragon, and St Jerome series of paintings in the lower hall of S. Giorgio degli Schiavoni and the St George and the Dragon in the Sala del Conclave at the Salute. The well-known Presentation at the Temple, a noble work, No. 44 in the Accademia (1510), is obviously inspired by Giovanni Bellini. The altar-piece in S. Vitale (1514) and three paintings in the Accademia, Nos. 89, 90, 91, painted in 1515, are later works telling all too plainly of declining power. Little is known of Carpaccio's life. He travelled in the East, was working at Venice in 1479, and died in 1525.

Sebastiani (Lazzaro Bastiani), his contemporary, worked with Gentile Bellini, Benedetto Diana and Mansueti in the decoration of the Guild of St John the Evangelist. The Offering of the Relic to the Brotherhood, No. 561 in the Accademia is by his hand. His works are rare. Three pictures in the Accademia; a Pietà in S. Antonino, much influenced by Squarcione; a more pleasing work, the S. Donato, at Murano—are all that Venice can show by this not greatly inspired artist. He was chosen by Giovanni Bellini, 1508, to value Giorgione's frescoes on the façade of the Fondaco dei Tedeschi, and died in 1512.

To Mansueti are due two of the Guild of St John pictures, rich in examples of Venetian costume and architecture, and two scenes from the life of St Mark painted for the guild of that name, now placed in the apse of Room XV. in the Accademia. He and his colleague Benedetto Diana, who painted one of the legends of the Holy Cross for the Guild of St John, were influenced by Gentile Bellini and Carpaccio. Benedetto's masterpiece, the Virgin Enthroned, an early work, is in the Accademia, No. 82. The much-disputed Christ at Emmaus in S. Salvatore has been attributed to him. Only scraps of the biographies of these two artists are known. The former was lame, and died in 1530; the latter once competed successfully with Carpaccio for the painting of a gonfalone for the Guild of Charity, of which he was a member, and died in 1525. Marco Marziale, a follower of Carpaccio, was much influenced by Albert Dürer during his stay at Venice, as may be seen in the Supper at Emmaus, No. 76, the only work by him in the Accademia. Little is known of his life. He was painting in the Ducal Palace in 1492, and still living in 1507.

Cima, Giovanni Battista, da Conegliano, son of a cloth-dresser (*Cimatore di panni*), a pupil of Alvise Vivarini, and one of the many painters from the mainland to whom Venetian art owes so much, is a great typical colourist of the Bellini School. To a feeling for colour he brings the expression of his love for natural scenery. The beautiful background of mountain landscape, the dignity and warmth of the saintly figures, the romantic architecture with tufts of the *erba della Madonna*[72] growing from its crevices, in his altar-piece in the Madonna dell' Orto, make it, though technically immature, one of the most delightful examples of Venetian art. Other maturer works by him are in S. Giovanni in Bragora and the Carmine. The Accademia possesses seven of his paintings. He was born in 1460, settled in Venice in 1490, and died about 1517. His Virgin and Child, with St Michael and St Andrew, now in the Parma Gallery, was long admired as a masterpiece by Da Vinci.

MADONNA DELL' ORTO—THE BAPTIST AND FOUR SAINTS
By Cima

Marco Basaiti, a pupil of Alvise, and influenced by Bellini, is a good colourist and a lover of natural scenery; but his work lacks refinement, strength and character. The Accademia has five of his works, of which the Agony in the Garden, No. 69, is the best; another and later one, Peter Enthroned, is in S. Pietro di Castello. He was working between 1490 and 1521.

Catena (Vincenzio di Biagio), yet another of Giovanni Bellini's school, is a sweet and graceful painter. The Martyrdom of S. Cristina in S. Maria Mater Domini is an early work of much charm. The church of S. Simeon Profeta has a picture by this master; two are in the Accademia and one in the Ducal Palace. The Judith in the Quirini-Stampalia and a Virgin and Child with the Baptist and a female saint, in the Palazzo Giovanelli are assigned to him by Mr Berenson. This noble and ingenuous artist has suffered much from the attribution of many of his best creations to Giovanni Bellini and Giorgione. He was working between 1495 and 1531.

Another of the mainland painters attracted to Venice by the fame of the Bellini was Andrea Previtali of Bergamo, of whose works the Accademia possesses two, a Crucifixion and a Nativity. He, like Cima and Catena, loves to introduce landscape, giving it, however, more prominence, and adding classic details. In the Sacristy of S. Giobbe is a good early work, the Marriage of St Catherine, formerly attributed to Giovanni Bellini. He died in 1525.

Bissolo, Pier Francesco, pupil and assistant of Giovanni Bellini, is a capable artist, the last of the school, whose best work, Christ offering the Crown of Thorns to St Catherine, is in the Accademia (No. 79) with three others. The Virgin and Child with St John and St Catherine in the Redentore, formerly attributed to Bellini, is now assigned to Bissolo. He died in 1554.

The advent of the romantic, almost mysterious, personality of Giorgione (Georgio Barbarelli) marks an epoch in the story of Venetian painting. Few artists in so short a life wrought so great a work. He lifted Venetian painting to the highest sphere of poetic inspiration and technical perfection, and influenced the whole of its subsequent progress. Yet paintings by his hand are rare. One alone, the Castelfranco altar-piece, is beyond dispute, and that, says Morelli, is daubed over by a Venetian restorer. Of the scores of works formerly put upon him in Europe few can now be safely defended, and of these few a bare half-dozen are allowed to Italy. The unstable position of expert opinion may be exemplified by the vicissitudes of the Miracle of St Mark, No. 516, in the Accademia, long since removed from its former position of honour and placed in a badly lighted corridor.[73] This, once assigned to Giorgione by Boschini, and at a later date generally attributed to Paris Bordone, is now esteemed by Mr Berenson to be one of Giorgione's greatest achievements. Crowe and Cavalcaselle doubt if the "inky and spacious canvas" was ever touched by Giorgione. The official catalogue of 1895 assigns it to Palma Vecchio, that of 1903 to Paris Bordone and restorers of the eighteenth century. We are on safer ground when we examine the Gipsy and Soldier in the Giovanelli Palace. Nothing can be seen at Venice to surpass this superbly beautiful composition for originality, poetic grace and romantic beauty. A fairly convincing work is the Apollo pursuing Daphne, almost ruined by a restorer's daubing, in the Seminario of the Salute. Of the many frescoes painted on Venetian palaces, especially those on the canal side of the Fondaco dei Tedeschi so eloquently described by Vasari, only a fragment remains, a head, torso and part of the arms, of a female figure. When Evelyn was at Venice in 1645, the frescoes seem to have been in good condition. The plague, or grief at the infidelity of his mistress, brought this great artist to a premature death in 1510. He was born about 1478. Passionately fond of music and song, his whole soul was attuned to impressions of inward and outward beauty. With him, romantic as distinguished from ecclesiastical painting leaps into being.

Alinari, Florence
S. MARIA MATER DOMINI—S. CRISTINA
By Catena

Titian (Tiziano Vecellio) is the complementary genius to Giorgione. In him is summed all that the Venetian school promised or attained to. Lacking perhaps the sunny radiance of Giorgione's temperament, his larger experience of life, his deep, strong nature give him a pathetic insight into the tragedy, as well as the beauty, of existence, so characteristic of great artists and poets. To judge fully of Titian's life-work one would need to travel over the greater part of Western Europe—to Madrid above all. Venice possesses but a score of his paintings, and these not the very greatest. Early works, attributed by some critics to Giorgione, are the Ecce Homo in the Scuola, and the Christ bearing the Cross, in the Church of S. Rocco. A somewhat later work, St Mark Enthroned, in the Sacristy of the Salute, painted in 1512, for S. Spirito, still bears traces of Giorgione's influence. The famous Assumption in the Accademia, first of the grand compositions of the later Venetian school and generally regarded as a masterpiece, was painted in 1518. A finer picture, painted in 1526 in the maturity of his power, is the Pesaro Madonna, in the Frari. The beautiful Annunciation in the Scuola di S. Rocco was painted in 1525. The Presentation in the Accademia, now restored to its original position, is a later work, 1538. The Tobias and the Angel, perhaps painted about 1537,[74] in S. Marziale, is a work composed with unusual simplicity and charm. We see the great master in one of his happy moods like a strong man bending to play with his children. In addition to Doge Grimani's ceremonial portrait there exists an unrestored fresco by his hand in the Ducal Palace. Many sacred subjects were painted late in life. In S. Salvatore are an Annunciation, a finely conceived work, and a Transfiguration, both executed when he was nearing ninety years of age. The grand old fellow died in harness. He failed to finish the Deposition, now in the Accademia, completed by Palma Giovane. "Titian is our standard-bearer," said Velasquez when he saw him in Venice, and when Vasari was there in 1566 he called on the veteran painter and found him, although eighty-nine years old, brush in hand. The friends had much converse together of their art and of the master's works. He died in 1576, wanting but one year to complete his century.[75]

With Titian, Venetian painting reached its meridian glory. Inspiration and technical mastery went hand in hand. He has been defined as the painter *par excellence* as distinguished from the draughtsman who colours. In his new manner, that became absolute painting which in the Bellini and Carpaccio was but coloured drawing.

Palma Vecchio (Jacopo Negretti), 1480-1528, Titian's contemporary, is the third of the dominant sixteenth-century painters. Without the finely endowed nature of his two fellows, he works with much energy and freshness, is masterly in his use of colour, and has a breadth and serenity of style which make of him a great, but not a paramount artist. The well-known St Barbara in S. Maria Formosa is the most grandiose and majestic female figure in Venetian art. The recently acquired Santa Conversazione, No. 147 in the Accademia, is an excellent example of a mode of composition which Palma brought to its ultimate form. He was the creator of that opulent type of female beauty with "marmoreal neck and bosom uberous" so characteristic of Venetian art.

ACCADEMIA—THE DEAD CHRIST
By Titian

Sebastiano del Piombo (Sebastiano Luciani), 1485-1547, a pupil of Giorgione, was a younger painter of the school, a competent but not very gifted interpreter of the prevalent type of sensuous beauty. The painting on the high altar in S. Giov. Crisostomo is a fine example of his early style and in Vasari's time was attributed to Giorgione. There is an early Pietà in Lady Layard's collection and a doubtful Visitation in the Accademia. Early in his career he went to Rome and won the friendship of Raphael and Michel Angelo by whom his later style was profoundly influenced. This period of his activity belongs to Roman rather than to Venetian art.

Lorenzo Lotto (1480-1556), pupil of Alvise Vivarini, is a highly gifted but unequal painter, who was working in Venice early in the sixteenth century. He is one of the more original of the contemporaries of Titian. Much attention has recently been given to this artist, especially to his portrait work, by Mr Berenson, who gives him high, but perhaps somewhat exaggerated praise, as the first painter who sought to interpret the varying moods of the individual human soul; as an artist of penetrating sympathy and charity, preserving for us in his portraits the lineaments of the more gentle and refined of his contemporaries. These, however, must be sought anywhere but in Venice. One fine altar-piece, painted in the maturity of his powers, may be seen in the Carmine, St Nicholas in Glory, a work of real poetic feeling; another, better preserved, the Apotheosis of S. Antonino, is in S. Zanipolo. A later work, the Virgin and Child with Saints, is in S. Giacomo dall' Orio.

A room in the Accademia is devoted to examples of the works of the Friulian school, a group of painters working in the capital, Udine, and other towns and villages of the northernmost Venetian territory during the second half of the fifteenth and first half of the sixteenth centuries. Of Martino da Udine (Pellegrino da S. Daniele), the Accademia possesses three examples. No. 151, an Annunciation, is a replica of the same subject in his best work, the series of frescoes in the church of S. Antonio, at S. Daniele, near Udine. Pictures by him have been assigned to Giorgione.

A greater man than Martino came to Venice from Pordenone, about thirty miles from the capital, his pupil Giov. Ant. Sacchiense, known as Pordenone. He was an artist of power, but who showed that pride in technical skill so characteristic of a declining art. He parades his anatomical knowledge and science of foreshortening, with all Michael Angelo's daring, but with none of his genius. Most of his works are on the mainland, but one characteristic altar-piece, No. 316, and three other paintings are in the Accademia in Venice. In the cloister at S. Stefano are some frescoes (in which medium he excelled), now almost ruined, and a St Sebastian, better preserved, in the church of S. Rocco, where also is a fine painting of St Christopher and St Martin. Another good work is the altar-piece—S. Rocco, St Sebastian and St Catherine—in S. Giov. Elemosinario. His Entombment, in the Monte di Pietà at Treviso, has been ascribed to Giorgione. He was working in Venice in the early half of the sixteenth century, and died at Ferrara in 1539.

The name of Bonifazio is associated with a remarkable revolution and counter-revolution in the history of criticism. Vasari and the older writers knew but one painter of that name, who was called by some Bonifazio of Verona, by others, of Venice. In 1864 Bernasconi, by the aid of documentary evidence, discovered two Bonafazios; and in 1877 Morelli,[76] by applying his famous method (the shape of the ears, outline of the bodies and other similar criteria) evolved three, who were distinguished as Bonifazio I., II., and III. With few exceptions the whole of the works in European Galleries, including the Accademia of Venice, formerly attributed to one Bonifazio, were then grouped under these three heads, and re-catalogued.

ON THE STEPS OF THE REDENTORE.

Vasari's accuracy has, however, been vindicated by the recent publication[77] of Gustav Ludwig's patient and conclusive researches, which demonstrate (1) that Bonifazio Pasini of Verona (1489-1540), the so-called Bonifazio I., could never have left Verona for any length of time between 1515 and his death, and that nothing is now known of his works: (2) that Bonifazio di Pitati of Verona (1487-1553), Morelli's Bonifazio II., came, a youth of eighteen, with his father, a soldier, to settle in Venice in 1505; learned his craft at Palma Vecchio's workshop; married a basketmaker's daughter; became one of the most famous painters in Venice; in 1530 was commissioned to decorate the Palazzo de' Camerlenghi (Treasury offices); and died, childless, in 1553, leaving the work to be completed by Tintoretto, who for a period adopted Bonifazio's style: (3) that Bonifazio III. is a mere phantom of Morelli's imagination. Bonifazio, like all the successful painters of the Renaissance, kept a large number of assistants and pupils to supply the demands of his clients at home and abroad, himself executing the more important parts of his productions, and supervising the work done in his atelier. The paintings assigned to Bonifazio I., such as the Rich Man's Feast, number 291 in the Accademia, and the Virgin and Child with SS. Omobono and Barbara in the Palazzo Reale, are those executed by Bonifazio di Pitati's own hand in the days before prosperity had rendered personal execution of the whole of his work impossible. The paintings attributed to Bonifazio II., such as the Woman Taken in Adultery, No. 278 in the Accademia, the Massacre of the Innocents, and the Fall, in the Palazzo Reale, works which betray a falling off in vigour and firmness of drawing while retaining the old brilliancy of colour, are those which were partly executed by his assistants. The paintings allotted to Bonifazio III., feeble work, such as the Last Supper in S. Maria Mater Domini, and most of the panels with figures of two or more saints, of which the Accademia possesses so many examples, were painted wholly by assistants during Bonifazio's lifetime, or after his death. Nearly the whole of those in the Accademia formerly attributed to Bonifazio III., many of which have been post-dated owing to a vicious theory of interpretation, were side panels painted for more important central compositions in the Treasury Offices. The 1903 (Italian) edition of the official catalogue adopts Ludwig's conclusions.

Bonifazio, who always signs himself "da Verona," is an eminently naturalistic painter. With perfect art he portrays for us the sensuous magnificence of the Venetian patrician's life: his luxurious home; his well-nurtured body; his powerful, sagacious intellect; his love of the country; his gorgeous costume; his pet animals; his ideal of female beauty.

A talented pupil of Titian who came under Michael Angelo's influence was Paris Bordone (1495-1571). He has the distinction of producing the finest of Venetian ceremonial paintings, No. 320 in the Accademia. No picture will evoke in the beholder a deeper sentiment of the peculiar charm of Venice. The magnificent architecture; the dignified Fathers of the State in their rich costumes; the romantic legend it illustrates; the warm, golden, sunny atmosphere in which the whole composition is bathed, make this the most essentially Venetian picture in the world. The Accademia has other works by this artist—the Paradise, No. 322, a poor canvas, and a small panel, No. 311.

Two great artists preserved the power and grandeur of the Venetian school during a time when elsewhere in Italy painting had sunk to nerveless mannerism and mawkish sentimentality.

Alinari, Florence
ACCADEMIA—PRESENTATION OF ST MARK'S RING TO THE DOGE
By Bordone

Tintoretto (Jacopo Robusti), 1518-94, a pupil of Bonifazio, and much influenced by Titian and Michel Angelo, is a painter who may only be studied at Venice. A fine example of his early work painted under Titian's influence, is the Adam and Eve, No. 43 in the Accademia. In 1552 he painted two panels for the Palazzo Camerlenghi, in continuation of Bonifazio's work, now in the Anti-Chiesetta of the Ducal Palace; and, a year later, the dramatic Miracle of St Mark, Accademia No. 42. This central work admirably displays the qualities of his genius. The composition is grandly conceived; the drawing stupendously clever and virile. But the craftsmanship is too insistent. The artist aims at displaying his triumph over difficult but non-essential problems of foreshortening and perspective. The whole scene is characterised by that "bustle and tumult" which Reynolds complains of in his criticism of

Tintoretto's work. Other paintings that may be noted are the Marriage of Cana in the sacristy of the Salute; two large and confused canvases, the Last Judgment and the Golden Calf, in the choir of the Madonna dell' Orto; the charming Ariadne and Bacchus, with its companion pictures, and the colossal Paradise in the Ducal Palace. His last work, S. Marziale, is in the church of that name. Admirers of Tintoretto may sate themselves at Venice. The Accademia and the Ducal Palace are rich in his works. The Scuola of S. Rocco alone is a veritable Tintoretto museum. The sixty-two compositions there, exhibit the painter's characteristics fully developed, his weakness as well as his strength. Never had sacred history been treated with such uncompromising realism. No one can contemplate these tremendous scenes without being impressed by the power of the genius that conceived them; none can turn away without a feeling of regret that so greatly endowed an artist should, in his later career at least, have been wanting in reverence and in the *incredibile diligenza*, which Vasari noted in all Titian's work. He was a passionate, impatient worker, too often unconscionably superficial. His bold, vigorous, rapid execution is such that the practice of painting in his hands seems to partake of the nature of physical exercise. When Goethe was frequenting the official picture-restorers at S. Zanipolo in 1790, it was discovered that Tintoretto had been in the habit of leaving spaces for the more important heads in the large compositions executed *in situ* (probably by pupils), which he would paint at home and stick on the canvas afterwards. How *presto e resoluto* he was may be learned from the story told by Vasari of the march he stole upon his competitors for the decoration of a room in the Scuola di San Rocco. He had already painted his masterpiece, the Crucifixion, for the Sala dell' Albergo, and the guild determined to decorate the hall with something *magnifica ed onorata*. Salviati, Zucchero, Veronese and himself were selected to send in designs. While his rivals were diligently at work, Tintoretto had taken the measurement of the space to be filled, painted his canvas with incredible rapidity and secretly fixed it in its place in the hall. When the masters of the guild met to examine the designs they found his work already finished. To their angry remonstrances the artist coolly replied that that was his way of competing, and if they did not care to pay him he would make them a present of the painting. Even in 1790 much of Tintoretto's work had become dull, almost leaden in colour, due, Goethe thought, to the artist's habit of painting *alla prima* without ground colours, or simply on red paint. Tintoretto left many followers, who neither sounding the depths of his knowledge nor possessing the magnanimity of his style, imitated him in his "splendid negligence" and contributed to the final decadence of painting.

S. CATERINA—THE MARRIAGE OF ST CATHERINE
By Veronese

His younger contemporary Veronese (Paolo Caliari), 1530-88, reverts to and develops to an even higher degree the warmer and more brilliant colour of the school. He is the unsurpassed interpreter of the festal pomp of Venetian society. Without possessing the elemental force of Tintoretto he is a more careful artist. How nobly and gently he could conceive, may be seen in the decoration of the church of S. Sebastiano, painted 1555-65, and in the marriage of St Catherine at the church of that name, his most tender and beautiful work. Of his well-known banquet compositions, the Accademia possesses the finest specimen, the Supper at the House of Levi, No. 203. In this magnificent painting, with its marvellous drawing and spacious architecture, the artist revels in his power of expressing the joy of man in the satisfaction of material existence. This glorification of the pomps and vanities of the world, painted for the refectory of the Dominican friars at S. Zanipolo, did, however, shock the Church, and the head of the Holy Office called on the Prior and severely criticised the picture. On the 8th of July 1573, Master Paolo Caliari was cited before the tribunal of the Inquisition. Being asked his profession, he answered, "I invent and draw figures." The inquisitor objected to the absence of Mary Magdalene and ordered that she should be substituted for the dog in the foreground; to St Peter carving a lamb; to a fellow dressed like a buffoon, with a parrot on his wrist; to another using his fork as a toothpick, and other indecencies. The artist defended himself stoutly and was ordered to reform his picture within three months. Veronese substituted the name of Levi for that of Simon and altered no more. Veronese was a noted house decorator of his time. None of his work survives at Venice, but visitors to Castelfranco may by a short detour see in the Villa Giacomelli, near Maser, some of the artist's best fresco work on the walls of a characteristic Palladian country-house.

With the works of the Bassani we reach the beginnings of modern painting. They are moderns not only in their dominant love of landscape, but in their touching affection for lowly peasant life and for the flocks and herds of their native hills. The family consisted of Jacopo da Ponte (1510-92), the father, and his sons Francesco (1549-92) and Leandro (1558-1623). The Accademia has good examples of their work, but to appreciate fully these homely and sympathetic artists one must travel to their native city Bassano, in the beautiful hill country north of Venice.

Palma Giovane, 1544-1628, son of Antonio Negretti and of Bonifazio's niece Giulia, is the last in whom the great traditions faintly survive. Besides his pictures in the Accademia some of the best of his work may be seen in the Oratorio dei Crocifissi. The school is now decadent; its productions feeble and mannered.

Giov. Battisto Tiepolo, 1696-1770, was a famous painter of his time: in the eyes of his contemporaries the equal of Veronese. He was a fine colourist, a bold and skilful draughtsman, with a broad and facile style, an excellent interpreter of the decadent splendour of Venetian life. He was in much demand as a decorator of palaces and churches. His best work may be seen in the frescoes executed for the Palazzo Labia. Among other churches, the Scalzi and the Gesuati have examples of his work in ceiling decoration, and there is a good altar-piece by his hand, St Lucy, in the SS. Apostoli.

Pietro Longhi, 1702-85, is a painter of scenes of intimate Venetian life in the eighteenth century with its trivial artificiality and social inanities. He has been aptly called the Goldoni of Venetian painters. Of Antonio da Canale (Canaletto), 1697-1768, and Francesco Guardi, 1712-93, Venice has few and poor examples. They were patient, excellent craftsmen but without inspiration, who have faithfully transmitted to us the Venice of their day.

Most ancient and important was the art of the glass-worker, peculiarly favoured by the abundance of fine sand and of a marine flora rich in alkaline products. In the thirteenth century so great was the expansion of the industry that it was deemed prudent to transfer the many furnaces working night and day from Rialto to Murano. It was a jealously guarded monopoly. In 1459 the Ten took over the control of the art and forbade under severe penalties (in some cases death) the emigration of workmen or the divulging of the secrets of the craft to foreigners. The craftsmen had their own *libro d'Oro* and ranked with patricians. Some beautiful examples of the masters, whom the genius of Marion Crawford[78] has invested with such dramatic interest, Zorzi il Ballarin and the Berovieri, may be seen at the Murano Museum, and an exquisite blue nuptial goblet in Room XII. at the Correr Museum in Venice. Wondrous stories are told of the subtle art of the craftsmen who were famed to make goblets so sensitive that they would betray by fracture the presence of poison.

The Venetians were great bibliophiles and readers. Soon after the discovery of the art of printing, Venice became its most important centre in Italy. By the end of the fifteenth century more books had been published in Venice than in Rome, Milan, Florence and Naples put together. In 1469 the Senate authorised John of Spires to print books for a period of five years. In 1470 Nicolo Jansen was issuing the Latin classics; in 1471 he published an Italian translation of the whole Bible, and in 1476 an edition of Pliny in the vulgar tongue. In 1490 the great humanist, Teobaldo Pio Manuccio of Rome (Aldus Manutius, or, as he wrote himself, Aldus Romanus), chose Venice as the most appropriate city for the achievement of his stupendous design of editing and printing the whole of the Greek classics. He gathered round him the greatest scholars of the age. Cretan Greeks were employed as designers of his types and compositors. Latin and Italian classics were printed in the type first used in the Virgil of 1501 and known as italics or *aldino*. It is said to have been modelled on Petrarch's handwriting and executed by Francia. Erasmus acted for a short time as editor and reader, and the great Dutch humanist had his translations of Euripides and his *Adagia* printed there. Erasmus and Aldus were good friends and would have been better if the fare provided at dinner had been less Lenten. The scholar's heart to-day warms to Aldus, whose steady, glowing enthusiasm carried him through his great task amid all the stress of the wars of the League of Cambrai. He founded at his house the famous *Accademia di Aldo*, where a symposium of humanists met for the study and emendation of the Greek classics. The rules were drawn up and the discussions conducted in Greek. Before Aldus died, in 1515, he had published twenty-eight *editiones principes* of the Greek masterpieces. He was the first of modern publishers, the first to break down the monopoly of the rich in books. His charming little octavo volumes with their familiar device of the anchor and the dolphin, so precious to the modern bibliophile, were sold at prices averaging about two shillings of our money. They were well read, for of the 24,000 copies printed of Erasmus' "Praise of Folly," only one copy has survived, and that in an imperfect state. He died a poor man and his kinsmen and descendants carried on the good work for a century.

If we turn from printing to literature we are met by a remarkable and impressive fact. Alone among the nations of Europe, Venice has given birth to no great literature. Save her crumbling architecture all that she conceived of the beautiful is expressed in painting. It is a great inheritance and immortalises a people of merchant princes, proud, sensuous, resourceful, with a firm grip of the realities of life, deeply religious in its own way, but without the spiritual idealism of the Tuscan. Through the millennial tale of her existence as a State, no great poet, no great thinker, no great dramatist meets us; none save a fluent and graceful writer of comedies of the Decadence, who was descended from a Modenese, and whose best work was written in a foreign tongue for a foreign capital.[79]

A VENETIAN WOMAN.

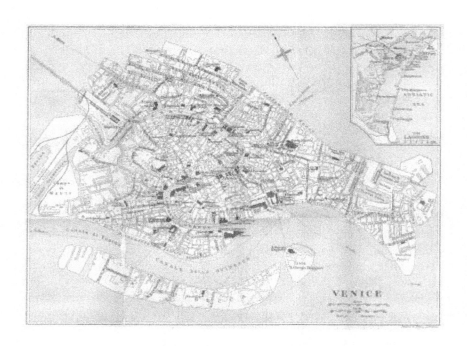

PART II

"They might chirp and chaffer, come and go
For pleasure or profit, her men alive—
My business is hardly with them I trow,
But with the empty cells of the human hive;
—With the chapter-room, the cloister-porch,
The church's apsis, aisle or nave,
Its crypt, one fingers along with a torch,
Its face set full for the sun to shave."
—*Browning.*

SECTION I

Arrival—The Piazza

THAT traveller will best attune himself to the peculiar charm of Venice, who arrives after sunset, when evening has veiled the somewhat unlovely approach to the city by railway. For the great lagoon State ever set her face to the sea and adorned herself to welcome her guests as they were rowed from Fusina, or as they sailed up from the Adriatic, to land at the Molo, the chief landing-stage by the Piazzetta. The modern visitor arriving by train is like one who should enter a stately mansion by the stables. Once, however, in his gondola, the "black Triton" of the lagoons, gliding along the waterways to the strangers' quarter by lines of houses and palaces, whose walls, timeworn or neglected, sometimes degraded, will be mellowed under the dim light of the infrequent lamps, he will be caught by the spell which Venice casts over those who come to her.

But there are two Venices: the Venice of the canals and the Venice of the streets. The traveller will do well therefore to go on foot to some of the sights he would see, for by no other means can he do justice to the varied beauty of the streets, the quaint fragmentary remains of ancient architecture, the brilliant patches of colour, the little shrines, and all the countless details that go to make the by-ways of the city so full of surprise and pleasure to the pedestrian. The difficulty of finding one's way from point to point has been greatly exaggerated. Anyone with a map and a normal sense of direction can with a little patience reach his destination. The churches are usually situated on or near a *campo*; a stream of people will generally be found passing along the streets and over the bridges between the *campi*, and a well-worn track marks the more frequented ways. If he should find himself blocked by a canal or a blind alley, a short deviation to the right or left will generally lead to one of the 380 bridges by which, to use Evelyn's picturesque phrase, the city is tacked together. Even if hopelessly lost, a *soldino* given to a boy will soon bring him to where he would go. The waterways, 150 in all, are divided into *canali* and *rii*. The *canale* is the broader, the *rio* the narrower stream. The *rii* are by far the greater in number. But the pedestrian is more concerned with street nomenclature. A *fondamenta* is a way alongside a *canale* or *rio*; a *calle* is a street with houses on either side; *ruga* or *rughetta* (French *rue*, *ruelle*) was first applied to streets with a few new houses here and there; the appellation was retained in later times when the houses or shops became continuous; a *salizzada* is one of the earliest of the paved streets, generally near a church; a *rio terra*, a *rio* filled up and paved; a *piscina*, a fish-pond treated in the same way; a *ponte*, a bridge; a *campo*, a paved, open place, formerly a field; a *campiello*, a smaller *campo*; a *corte*, a court. Avoid a *vico cieco*, or a *viccolo cieco*, which have no thoroughfare. The city is divided into six *sestieri* or wards, subdivided into *parocchie* or parishes. The houses are numbered by *sestieri*, the numbers reaching to thousands. The Merceria, a crowded thoroughfare, leads from under the Clock Tower in St Mark's Square, after many kinks and turns, to the Rialto bridge over the Grand Canal, which is spanned by two other bridges about equidistant from the Rialto bridge. E. and W. of the Rialto, in addition to these bridges, numerous ferries (*traghetti*) make either bank of the Grand Canal easy of access, and small steamers (*vaporetti*) call at frequent piers the whole length of the chief waterway. Travelling by gondola, therefore, is to be regarded as a luxury rather than a necessity. The gondola bears the same relation to Venetian life as does the cab or carriage to the dweller in an ordinary town. The average tide is about twenty inches: on exceptional occasions, the difference between high and low tides has been six feet.

La Piazzetta

The Piazza of S. Marco offers to the traveller a scene of unparalleled interest. Eastwards it is adorned by the most wonderful group of Byzantine and Gothic architecture in Europe. To the N. is the rhythmic symmetry of Pietro Lombardo's Procuratie Vecchie, ending with the Clock Tower[80]; to the S. are the Procuratie Nuove, Scamozzi's tasteless elaboration of Sansovino's lovely design for the Libreria Vecchia on the Piazzetta. Westward is the baser structure of Napoleonic times. Opposite the Porta della Carta of the Ducal Palace stood for a thousand years the old Campanile, like a giant sentinel set towards the lagoons to watch over the city. On the morning of July 14th, 1902, to the stupefaction of the Venetians, the huge tower, which in its massive strength seemed to defy the tooth of time, gently collapsed, as though weary of its millennial watch, crushing in its fall Sansovino's beautiful

Loggetta and the N. side of the Libreria Vecchia, but miraculously doing no further hurt. When the Venetians recovered from the shock and learned how mercifully exempt from toll of human life the disaster had been, and that St Mark's and the Ducal Palace were unscathed, they remembered their protector and said: *È stato galant'uomo S. Marco* (St Mark has been a good fellow). Ten months later, when the King and Queen of Italy, during their visit to Venice, turned to look at the site of the old tower, a lament was heard in the crowd of people: *I varda dove gera el nostro pavaro morto* (They are going where our poor dead one lies). The foundations laid a thousand years before, were found to be as sound as ever, and a new Campanile has now been raised to replace, though it cannot restore, the old one, which, with all its dramatic history and romantic associations, has disappeared for ever.

It is not by accident that the chief buildings of Venice stand where they do, for this part of the Rialtine islands, called *il Morso*, offered a soil harder[81] and more tenacious than any other. In early ages the Piazza was a grass-grown field, called the Broglio or Garden, scarce a third of its present area, and a large elder tree flourished on the site of the Campanile. It was bounded on the W. by a rio which ran from N. to S. a few yards beyond the Campanile and discharged into the Grand Canal to the W. of the present Zecca (mint). On the W. bank of the rio, facing the basilica of St Mark, stood the old church of S. Giminiano. In 1176 Doge Ziani filled up the rio, razed the fortifications and extended and paved the Piazza, to its present boundary westward. The church of S. Giminiano was rebuilt at the W. end. It was again rebuilt by Sansovino in 1556 and finally demolished by Napoleon I. to extend the Royal Palace. Houses on the S. abutted on the Campanile. The Piazza was enclosed by stately mansions with columns and arcades on the first floor, "where one walked round as in a theatre."[82] When Scamozzi built the Procuratie Nuove in 1584, the houses on the S. were demolished and the Piazza set back to its present line. If we would restore its aspect in the fulness of Venetian prosperity, we must imagine a scene brilliant with colour. The archivolts, capitals, friezes and sculptures generally of St Mark's and the Ducal Palace were richly decorated with gold and vermilion and blue. The Porta della Carta glowed so with gold that it was known as the *Porta dorata* (the gilded portal). The bronze horses were gilded; so was St Mark's Lion and St Theodore in the Piazzetta. From Leopardi's beautiful bronze sockets three tall masts upheld the standards symbolising dominion over Greece, Cyprus and Crete.

A throng of merchants and strangers from all the corners of the earth, an ever-changing pageant of quaint and gorgeous costumes, passed and repassed. So many strange tongues would you hear, says an old writer,[83] that the Piazza might not inaptly be called the *forum orbis non urbis*—not the market-place of a city but of the world. Strange tongues are still heard in the Piazza, but of those who come for the pleasure, not for the business of the world: the heart of commerce no longer beats at Venice. The Piazza is, however, a scene of much animation on public holidays when the band is playing. We will sit outside Florian's coffee-house, as a good Venetian should, and observe the women of the people passing, with their graceful carriage and simple costume, their wealth of hair so charmingly treated; the gondolier, lithe of body and superb in gait; the *signore* and *signorine* with their more modern finery; the fashionable youth, dressed, as he fondly imagines, *all' inglese*; rich and poor, *borghese* and *popolano*, bearing themselves with that ease of manner, vivacity of spirit and social equality so characteristic of the Venetians. In the height of summer, when the rich merchants of Milan and other cities of North Italy with their women folk come to Venice for the Italian season, the Piazza after dinner and far into the night becomes one vast open-air salon, crowded with visitors in the most *chic* of costumes, many of the ladies promenading in evening dress. As one sits in the Piazza at setting sun, the atmosphere, exquisitely delicate and clear, changes from pale blue to amethyst, pink, turquoise, dark blue and indigo; and the night is lovelier than the day.

SECTION II

The Basilica of St Mark

FEW things in the history of art are more remarkable than the revulsion of taste that has taken place with regard to the architecture of Venice. In the early part of the nineteenth century, before Ruskin wrote "The Stones of Venice," an English architect,[84] giving expression to the professional judgment of the age, speaks of "the lumpy form of the Cathedral which surprises you by the extreme ugliness of its exterior; of the lower part built in the degraded Roman we call Norman; of the gouty columns and ill-made capitals, all in bad taste." "The Ducal Palace is even more ugly than anything previously mentioned," vastly inferior to Palladio's churches of S. Giorgio and the Redentore. Disraeli echoes in "Contarini Fleming" the conventional lay praise of Palladio, and writes of the "barbarous although picturesque buildings called the Ducal Palace." Even to-day the stranger fresh from the North with memories of the massive towers and lofty spires of his own architecture will hardly escape a sense of disappointment as he stands before St Mark's. The fabric will seem to lack majesty and to be even less imposing than the Ducal Palace. It must, however, be remembered that the raising of the level of the Piazza has somewhat detracted from the elevation of both the basilica and the Palace. Fynes Moryson notes in his Itinerary (1617) that "there were stairs of old to mount out of the market-place into the church till the waters of the channel increasing they were forced to raise the height of the market-place."

A GONDOLIER.

Whether there were any such intention in the minds of the builders is doubtful, but in all communities where the sense of municipal liberty or of secular independence is strong, the dominant civic power is actualised in architecture. In Flemish towns the Hôtel de Ville and not the cathedral is often the more important structure; even so in Venice the subordinate position of the church is marked by the accessory character of the ecclesiastical building, which in its origin indeed was but the official chapel of the Doge, and only became the Cathedral in 1807, when Napoleon transferred the patriarchate from S. Pietro in Castello—itself a poor thing architecturally—to St Mark's.

Joseph Woods gave a shrewd criticism of Venetian architecture when he characterised it as showing riches and power rather than just proportions. St Mark's was erected by a merchant folk, with all the merchant's love of display of wealth. Their taste was for costly material rather than for nobility and grandeur of design. For centuries the East was ransacked for precious stones to adorn the sanctuary of their patron saint, and the captain of every ship that traded in the Levant was ordered to bring home marbles or fine stones for the builders. St Mark's is a jewelled casket wrought to preserve the Palladium of the Venetian people.

S. MARCO—MAIN PORTAL

The fabric dates from the early eleventh to the late fourteenth centuries. Its core is of brick, of which most Venetian churches are built, and it is veneered with marble[85] and decorated with mosaic and sculpture. When the eye turns from the whole to examine details, the façade is seen to be composed of two tiers of arches—the lower of seven, the upper of five spans. Of the seven, two form the N. and S. porticos; five the western doors, whose recesses are enriched with rows of columns wanting in unity of design, but of exceeding richness and variety of material. They are mainly the spoils of Eastern churches, and, if closely scrutinised, will be found to be incised with Eastern crosses and curious inscriptions in Greek and oriental characters.

The capitals flanking the main portal, with carving of leaves blown by the wind, are probably from the East, their prototype being at the Church of St Sophia in Thessalonica, built in the later years of Justinian's reign. The main portal is spanned by an inner triple archivolt and an outer main one. The under side of the inner arc of the former, over the relief of St Mark and the Angel, is wrought with sculptures, whose subjects are symbolical, and will be met with again and again in early Venetian decoration: a naked man and woman seated on dragons; a child in the open jaws of a lion; an eagle pecking at a lamb; a lion devouring a stag; camels and other animals, wild and tame, in various groups. On the outer face are similar carvings of boys fighting and robbing birds' nests; men shooting birds with bows and arrows, and hunting wild beasts. The work is exceedingly quaint, and affords a fruitful theme for interpretation.

S. MARCO—DETAIL OF ARCHIVOLT

The sculptures on the under side of the outer arc symbolise the months of the year, with their appropriate celestial signs. May, a seated figure holding a rose and crowned with flowers by two maidens, is most beautiful and original in treatment.

On the outer face of the archivolt are represented the Beatitudes and the Virtues, eight on either side of the keystone, which symbolises Constancy.

On the under surface of the main archivolt are fourteen most beautiful carvings, representing the chief guilds and crafts of Venice. To the L.,[86] at the bottom, is a seated figure with finger on lip, said by Ruskin to represent the rest of old age; by tradition it is the portrait of the architect of the building, of whom the following story is told. When Doge Pietro Orseolo determined to restore the church after the fire of 976, a queer, unknown man, lame in both legs, offered to make St Mark's the most beautiful structure ever erected, if, on completion, his statue were placed in a conspicuous part of the building. His terms were accepted, but after the work had progressed some time, the stranger incautiously let fall a remark to the effect that the church would have been much more magnificent if certain difficulties had not intervened. Word was sent to the Doge, and the statue was set in its present obscure position.

S. MARCO—DETAIL OF MAIN DOOR

On either side of the main portal are two doorways, spanned by richly decorated Byzantine arches; that to the L., has the figure of Christ in the keystone and two prophets with scrolls in the spandrils; that to the R. has the keystone defaced; in the spandrils to the R. and L. are the archangels Michael and Gabriel. The lateral doorway to the L. has in the lunette a winged figure on horseback and symbols of the Evangelists; on the lintel are some fine Gothic reliefs. The pierced screen-work in the lunette windows should be noted, for in olden times the whole of the window spaces in the domes were thus treated. The corresponding doorway to the R. has in the spandrils, carvings of two archangels, and on the keystone the Virgin and Child.

The beautiful lily capitals are at either end of the façade, and support the arches that span the N. and S. porticos.

The late fifteenth-century Gothic additions consist of pinnacles and gables of no structural value. They are seen in Gentile Bellini's picture,[87] dated

1496, of the Procession in St Mark's Square, but are absent in the extant thirteenth-century mosaic on the façade.

The mosaics in the lunettes of the five doorways are, with one exception, poor in craftsmanship, but interesting in their storiation. That of the central portal is a feeble representation of the Last Judgment. Salandri, who executed it in 1836-38, had already been mulcted for bad workmanship. The remaining four tell of the discovery and translation of the body of St Mark. In the fifth porch, to the N., the body of the saint being carried into St Mark's, though largely renewed, is a precious relic of the beautiful thirteenth-century mosaics that covered the front in Gentile Bellini's time, as may be seen from the picture already referred to. The four mosaics in the lunettes on either side of the great window above, represent the Deposition from the Cross, the Descent into Hades, the Resurrection, the Ascension—all seventeenth-century work. Beneath the great window stand the four bronze horses, part of the spoils sent from Constantinople by Enrico Dandolo in 1204. They are said to be Greek work of the fourth century B.C., and to have been sent from Rome to the new capital of the Empire by Constantine. They remained in their present position until 1797, when the "gran ladrone," Napoleon I., sent them to Paris to adorn the Arc du Carrousel. In 1815 they were restored to Venice by Francis I. of Austria, as the Latin inscription under the archivolt beneath tells. A magnificent festa was organised when they were raised to their old position in the presence of the Austrian. The Piazza was bright with gorgeous decorations; a superb loggia erected for the Imperial family; an amphitheatre for the Venetian nobility. Nothing was wanting—but an audience. The amphitheatre was empty; a few loungers idled about the square. Cannons were fired; the bells rang a double peal; the music played; the horses were drawn up—but not a cheer followed them. The Emperor and his suite had the show to themselves.

N.E.
BYZANTINE RELIEF, NORTH SIDE, S. MARCO

In the lunette of the N. portal, which gives on the Piazzetta dei Leoni, with its two double cusped inner arches, is an early relief of the Nativity, a work of great beauty, framed by the vine decoration so beloved of the early sculptors. Among the many Byzantine reliefs with which this façade is jewelled the most perfect is that of the Twelve Apostles, symbolised as sheep, with the Lamb enthroned in the centre and palm trees on either side. This exquisite carving will be found in the last recess R. of the doorway.

BYZANTINE RELIEF FROM SOUTH SIDE, S. MARCO

The S. façade, looking as it does towards the Molo, would in olden times arrest the eye of the traveller as he entered the city. It is most lavishly decorated. The reliefs and marble facings towards the Porta della Carta are some of the finest that remain of the ancient basilica. Their lowly position seems to have preserved them from the restorer's hand. At the angle is a rude Greek relief in porphyry, probably from Acre, of two pairs of armed figures clasping each other. They are said to represent Greek emperors who shared the throne of the East early in the eleventh century. In the foreground stand the two beautifully decorated marble door-posts brought from St Sabbas in Acre. They should, however, change places to occupy the relative position they formerly held in the church. Below the mosaic of the Virgin and Child in the smaller arch above the gallery two lamps burn nightly in perpetual memory of an act of injustice perpetrated by the Ten in 1611, when an innocent man, Giovanni Grassi, was executed. The short porphyry column at the S.W. corner is the old edict stone where the official notices and laws of the Republic were proclaimed to the people.

CAPITALS, ATRIUM, S. MARCO

At our feet, as we enter the atrium by the main portal are three slabs of porphyry which mark the legendary, but not the actual, spot where the reconciliation of the Pope and the Emperor Barbarossa took place. The shafts and capitals of the columns in the atrium are among the richest in the basilica. The mosaics, designed to instruct and prepare the catechumen, illustrate Old Testament history, and for their simple beauty will repay perusal.

I TRE PONTI.

In the south cupola are three concentric zones of mosaics which illustrate the six days of Creation, the Institution of the Sabbath, the Fall and the Expulsion from Eden. The number of the day is indicated by a corresponding number of angels standing beside the Creator with hands uplifted in praise. At the institution of the Sabbath the Lord is seen resting from His work with three angels on either side; the seventh kneels receiving the Lord's blessing.[88] There is a quaint portraiture of the Lord clothing Adam and Eve,—Adam most uncomfortable, and Eve looking reproachfully at the ill-fitting garment.

Five mosaics in the three lunettes under the cupola tell the story of Cain and Abel, and under the vaultings between the first cupola and the central vestibule is the story of Noah.

On the W. side of the next vaulting is the story of the Tower of Babel. Below is the tomb of the Dogaressa Felicia, the young wife of Vitale Falier, who, as the inscription tells, was a true servant of God and of the poor, and who spurned luxury (*calcavit luxurium*).

The second cupola contains scenes from the life of Abraham. In the lunette over St Peter, above the inner door, Abraham receives the three angels and entertains them. Behind is Sarah at the door of her tent laughing at the promise that she should bear a son. The third cupola tells the story of Joseph, which is continued on the fourth and fifth cupolas to the N. The sixth cupola deals with the story of Moses. In the recess opposite the lunette to the R. once lay the remains[89] (whence they were taken and brought to England) of Thomas Mowbray, Duke of Norfolk—

"Who at Venice gave
His body to that pleasant country's earth,
And his pure soul unto his captain, Christ,
Under whose colours he had fought so long."
—RICHARD II., iv. I.

Returning to the main portal of the atrium—in the lunette is St Mark, executed by the brothers Zuccati in 1545 from a cartoon by Titian. Below in seven niches are the Virgin and Child and six Apostles; lower down on either side of the portal, the four Evangelists. In the lunette, R., Raising of Lazarus; lunette over the outer portal, Crucifixion; lunette L., Burial of the Virgin. These, which are among the finest mosaics of the period, formed part of the work that the Zuccati had to answer for in 1563. They were charged by the Bianchini and Bozza with having used the methods of painting and not of true mosaic to produce certain effects. The most famous tribunal ever brought together in the history of art sat to try the case. It was composed of Titian, Paul Veronese, Tintoretto, Jacopo da Pistoia and Schiavone. Although the Zuccati were condemned to remove and replace at their own cost the work that had been gone over with the brush, the honours of the trial rested with them, Titian frankly eulogising their craftsmanship.

No sense of disappointment will be felt at the first view of the interior. The symmetry of the architecture, the gorgeous mosaics, the rich pavement, the precious marbles covering the walls, the manifold variety of the columns, and (if the traveller have the fortune to be present on Easter or St Mark's Day) the dazzling brilliancy of the Pala d'Oro glittering with jewels make a scene of oriental splendour not easily forgotten. In earlier times, when the windows were filled with pierced screen-work of marble, the church was much darker, for, says Moryson, "the papist churches are commonly dark to cause a religious horror." Evelyn in 1645 found the interior dark and dismal.

Merely to name the subjects of the 40,000 square feet of mosaics in the interior would weary the reader. We do but indicate the more important and more interesting. The general scheme is designed to illustrate the mysteries of the Christian faith and the story of the patron saint. Over the main entrance is the oldest of the mosaics, probably an eleventh-century work— Christ enthroned between the Virgin and St Mark. In the book held by the Redeemer are the words in Latin, "I am the Door; if any man enter by Me he shall be saved and find pasture." A similar inscription exists to this day over the Porta Basilica which opens into the nave of St Sophia at Constantinople. In the half dome of the apse the colossal seated figure of Christ in the act of blessing meets the eye of the worshipper as he enters the church and walks towards the sanctuary, even as it did in the apse at St Sophia.[90] In the centre of the dome over the high altar is again the figure of Christ, and, above the windows, the Virgin, and the prophets who foretold Christ's coming, bearing scrolls inscribed with their testimony. The pendentives bear symbolic figures of the Four Evangelists, that of the Lion of St Mark with a strangely human face, being designed with admirable force and dignity. Scenes in the life of Christ are portrayed on the vault between this and the central dome; the Passion and Resurrection on the vault between the central and western domes. The great central dome is treated with profound thought and fertile invention, and executed with infinite care. In the apex is the glorified Christ seated on a double rainbow, surrounded by exulting angels. Below are the Virgin, the Apostles and the Evangelists alternating with olive and palm trees. The beautiful figure of the Virgin stands between two angels. In the spaces between the windows are the Virtues and the Beatitudes. They may easily be distinguished by their inscriptions and symbols.

The W. dome treats of the Descent of the Holy Ghost. A white dove standing on a book placed on a throne fills the centre, and from this emblem of the Holy Spirit twelve streams of fire descend upon the figures of the Twelve Apostles circling the dome. The men of every nation to whom they spoke, each in his own tongue, are figured at the Apostles' feet between the windows.

In the dome of the N. transept is figured a Greek cross, in the centre of which are eight Greek letters set in a circle, whose meaning is doubtful. Near this centre, N. and S., is an alpha; E. and W., an omega. On the arms of the cross the Golden Rule is expressed in a curious rhyming Latin paraphrase, beginning on the E. and continuing on the W., N. and S. arms.

The dome of the S. transept bears figures of SS. Leonard, Nicholas, Clement and Blaise. In the pendentives SS. Erasmus, Euphemia, Dorothy and Thecla. While Vicenzo Sebastiani was finishing this last, he fell from the scaffolding and was killed. On the vaultings of the transepts are represented the parables and miracles of Christ. The vaulting to the E., between the S. and the centre domes, has delightfully naive and dramatic representations of the Temptation and the Entry into Jerusalem. On the western side are beautiful representations of the Last Supper and the Washing of the Disciples' Feet. On the vaultings and the walls of the aisles are stories of the martyrdom of the Apostles.

Modern mosaics illustrating the Book of Revelation, the Last Judgment, Hell and Paradise, cover the vaultings beyond the W. dome and over the W. gallery. They and many other of the mosaics are best seen from the galleries.

On the lower walls of the aisles are repeated the figures of prophets that foretold the coming of Christ bearing the usual scrolls. To the N. are Hosea, Joel, Micah and Jeremiah, with a beautiful representation of the youthful Christ in the centre. S. are Isaiah, David, Solomon and Ezekiel, with the Virgin answering to the figure of Christ.

The story of the patron saint begins on the vaulting of the N. organ loft over the choir, where scenes in his life and martyrdom are portrayed. They are, however, partly concealed by the organ. These, perhaps the oldest mosaics in the church, were largely restored in 1879 by the Venezia-Murano Company. Opposite, to the S., on the vaulting, is most quaintly told how the body of the saint came to Venice. The designers are very frank in their story of the Translation of the body. *Furenter*, "it is stolen" from Alexandria.

On the W. wall of the S. transept opposite the Chapel of the Holy Blood is told the story of the miraculous rediscovery of the body in 1094: The Doge, clergy and people, with solemn fast and prayer, implore divine aid, and a round column in the church opens and discloses the saint's body. Tradition, however, says that the body was found in the large pier called St Mark's pillar, to the left of the Chapel of the Holy Blood. An angel's head in full relief is carved above the spot, and a lamp burns below an inlaid cross. The line of cleavage is still seen. Tradition, however, would seem to be at fault in this matter, for when the pillar was recently stripped of the marble facing, the solid core had clearly never been disturbed.

The Baptistery and the Zeno Chapel, entered from the right aisle, originally formed part of the atrium. The mosaics in the Baptistery were executed by the order of Doge Andrea Dandolo (1343-54), but have been partly restored[91] by the Venezia-Murano Company. In the lunette above the altar is the Crucifixion. Weeping angels hover over the cross; L., are the Virgin and St Mark; R., St John the Evangelist and St John the Baptist. At the foot of the cross kneels Doge Andrea Dandolo; at the extreme ends kneel his Grand Chancellor, Riafano Caresini, and a Senator. The table of the altar is formed of a massive block of Egyptian granite from which Christ is said to have preached, brought from the siege of Tyre in 1126. In the centre of the cupola above is Christ enthroned; below is a ten-winged angel bearing on his breast the inscription—"Fulness of Wisdom." This is the first of the nine Intelligences circling the cupola, which in mediæval cosmogony ruled over the nine heavenly spheres.

The story of the Baptist's life is told in the lunettes and on the walls. The mosaic of the Burial of the Saint's Body is said by Ruskin to be the most beautiful design of the Baptist's death that he knew in Italy.

In the centre of the cupola over the font is a figure of Christ seated on a double rainbow and holding a scroll on which is inscribed the injunction to the Twelve to go and preach the gospel to all creatures. Beneath, each is seen obeying the command in that country where tradition places his martyrdom. Quaint local costumes are introduced, and converts are being baptised.

Opposite the entrance is the tomb of Andrea Dandolo, the last Doge buried in St Mark's. On the workmanship of this beautiful example of fourteenth-century monumental art Ruskin has lavished ecstatic praise. Beneath the noble, peaceful figure of the Doge are the Virgin and Child, two scenes from the Martyrdom of St John the Baptist and of Andrew, the Doge's patron saint, and an Annunciation. The long Latin epitaph has been attributed to Petrarch.

The vault of the vestibule of the Cappella Zen is decorated with scenes from the life of Christ before His baptism. The tomb in the recess is that of Doge Giovanni Soranzo (1328). The Cappella Zen contains the monument of Cardinal Zeno, executed at the beginning of the sixteenth century. The altar is dedicated to the Virgin of the Slipper, whose figure in bronze has a gilded shoe, in perpetual memory of the miraculous alchemy by which her slipper, given to a poor votary, was changed to gold. The Zeno tomb is a fine Renaissance work in bronze which, together with the altar, was designed by the Lombardi and Aless. Leopardi (p. 191). The walls of the chapel are decorated with the history of St Mark.

S. GIORGIO MAGGIORE

In the little chapel of the Madonna dei Mascoli at the W. angle of the N. transept, where of old a guild of men used to assemble, are some fine fifteenth-century mosaics by Michele Giambono. They are unhappily injured by restoration, but in the main the early Renaissance feeling has been preserved and the more natural modelling of the figures and fuller architectural detail form a pleasing contrast to the stiff and sometimes hard design of the Byzantine workmen.

East of this is the richly decorated chapel of St Isidore founded by the same Doge and scholar who decorated the Baptistery. The work was not, however, completed until 1355 under Dom. Gradenigo. The inscription over the altar tells that the body of the Blessed Isidore was brought from Chios in 1125 by Doge Dom. Michiel and now rests in the tomb below. The sculptured figure of the saint and the reliefs to left and right representing his martyrdom are fine work. The fourteenth-century mosaics so faithfully wrought by the artists of that great epoch have needed but slight repair and remain practically as they left them. Over the altar is Christ seated between S. Mark and Isidore, and balancing this at the opposite end are the Virgin and Child, the Baptist and St Nicholas. The legend of the saint is illustrated on the walls. In this chapel we are standing within part of the actual fabric of the old church of St Theodore. When the S. wall of the chapel was peeled in 1832 it was found to be blackened by exposure to the weather and pierced by a window with an iron grille.

The group of worshippers ever before the altar to the left as the visitor leaves this chapel will tell him that he is approaching the shrine of the Virgin. Under a canopy is the miraculous Nicopeian icon of the Virgin which was captured from Murzuphles and formed part of the spoil of Constantinople. Doge Dandolo sent it to Venice in a specially appointed ship, and in 1618 the present altar was raised by Doge Giov. Bembo. The image (only exposed on Saturdays) was traditionally painted by St Luke. It is lavishly decorated with precious stones and surrounded by ex-votos.

Passing the altar of St Paul, bearing a statue of the saint and a fine relief of the scene of his blindness, the chapel of St Peter is reached. In front is a screen with statues of the Virgin and Child and four women saints, the Massegne. In the apse of this chapel is the entrance to the Sacristy, one of the most beautiful chambers in Europe. The magnificent mosaic ceiling designed by Titian and wrought with perfect art; the rich marble decorations; the symmetry and proportion of the architecture; the chastened glow of colour will not fail to impress the spectator.

Beyond the altar of St Paul is the great N. pulpit. It is one of the finest architectural features in the church and rich in historical memories. Here Enrico Dandolo and other great Doges and prelates addressed the people in national crises. Another pulpit smaller and simpler in style stands to the S. of the choir screen, and an altar to St James balances that to St Paul on the N. On the architrave of the screen stand the crucifix, statues of the Virgin, St Mark and the Twelve Apostles by the Massegne, signed and dated 1394-97. On either side of the choir are three reliefs in bronze by Sansovino. The great bronze-doors by the same master lead from the L. of the choir to the Sacristy. The canopy of the high altar is borne by four marble columns with reliefs (p. 187). The rude timeworn figures tell the story of the life of the Virgin on the N.E. pillar and the life of Christ on the remaining pillars, reading N.W., S.E. and S.W.

The gorgeous Pala d'Oro is exposed to view on Easter Eve and Day, and St Mark's Eve and Day. It may be seen on other days between twelve and two on payment of 50 centesimi. This magnificent example of the goldsmith's art was made to the order of Ordelafo Falier by Byzantine craftsmen at Constantinople in 1105. It was added to and restored by Gothic artists under Pietro Ziani in 1209, and under Andrea Dandolo in 1345. The gold, estimated to weigh thirty, the silver three hundred pounds, is set with some 1200 pearls and a like number of precious stones. Most of the jewels were, however, looted by the French in 1797 and are replaced by inferior modern stones, which may be detected by the fact that they are cut in facets. The upper compartment has in the centre St Michael surrounded by sixteen medallions of the doctors of the Church. To the L. are three panels: The Feast of Palms, Descent into Limbo, Crucifixion; to the R., other three, the Ascension, Pentecost, Death of the Virgin. The lower and larger compartment is framed on three sides by twenty-seven small panels whose subjects are taken from the lives of St Mark, Christ and the Virgin. In the middle is a large panel with the figure of the seated Christ and four smaller figures of the Evangelists; above are two archangels and two cherubim. On each side of the large panel are two sets of six medallions, the upper and smaller of archangels, the lower and larger of the Apostles. Beneath the figure of Christ in the large panel are three plaques: the centre contains the figure of the Virgin; L. of her is a crowned figure, which a Latin inscription tells is that of Doge Ordelafo Falier; R. of the Virgin is a crowned figure with a Greek inscription stating it to be the Empress Irene. If, however, the observer will scrutinise the figure of the Doge it will be seen that his head has been substituted for that of the Empress's consort, John Comnenus. On each side of these three central figures are inscriptions which give the history of the Pala d'Oro and six prophets bearing scrolls. The technique of the gold *cloisonné* enamels is admirable. They are glorious in colour, partly translucent, and allow the backing of fine gold to shine through.

Behind the high altar is the altar of the Holy Cross, adorned with six columns of precious marble. The two spiral, semi-transparent ones were reputed to come from Solomon's Temple. The chapel to the S. of the high altar is dedicated to St Clement. Beneath the cornice whence springs the vaulting of the apse is a stern minatory inscription in Latin that met the eye of the Doge, as he entered from the Ducal Palace through an ante-room opening on this chapel. It is now but dimly seen, and runs thus: *Love justice, give all men their rights: let the poor and the widow, the ward and the orphan, O Doge, hope for a guardian in thee. Be compassionate to all: let not fear nor hate nor love nor gold betray thee. Thou shalt perish as a flower: dust shalt thou become, and, as thy deeds have been, so after death thy reward shall be.*

In the S. transept, answering to the Lady Chapel, is the chapel of the Holy Blood, formerly dedicated to St Leonard.

The old and new crypts open to the public on St Mark's Day, and at other times on payment of 50 centesimi, are of great interest. In the centre of the new crypt, that of Contarini's church, is the empty tomb, reaching to the roof, where lay St Mark's body from 1094 until 1811, when it was removed to the high altar where it now remains. Three steps, topped by a slab of stone worn by pilgrims' feet, lead to a semi-circular cell with a small window once filled with pierced stone-work. The ancient capitals of the columns of this crypt are of great beauty. The older crypt with its rude brick vaulting that formed part of the ninth-century basilica of Giov. Participazio, was drained and cleared of rubbish, as the inscription tells, in 1890.

The chief object of interest in the Treasury, entered at the W. angle of the S. transept, is the so-called chair of St Mark, wrought from a block of Cipollino marble, said to have been sent to Aquileia from Alexandria by the Empress

Helena and to have been carried thence with the other relics to Grado at the time of the Lombard invasion. Some beautiful book-covers from St Sofia; a number of Byzantine chalices made of precious stones; two fine candelabri attributed to Cellini; a ring used at the Wedding of the Adriatic, are among the exhibits. The Treasury was looted at the same time as the Pala d'Oro by the French. The room itself, outside the fabric of the church, is of interest inasmuch as it originally formed part of the tower of the old Ducal Palace. The body of St Mark is said to have lain there from 829 until 832, when the church was ready to receive it.

Before we quit the interior, the old rich mosaic pavement with its quaint and beautiful Byzantine designs is worth notice. The uneven, wavy form is due, not to any intent of imitating the waves of the sea, but to the fact that the pavement is supported by the crypt and has settled into hollows corresponding to the cells of the vaulting which, being filled with loose material, are less rigid than the crown where no settlement has taken place.

SECTION III

The Ducal Palace

TO turn from the fair temple of the Christian faith in Venice, warm with the affection and the presence of her people, to the empty splendour of the Palace where her secular princes sat in state, is to turn from life to death. If a patrician of the great days were to revive and enter St Mark's he would find the same hierarchy, the same ritual, the same prayers and praise uttered in the same language to the God he knew. But if he sought to enter the Ducal Palace, the servant of a then petty dynasty would demand a silver coin before he were permitted to ascend the Golden Staircase. There, on steps once trod by those alone whose names were inscribed in the Book of Gold, he would meet a strange company. He would find the great palace of Venice a museum; her millennial power a memory; and the gorgeous halls that once echoed to the voices of the masters of land and sea occupied by a crowd of sightseers, alien in race and creed, gazing curiously at the faded emblems and pictures which tell of her pride, her glory and her imperial state.

The earliest official residence of the Tribunes of Rivoalto was situated by the church of the Holy Apostles near the Rio dei Gesuiti, whose northern mouth is opposite the channel leading to Murano. The remains of this fortified building, which was furnished with a great gate, always kept closed, and a guarded postern, still existed towards the end of the sixteenth century, and then served as a prison. In 820, Doge Angelo Participazio built another feudal-like structure on the site of the present Ducal Palace, near the church of St Theodore. Nothing could be less like the *palazzo fabbricato in aria* we know to-day. It and the whole of the Piazza, then but a third of its present area, were enclosed by a strong wall with Ghibelline battlements. One of the old towers is incorporated in the masonry, at whose corner now stand the four figures in porphyry referred to on p. 229.

Angelo's structure was destroyed by fire during the riots which attended the murder of Doge Pietro Candiano in 976. The rebuilding was undertaken by his successor, Pietro Orseolo, and completed towards the end of the eleventh century by Doge Selvo, who adorned the exterior with marble columns and the interior with mosaics. Doge Sebastiano Ziani extended the buildings in the late twelfth century. Early in the fourteenth, the E. portion of the S. façade was begun under the direction it is believed of the chief mason (*Prototaiapiera*), Pietro Basseggio, and in the course of about a century the S. wing was completed and the W. façade carried so far as the boundary of Ziani's building. About 1365 Doge Marco Cornaro had the walls of the Hall of the Grand Council, the necessity for which had been the chief cause of the new buildings, painted with scenes from the story of the reconciliation of Pope Alexander and the Emperor Barbarossa, and the cornice decorated with portraits of the Doges so arranged that his own came exactly over the ducal chair. The Gothic additions made the simple edifice of Ziani look poor in comparison, and a strong desire was evoked to rebuild the old palace; but the Senate, chary of adding to the public burdens, forbade any member to make such a proposal under a fine of 1000 ducats. In 1419 fire injured the old edifice, and the good Doge Tomaso Mocenigo offered to pay the fine, and thus carried a proposal to rebuild Ziani's portion of the Palace, which reached from the present Porta della Carta to the sixth arch and seventh column N. of the Adam and Eve angle. The Gothic building was completed between 1424 and 1439, under Doge Francesco Foscari, whose kneeling figure (restored) is carved over the Porta.

The ornate façade on the east side, best seen from a gondola or from the Ponte di Canonico, is by Ant. Riccio, and was erected between 1483 and 1500.

After the great fire of 1577, when the conflagration seemed "like Etna in eruption," the whole structure narrowly escaped demolition to make place for a new building of Palladian architecture. The strenuous opposition of the architects Giovanni Rusconi and Antonio da Ponte alone saved it. The latter's plans were accepted and the ruin was repaired and redecorated.

The Bridge of Sighs is a later addition by Ant. Contino, about 1600. It is a commonplace structure, and none but commonplace criminals ever crossed it to their doom.

The brick core of the palace may still be seen in the Cortile and from the Ponte della Paglia, on the eastern façade, where Riccio's beautiful work ends.

The sculptures at the three free angles, the Drunkenness of Noah, the Adam and Eve, and the Judgment of Solomon are placed S.E., S.W. and N.W. The group of the Judgment of Solomon is by two Tuscan sculptors, Pietro di Nicolo di Firenze and Giov. di Martino da Fiesole.

The S. façade, like the W., is composed of a lower arcade and an upper gallery whose columns support the massive walls of the upper storeys, a daring inversion of architectural tradition which is not wholly satisfying. The marble lozenge-shaped incrustation, however, relieves the heaviness. Indeed, from a fourteenth-century drawing[92] in the Bodleian Library, Oxford, it is possible the upper storeys may have been originally set back.

The squat appearance of the columns of the arcade is due to the raising of the level of the Piazzetta, which in the days when the palace was built was some thirty inches below the present pavement.[93] The original building was approached by a stylobate of three steps which greatly added to its dignity and proportion. Under this arcade the Venetian nobility were accustomed to meet and talk of public affairs, for meetings in their own houses would have roused the suspicion of the Ten. When the patricians, as they paced up and down, raised their eyes to the capitals just above their heads they saw a series of sculptures which for beauty of design, richness of invention and craftsmanship were unsurpassed in Europe. Even to-day, largely renewed as they are, they will repay careful inspection. The subjects are of the usual symbolical types: children, birds, famous emperors and kings, the virtues and sins, the signs of the Zodiac, the crafts, the seven ages of man under celestial influences, the months and seasons, famous lawgivers—all treated with the *naïveté* and didactic purpose so characteristic of Gothic artists. Most of the carvings bear inscriptions which make the interpretation of the subjects comparatively easy. The artists, however, who wrought the fifteenth-century capitals on the W. façade seem to have been lacking in invention, for of the thirteen columns southwards from the Porta della Carta, six are copied from those wrought by the fourteenth-century masons on the S. façade.

PONTE DEI SOSPIRI.

The gallery above is beyond criticism; for originality and grace it is unique in Europe. The eye never tires of its beauty; it adds distinction to the whole structure, and it gives an element of peaceful repose and conscious security so markedly in contrast to the grim civic fortresses of Florence and Siena and other faction-ridden Italian States. The four raised windows of the main storey on the S. are due to the fact that the builders of the Hall of the Great Council cared less for external symmetry than for internal convenience. The two balconied windows, one in each façade, were added soon after the completion of the Porta della Carta. Before 1577 all the windows of the great chamber were decorated with Gothic triforia. It is now proposed to restore them, though the project meets with much opposition.

We pass through the Porta della Carta, enter the Cortile and turn to examine Riccio's famous statues of Adam and Eve opposite the Giant's Staircase. The inner façade was begun on the E. side by Riccio and continued by Pietro Lombardo and Scarpagnino. The two cisterns of bronze are fine Renaissance work of 1556-57.

We ascend the stately Scala dei Giganti and pass Sansovino's statues of Mars and Neptune at the top. Here, between the two pagan deities, the later Doges were crowned. The Doge stood surrounded by the electors, and was acclaimed by the people below in the courtyard; a line of ducal guards kept the staircase.

We mount[94] the Scala d' Oro to the chambers where the rulers of the Republic held their meetings. Nearly the whole of the architectural decorations and paintings we shall see are later than 1577, when the disastrous fire occurred which destroyed the priceless works of Gentile da Fabriano, Vittore Pisano and the Bellini. With few exceptions they are all by the later Venetian masters, characterised by vigour and breadth of treatment rather than careful execution and reverent feeling. It was a time when the rulers of Venice, their initiative and courage gone, lived on the traditions of a great past, for Lepanto was but a magnificent episode. In few cases was the artist contemporary with the events he depicted. The paintings do, however, enable us to realise the costumes and architecture of the declining Venice of the sixteenth and seventeenth centuries. They have suffered much at the hands of the restorer. When Goethe was examining Titian's Death of Peter Martyr in S. Zanipolo in 1790, a Dominican friar addressed him and asked if he would like to see the artists at work above. There in the monastery he found an academy of picture restorers established by the Republic working under a director on the paintings of the Ducal Palace. In 1846 Ruskin saw a picture by Paul Veronese, lying on the floor of a room in the palace, in process of restoration. The restorer was working on the head of a white horse, using a brush fixed at the end of a five-foot stick which he dipped into a common house-painter's pot.

In the vestibule (Atrio Quadrato) is a fine ceiling-painting by Tintoretto, Doge Lorenzo Priuli receiving the Sword of State from the Hands of Justice, one of a series of allegorical and devotional pictures, the main feature being the portrait of the Doge, which we shall meet with again and again in the decoration of the palace. The walls are hung with portraits of Procurators of St Mark by the same master, who was their official portrait painter. To the R. is the Hall of the Four Doors (Sala delle Quattro Porte), designed by Palladio. On the R. wall is a late work by Titian, Doge Antonio Grimani kneeling before Faith, a beautiful creation: the figures on either side are by his nephew, Marco Vecelli. Historical and allegorical scenes cover the remaining walls.

DUCAL PALACE—THE MARRIAGE OF ST CATHERINE
By Tintoretto

The door opposite the entrance leads to a small ante-room (Anti-Collegio) containing some of the most charming pictures in the palace—Tintoretto's Ariadne and Bacchus, Minerva repelling Mars, and Mercury with the Graces, painted 1578. Sensuous beauty and poetry of line are their main qualities. A famous painting by Veronese, The Rape of Europa, and Jacopo Bassano's Return of Jacob are on the wall opposite the windows. A foreshadowing of modern naturalism in the treatment of the sheep and horse in the last picture is especially noteworthy. We now enter the room where the Signory received foreign ambassadors (Sala del Collegio). Over the entrance is a portrait of Doge Andrea Gritti kneeling before the Virgin; over the door of exit, the Marriage of St Catherine, with a ceremonial portrait of Doge Francesco Donà, elaborated with the usual accessories, the figure of the Doge's name saint, in this case St Francis, is common to all these compositions; to the L. is a portrait of Doge Nicolo da Ponte, with the Virgin in glory; farther on, Doge Alvise Mocenigo adoring the Saviour. All these are by Tintoretto; the figures of the Virgin and of St Catherine in the second and third of these pictures are from his favourite model and in his most gracious manner. Over the throne, Doge Sebastiano Venier returning Thanks for the Victory of Lepanto, is by Veronese. The ceiling, designed by Ant. da Ponte and painted by Veronese in his grandiose style, is considered by Ruskin to be the finest in the palace. Parallel to the last two rooms is the Senate hall (Sala del Senato). The paintings here are of but secondary interest: ceremonial portraits of Doges by Palma Giovane, Marco Vecelli and Tintoretto. The central panel of the gorgeous ceiling—Venice, Queen of the Sea—is by Domenico

Tintoretto, son of Jacopo. A door R. of the dais gives access to the vestibule of the Doge's private chapel (Anti-Chiesetta). Here are the two pictures painted by Tintoretto for the Camerlenghi in 1552; over the entrance door, SS. Jerome and Andrew; opposite, St Louis of Toulouse and St George. Two early Madonnas in the chapel are doubtfully attributed to the schools of Boccacino and Bellini. Christ in Limbo and the Israelites crossing the Red Sea are attributed by Mr Berenson to Previtali. These and other paintings in the chapel afford fruitful themes for critical ingenuity.

Returning through the Senate-hall we cross the Sala delle Quattro Porte, and traverse a small ante-room to the Hall of the Ten (Sala del Consiglio dei Dieci). The ceiling pictures are by Veronese and his pupils. An oval panel, The Elder and the Fair Lady, is a famous painting by the master. We enter next the ante-room of the three Inquisitors of State (Sala della Bussola), formerly a guardroom occupied by the captain of the police and by the guards of the Ten. An opening in the wall was formerly decorated with a lion's head in marble (*bocca del leone*). Here secret denunciations were placed from the outside. The delators would ascend the Scala dei Censori and cast their accusations in the opening on the L. at the top of the staircase. The custom of receiving secret information was common in the Republic. To this day similar *bocche di leoni* remain in various parts of Venice—on the Zattere for denunciations of breaches of sanitary regulations with the inscription: D□ÑCIE CONTRA LA SANITA PER IL SESTIERE DE OSSODVRO; another in front of St Martin's Church near the arsenal invites secret denunciations against blasphemers and brawlers in churches.

DOGE'S PALACE—THE CORTILE

To the R. of the Sala della Bussola is a small chamber (Stanza dei tre Capi del Consiglio) where sat the three chiefs of the Ten. The room contains a simple, refreshing picture by Catena, Doge Leonardo Loredano kneeling and presented by St Mark to the Virgin, a St Christopher by Bonifazio, a Pietà by Giovanni Bellini, hard and realistic in treatment, and portraits of three Senators, by Tintoretto. Returning to the Sala della Bussola (the Sala dei Inquisitori di Stato is not shown), we descend the Scala dei Censori to the lower floor. Here we enter the huge Hall of the Great Council (Sala del Maggior Consiglio), on which the later artists of the Republic lavished all their powers of sumptuous decoration. The entrance wall over the throne is covered by Tintoretto's famous Paradiso—a tremendous conception which at first almost dazes the spectator by its daring, then leaves a profound impression of the master's gigantic but unchastened power. After patient contemplation, groups and individuals stand out from the bewildering crowd of figures—Christ and the Virgin in glory; the Archangels; the Intelligences that preside over the heavenly spheres; the Evangelists with their symbols;

prophets, saints and martyrs, an exultant host, treated with originality and force, sometimes even with tender grace. But the composition is too vast; it lacks symmetry, and Domenico's feebler hand is all too evident in parts. The eye wearies of seeing, and none but admirers of the *piu terribile cervello che abbia mai avuto la pittura*[95] will care to read the canvas in all its details. Tintoretto was seventy-five years of age when commissioned to execute the work. Ruskin estimated the number of figures to be not less than 500. To L. and R. the walls are filled with scenes from the heroic times of Venetian history. Here again the crowded canvases, the conscious straining after effect weary the spectator, and few are they who do not soon turn from detailed examination of the pictures, to rest eye and brain on the beautiful scene that opens out from the loggia on the side of the hall—the island of S. Giorgio; the Giudecca; the waters laughing in the sun; the peaceful lagoon; the Lido far away with its line of trees. The series of paintings on the N. wall represent scenes, mainly legendary, in the story of Pope Alexander III. and the Emperor Barbarossa, mostly by inferior artists. The S. wall is decorated with scenes in the epic story of the conquest of Constantinople under Enrico Dandolo; a single canvas, at the end of the hall opposite the Paradiso, by Veronese, has for its subject the return of Doge Contarini after the defeat of the Genoese at Chioggia. The panels of the magnificent ceiling were painted by Veronese, Tintoretto, Palma Giovane and F. Bassano. Veronese's Apotheosis of Venice and Tintoretto's Doge Nic. da Ponte with the Senate and envoys from conquered cities paying homage to Venice are stupendous works of their kind. On the frieze are portraits, mostly imaginary, of seventy-six Doges, by Tintoretto and his assistants, the place of Marino Falier being filled by a black tablet with the inscription: *Hic est locus Marini Faletri decapitati pro criminibus.* A door to the R. leads to the Hall of the Scrutineers (Sala dello Scrutinio). This, which almost rivals the Hall of the Great Council for magnificence, was the chamber where the Doges and other officers of State were elected. The S. end is filled with an ambitious Last Judgment by Palma Giovane in which that very second-rate artist tried to emulate Tintoretto's Paradise. The E. and W. walls are decorated with scenes in the history of Venice of small artistic merit. When Garibaldi was at the Ducal Palace his attention was arrested by the resemblance to himself of the figure of Admiral Sebastiano Venier in Vicentino's Battle of Lepanto. Thirty-nine portraits of Doges complete the line from the Hall of the Great Council ending on the W. wall with Ludovico Manin. At the N. end is the monument to Doge Francesco Morosini.

We retrace our steps to the Scala dei Censori, beyond which is a suite of rooms, once the private apartments of the Doges, now used as an archæological museum. In the corridor are two fine allegorical pictures of St Mark's Lion by Jacobello del Fiore and Carpaccio; and Bart. Buoni's remarkable head of Francesco Foscari. The beautiful rooms with their gilded ceilings and fine chimney-pieces by the Lombardi, contain Greek, Roman and Venetian sculpture, Renaissance bronzes, coins, old maps and other objects, many of them of high merit but only of interest to the more leisured student. In the Stanza degli Stucchi are a voting urn from the Scuola della Carità, and another from the Great Council. Before he leaves this room the visitor should ask to be shown one of the most interesting paintings in the palace—an unrestored fresco by Titian of St Christopher, with a view of Venice in the bottom background, at the foot of the staircase leading up to the Doge's chapel. The Piombi have long since disappeared owing to structural alterations; such of the Pozzi and other cells that are shown may well be left unvisited.

Before descending the Giant's Staircase permission may be had, on application to the "Ufficio Regionale per la Conservazione dei Monumenti del Veneto," to inspect the "Cobden Madonna" at the E. end of the S. gallery overlooking the Grand Canal. It is a fine marble relief of the Virgin and Child with attendant angels, wrought probably by Pietro Lombardo to commemorate the reduction of the duties on corn during a severe famine in the reign of one of the Mocenighi towards the end of the fifteenth century. When Richard Cobden was in Venice in 1847, during the course of his triumphant journey through Europe, he wrote his name, which is still visible, over one of the ears of corn beneath the Latin inscription.

SECTION IV

The Accademia

AFTER the fall of the Venetian Republic the French government expropriated a group of buildings belonging to the church, monastery and guild of S. Maria della Carità, and there housed the collection of paintings selected from the public offices, the suppressed religious orders, guilds and churches of Venice, by their commissioner, Peter Edwards, who had formerly been chief picture restorer to the Republic. Some conception may be formed, after visiting the Ducal Palace and the magnificent collection treasured in these rooms, of the enormous wealth of paintings existing in the city in the latter half of the eighteenth century; for the commission then appointed to overhaul the artistic possessions of the government decided to restore only the best and allowed the remainder to rot. The Guild of Our Lady of Charity, the earliest of the six greater *Scuole*[96] of Venice, was founded in 1260 to ransom Christian captives from the Moors and other pirates. Over the portal of the outer cloister are three early reliefs in stone, St Leonard, patron of captives and slaves; the Virgin and Child with kneeling guildsmen; and St Christopher. In the inner court, entered from the corridor of the Istituto delle Belle Arti, may be seen Palladio's unfinished cloisters, one of the most beautiful examples of the use of brick in N. Italy. Of the old rooms of the guild two only remain, Room XX., the former Guest Chamber, and Room I. Both have magnificent fifteenth-century ceilings; that of the latter is by Giampietro of Vicenza, a famous wood-carver whose figures of eight-winged cherubs have been ingeniously but erroneously interpreted as a rebus on the name of a supposed brother, Cherubino Aliotto (eight-winged), who was believed to have paid for the decoration of the ceiling.

We enter Room I., which is filled with admirable examples of the work of the earliest Venetian masters, Jacobello del Fiore, Giambono, Lorenzo Veneziano, Simone da Cusighe, Andrea and Quirizio da Murano, all dominated by Byzantine models, and giving small promise of the future glories of the Vivarini and Bellini schools.

Before entering Room II. the eye will be arrested by Titian's famous Assumption, No. 40. A nearer view of this grandiose painting will serve to impress the beholder with the animation and force of the master's new style and the subtle artifice by which he attracts the eye of the spectator to the ascending Virgin, to whom the whole composition yearns. This great altar-piece created a vast sensation when exposed at the Frari, pregnant as it was with the future development of the grand school of Venetian painting:—its masterly group of a large and complicated subject, its breadth of treatment and habit of massing the warmer and mellower colours of the palette on the canvas. It must be remembered, however, that the features of the Virgin and the picture generally have been coarsened by restoration, for, unhappily, most of the old paintings which have come down to us have been restored more than once, more than twice, more than thrice, and the traveller will need to make allowances for the consequent debasement of the original creation in this and many other works by the old masters. In this room of masterpieces we are enabled, by the juxtaposition of three altar-pieces (38, by Giov. Bellini; 36, by Cima; 37, by Veronese) to compare the treatment of the same subject, the Virgin and Child and Saints, by three great masters. 41, The Death of Abel, by Tintoretto, is an admired work, powerful but sombre. It is considered by Ruskin to be one of the most wonderful works in the gallery and superior in many respects to 42, The Miracle of St Mark, the most popular of the master's paintings (p. 209). A Christian slave is tortured and ordered to be executed for his devotion to St Mark, who descends from heaven like lightning to rescue him. The executioner exhibits the broken hammer. A work of amazing science and originality which so perplexed the members of the guild[97] for whom it was executed and gave rise to so many discussions, that the impatient artist fetched it away and kept it in his atelier until it was better appreciated. 43, Adam and Eve, is an early work by the master. 44, Carpaccio, Presentation in the Temple, is, in Ruskin's estimation, the best picture in the Accademia. The painter wrought the work in emulation of his master's altar-piece (No. 38). All the Bellini features are here—the mosaic half dome, the Renaissance decoration, the sweet boy musicians with instruments almost too big for them to handle. The two paintings adorned the same church.

We pass Room III., which contains a miscellaneous collection of paintings of various Italian schools, and Room IV. (drawings by Italian masters), and reach Room V., where the dominant genius of the Bellini is manifested in the works of their contemporaries with which the room is hung. It contains, 69, The Agony in the Garden, the finest of Basaiti's paintings in Venice, and some excellent examples of Bissolo's warm colour and dignified figures. 76, The Supper at Emmaus, is a remarkable and unique work by Marco Marziale. Two powerfully wrought figures seated at the table betray the alien influence of Dürer over this painter. 82, The Virgin and Child enthroned between SS. Jerome, Benedict, Mary Magdalene and Giustina, is Benedetto Diana's last work. We pass to one of Bissolo's best productions, 79, Christ presenting the Crown of Thorns to St Catherine of Siena, and showing the crown of gold, her portion in heaven. Near 97, a typical plague picture by Mansueti, are two fine paintings by Lazzaro Sebastiani. 104, St Anthony of Padua enshrined in a tree, beneath which are St Bonaventura and another Franciscan saint, has much puzzled the critics. According to tradition St Anthony composed his last sermons while sitting on the branches of a tree. It is, moreover, an old custom to place shrines, with figures of saints, in the trees by the wayside in Italy. We have seen many such in the hill country of Venetia.

We enter Room VI., which contains a collection of Dutch pictures of no great merit, and cross to Room VII., devoted mainly to the Friulian painters. The chief attraction of this room is, however, 147, a magnificent Sacra Conversazione by Palma Vecchio. It is a late work by the master, and was probably left unfinished at his death.

At the farther end is the entrance to Room VIII., hung with Flemish paintings. Turning L. we ascend the steps which lead from Room V. to Room IX., which glows with the compositions of the sixteenth-century masters Veronese and Tintoretto. 203 is The Supper in the House of Levi (p. 211). Under a spacious Corinthian portico Christ is seated between St John and St Peter. The whole scene is dominated by the princely magnificence of the repast. The details objected to by the Inquisitor are untouched; Peter is still carving the lamb, and between two columns on the L. is the fellow picking his teeth with a fork. Four scenes from the story of S. Cristina, and the Virgin of the Rosary are characteristic paintings by the same master. 210, The Virgin and Child with SS. Mark, Sebastian and Theodore, and three officers of the Treasury, followed by their servants, was one of Ruskin's favourite Tintorettos. 213, The Crucifixion, by Tintoretto, is a sombre dramatic representation of the scene envisaged in his most naturalistic manner, another of Ruskin's favourites; he believed that neither the Miracle of St Mark nor the great Crucifixion in S. Rocco cost the artist more pains than this comparatively small work. 214, by Il Moro, is an interesting picture from the Admiralty; it is divided into two parts, (1) St Mark and three functionaries who are recruiting for the navy; (2) view of the Molo or chief quay of Venice, the Piazzetta and the Ducal Palace; gondolas and galleys are seen on the canal. 217, Tintoretto's Descent from the Cross, is another fine composition, almost Spanish in its gloom. Numerous portraits on the end walls are by the same master. R. of the door is an interesting picture, 243, Virgin and Child and four magistrates of the Salt Office in adoration. It was the custom of the chief civil servants of the Republic to leave as a souvenir of their term of office a picture of their patron saint with their escutcheon and initials painted on it. Most of the Bonifazios in Room X. are such, and came from various public offices; Tintoretto, in this picture, was the first to represent actual portraits. 255, a Crucifixion by Veronese, is painted in the frankly naturalistic style of the later school of Venice. 260, an Annunciation, is in the master's most spacious and stately manner.

ACCADEMIA—THE RICH MAN'S FEAST
By Bonifazio

Room X. is largely held by the creations of Bonifazio and his pupils. 281, The Adoration of the Magi, is a beautiful work, painted with great care, by the master, for the Ten. On the opposite wall, 319, The Slaughter of the Innocents is the companion picture. Bonifazio's receipt, dated 1545, for ten ducats on account of these two pictures still exists among the archives of the Ten. They were hung in their Financial Secretary's office in the Palazzo dei Camerlenghi. 291, The Rich Man's Feast (p. 207). For depth of feeling, sumptuous colour, variety and strength of characterisation, one of the most noteworthy creations of Venetian art. Dives[98] is seated in a Venetian country-house at table between two courtesans, one of whom he clasps by the hand. She, with a far-away look, turns aside listening to a woman playing on the lute, accompanied by a man with the bass viol. All the accessories of a rich man's establishment are present. Hawks are being trained, horses exercised. To the R., Lazarus is seen, a dog licking his sores, and in the background lurid flames forbode impending doom. 284, Christ Enthroned, is a richly coloured picture formerly placed in the chief office of the Customs. On the top line are twelve groups of saints,[99] painted in the Bonifazio atelier, and formerly assigned to Bonifazio III. 318, St Mark, skied among them, is however a finer work, probably by the master's hand. On the screen are The Judgment of Solomon, another masterly composition, painted in 1533 for the Salt Office, in the Palazzo dei Camerlenghi, and some portraits by Pordenone. 400, a Deposition, is Titian's last work, a pathetic canvas. An inscription tells that what Titian left unfinished, Palma Giovane completed, and dedicated to God. The Virgin bears the dead Saviour on her knees. To the R. kneels St Joseph of Arimathea; to the L., in an attitude of poignant grief, is St Mary Magdalen. 320, Paris Bordone: scene from the legend of St

Mark and the Fisherman (p. 121). The Doge, Bartolomeo Gradenigo, is represented enthroned in the midst of the Council, bending forward to receive the ring. 316 is Pordenone's masterpiece. The patriarch, S. Lorenzo Giustiniani, with Dantesque features, stands under a Renaissance chapel. Before him kneels S. Francis, behind whom is St Augustine and an acolyte. R., S. John the Baptist, with the muscular development of an athlete, behind whom is St Bernardine of Siena and a kneeling monk.

We turn by the Loggia Palladiana, hung with late Dutch and Flemish paintings, copies and school pictures of minor interest, and enter Room XI. on the R., which is given to some characteristic landscapes, scenes of peasant life and portraits by the Bassani. Rooms XII. and XIII. display work by artists of the seventeenth and eighteenth centuries, including some interesting genre pictures by Pietro Longhi. Room XIV. contains some Tiepolos, among them a fine ceiling painting, No. 462, the Invention of the Cross, three small Guardis, 704, 705, 706, two Canalettos, 463 and 494, and other works of minor interest. In Corridor I.[100] is the much debated, No. 516, The Tempest calmed by SS. Mark, George and Nicholas, illustrating the story of the Fisherman and St Mark.

We now turn to Room XV., where are exhibited the paintings illustrating the miracles of the Holy Cross which Gentile Bellini and his pupils were commissioned to execute for the decoration of the Hall of the Guild of S. Giovanni Evangelista about 1490. The room is specially constructed to display these important pictures to the best advantage. 561 by Lazzaro Sebastiani. A crusader, Filippo de' Massari, on his return from Jerusalem offers a fragment of the Holy Cross to the brethren of the Guild. 562 by Mansueti. The daughter of one Benvenuto da S. Polo is healed on touching three candles sanctified by contact with the relic. The scene is the interior of an old Venetian palace with costumes of the period. 563 by Gentile Bellini. Pietro de' Ludovici, sick of a fever, is healed by means of a candle as in the former miracle. We are here in the chapel of the guild with the brethren in their black and crimson robes in the foreground. 564 by Mansueti. The relic is brought over the wooden bridge opposite St Lio to accompany the remains of a brother who during his life had scoffed at its power. The procession which is to accompany the body to its last resting-place is thrown into confusion by the Cross containing the relic refusing to advance into the church where the body lies. The scene is most animated. Spectators look from the windows, from the housetops and from the streets. The gondola of the period is represented. The artist himself stands at the foot of the bridge to the left, holding a paper inscribed with his name, Giovanni Mansueti the Venetian, disciple of Bellini. 565, attributed to Benedetto Diana, is said to portray the healing by the relic of a child fallen from the top of the stairs. Neither the quality of the work nor the subject seems convincing. The woman seems to have slipped on the pavement with her child. If genuine it can be no more than a fragment of a larger composition referred to by the older writers as containing elaborate architectural details and groups of people similar to the other paintings of this series. 566 by Carpaccio. Casting out of a devil by the Patriarch Francesco Querini. The Grand Canal is crowded with gondolas. The old wooden Rialto drawbridge with its bascules and levers spans the canal. Above, L., the patriarch is seen in a loggia of his palace at S. Silvestre casting forth the evil spirit by holding out the relic. A most interesting presentation of old Venetian architecture. Two youths in the foreground, with their backs to the spectator, one of whom has a mermaid embroidered on his hood, are in Calza costume. 567 by Gentile Bellini, Procession in the Piazza. A merchant of Brescia whose son lay dying made a vow to the relic as the procession passed and his son was saved. In the ducal procession to the R. the Doge is seen under the State umbrella with the Procurators of St Mark, chamberlains and senators and trumpeters. This is one of the most precious pictorial documents for the aspect of the Piazza in 1496. The thirteenth-century mosaics of St Mark's are in their place; the Procuratie Vecchie are there but no Clock Tower; houses abut on the Campanile. The Porta della Carta and the façade of St Mark's are richly gilded. According to Vasari, Gentile surpassed himself in the next painting (568), which firmly established his reputation. During a procession to the church of St Lorenzo the reliquary falls from a bridge into the canal. Several persons plunge in to save it. To none but the warden of the guild, Andrea Vendramin, was it vouchsafed to recover the shrine. A vivid representation of a piece of old Venice. At the head of the Venetian ladies, kneeling to the L., is Catherine Cornaro, Queen of Cyprus, wearing her crown. This picture, and No. 567, the artist tells us, were painted in pious affection for the Holy Cross. 570, a faded work by the same artist, S. Lorenzo Giustiniani, with two kneeling canons and angels bearing his crook and mitre. In the apse are two important works painted by Mansueti for the Guild of St Mark. 569, St Mark heals the cobbler Anianus, wounded by his awl, a favourite legend; and 571, St Mark preaching at Alexandria.

Room XVI. contains Carpaccio's St Ursula series, painted 1490-95, for the Guild of St Ursula. The legend, familiar to those who have studied the paintings of Carpaccio's contemporary, Memling, on the shrine of St Ursula at Bruges, may be briefly summarised. Maurus, the Christian king of Brittany, had a daughter named Ursula (Little Bear), because she came into the world wrapt in a hairy mantle. The pagan king of England, Agrippinus, hearing of her wisdom, virtue and beauty, sent ambassadors to ask the maiden's hand for his son Conon. King Maurus, knowing his daughter's vow of perpetual chastity and yet fearing to anger a powerful neighbour by refusal, was in great distress. Just before dawn[101] of the next day, while Ursula lay in her chamber, the angel of the Lord appeared to her in a dream and bade her go to her father, and wisdom would be given her to counsel him aright. When day was fully come she went to his chamber and enumerated to the anxious king the conditions on which the suit would be accepted: For companions she required ten virgins of noblest blood, each with one thousand virgin attendants, herself another thousand virgins; they must be allowed to make a pilgrimage to Rome; the prince and his court to be baptised.

The envoys returned to England bearing such reports of the princess's beauty that Conon was fired with a desire to marry her, and the conditions were granted. Ursula and her maidens, Conon and his suite, set sail in eleven ships for Rome. Being arrived, the Pope and his clergy came forth to bless them. When they had performed their vows the pilgrims returned accompanied by the Pope and reach Cologne, then besieged by the Huns, who straightway massacred the pilgrims, the Pope and his clergy—all except Ursula, whose beauty destined her to be the bride of the king of the Huns. But she, defying his power, aroused his fury; he ordered her to be put to death.

The artist has illustrated this story in his most charming and dramatic manner, though, as the dates prove, no consistent plan of the series was drawn up. The most popular of the paintings is No. 578. Ursula is sleeping in her chamber and an angel, bearing in his right hand a palm-branch, the sign of martyrdom, appears to her in a vision. The early light of dawn streams through the open door. On the tassel of her pillow is inscribed, *Infantia*. Every detail in this virgin sanctuary, the little crown at the foot of the bed, the clogs placed side by side, the tidy over her head, the shrine and receptacle for holy water against the wall, betokens maidenly care and piety. The charm of these pictures is perennial. Zanetti[102] used to conceal himself in the hall where they were placed to watch the effect they produced on the ordinary spectator.

Room XVII. is chiefly taken up with pictures by the Vivarini and by Cima. 618 and 619, The Baptist and St Matthew, and 593, St Clare, are all fine examples of Alvise Vivarini's work; the last is one of his greatest achievements, a living portrait, full of character. 588, Mantegna's St George and the Dragon, is a precious possession, one of the great Paduan master's most careful works, painted about 1460. 584 and 585, SS. Mary Magdalen and Barbara, are late works (1490) by Bartolomeo Vivarini. 589, Christ bound to the Column, and 590, The Virgin in Meditation, have been ascribed to Antonello da Messina, but their genuineness is doubtful. Mr Berenson admits the former in his index to the works of the Venetian painters; the official catalogue attributes it to Pietro da Messina, and 590 to an unknown copyist working from an original at Munich. We now come to one of the most delightful and graceful compositions in this room, 600, a Marriage of St Catherine, by the Lombard master Boccaccino: before the Virgin and Child kneel St Peter and the Baptist; to the L. St Catherine holds forth her hand to receive the ring; to the R. stands the beautiful figure of St Rose; to the R. of the charming landscape background are portrayed the Wise Men and the Flight into Egypt. Then follow some guild pictures by Cima. 604, the last of the master's work in this room, is an early painting of much beauty, The Deposition with the Marys and Nicodemus.

Room XVIII., at the farther end, is the new Bellini room in which are collected the Bellinis formerly hung in XVII. This little treasury includes, 582, a unique example of Jacopo's work, The Virgin and Child. 596, Giovanni's famous Virgin of the Trees, has recently been peeled and some strata of repainting removed; it is dated 1487, but this date has been questioned by Morelli and other critics who believe it to be a maturer work painted about 1504. 610, The Virgin and Child between SS. George and Paul, is another popular work by the master; both are admirable for warmth of colour, and dignity and beauty of form. 613, The Virgin and Child between SS. Catherine and Mary Magdalen, is one of the most characteristic of Giovanni's productions; less virile perhaps than 610, but rich and warm in colour and gentle in feeling. We now turn to 595, a remarkable series of panels painted for a *cassone* or wedding chest; charming allegories on which the painter has lavished all his skill. Their interpretation still awaits an Œdipus, but the following suggestions by Ruskin will help the visitor: 1, Fortitude quitting the effeminate Bacchus; 2, Domestic Love,—the world in Venus' hand becoming the colour of heaven; 3, Fortune as Opportunity distinguished from the greater and sacred Fortune appointed by Heaven; 4, Truth; 5, Lust.[103]

Room XIX. contains a small collection of Muranese and Paduan school paintings, and others of no great importance. We descend to Room XX., originally the guest-chamber of the brotherhood. The carved and gilded ceiling, representing Christ in the act of blessing, and the four Evangelists, each in his study, is one of the most beautiful schemes of decoration in Venice. It was here that Titian, between 1534 and 1538, painted the Presentation, now restored to its original place. The high-priest stands before the temple at the top of a grand staircase to receive the little maid who seems somewhat too conscious of her pretty blue frock. A group of richly attired Venetian ladies and gentlemen look on. At the foot of the stairway sits an old, coarse-featured peasant woman with a basket of eggs; the mountains of Cadore are in the background. According to Ruskin, the most stupid and uninteresting work ever painted by the artist. 625, Giov. d'Alemano and Ant. da Murano, Virgin and Child enthroned, and four Latin fathers of the Church, was also executed for the very wall space it now covers. It is obviously much repainted. On a screen is 245, a portrait of Jacopo Soranzo by Titian. Above, on a swing panel, is 316, St John the Baptist, painted when the master had passed his eightieth year.

SECTION V

The Grand Canal and S. Georgio Maggiore

SECOND only in architectural interest to St Mark's and the Ducal Palace are the patrician mansions that line the chief artery of Venice, known to Venetians as the Canalazzo. No more luxurious artistic feast can be enjoyed in Europe than to leisurely examine from a gondola the architectural details of the Grande Rue that so excited the admiration of Philippe de Comines. We begin on the L. side opposite the Piazzetta. The DOGANA (Custom House) is a late seventeenth-century structure, low in elevation, in order not to obstruct the view of Longhena's SALUTE. This church stands on the most magnificent site in Venice, and despite the baseness of many of its details is, when regarded in the mass, an impressive edifice and one of the architectural features of the city. The noble flight of steps and the symmetry of the domes are most effective and pleasing. The anniversary of its consecration in 1687 is still a great popular festival, and yearly on November 21st a bridge of boats is thrown across the canal to facilitate the foot traffic. On the further side of the rio della Salute is seen the apse of the fine Gothic abbey church of S. GREGORIO. We may disembark at the square portal, with a relief of St Gregory over the lintel, which opens on the Grand Canal just beyond the rio. It gives access to one of the most picturesque spots in Venice—the fourteenth-century cloister of the monastery. We continue our voyage, and, passing the rio S. Gregorio, note the PALAZZO[104] DARIO (fifteenth century), beautifully decorated with discs of porphyry and serpentine in the style of the Lombardi. This fine mansion has altered little since the time of De Comines. The huge ground-floor beyond is the unfinished PAL. VENIER, begun in the eighteenth century. Farther on is the PALAZZO DA MULA, a fine Gothic building of the early fifteenth century, adjacent to which is the PAL. BARBARIGO, with its brazen mosaics, now the property of the Venezia-Murano Glass Co. We pass on, and next to a garden note the PAL. MANZONI (1465) by Tullio Lombardi, somewhat later in style than the Pal. Dario. Passing the Accademia and a few houses, we reach the two PALAZZI CONTARINI DEGLI SCRIGNI (Contarini of the Coffers), the first by Scamozzi (1609), the second fifteenth-century Gothic. The Contarini were a wealthy family pre-eminent in the nobility of their ancestry, and owned many palaces in Venice. The last of the race died in 1902 in lodgings. They had given eight Doges and forty-four Procurators to the Republic. Beyond the rio S. Tomaso is the fifteenth-century Gothic PAL. DURAZZO or dell' Ambasciatore, once the German Embassy. The two statues on the façade are probably by one of the Lombardi. We pass two rii and reach the imposing PALAZZO REZZONICO, where Robert Browning died. It was built about 1680 by

Longhena; the upper storey is, however, a later addition by Massari (1740). We soon come to a magnificent group of three Gothic palaces in the style of the Ducal Palace and attributed to the Buoni. They once belonged to the powerful Giustiniani family, but the last (now the School of Commerce) was bought and enlarged by Francesco Foscari in 1437 and still bears his name. The iron lamp at the corner is modern. Facing us at the farthest corner of the rio Foscari is the PAL. BALBI by Aless. Vittoria (1582). It is now Guggenheim's shop. We pass on to the rio S. Tomà, at whose farther corner is the PAL. PERSICO (formerly a Giustiniani) in the style of the Lombardi. A few houses beyond is the Gothic PAL. TIEPOLO. Next but one stands the PAL. PISANI, fifteenth-century Gothic. At the farther corner of the rio S. Polo is the PAL. CAPPELLO-LAYARD with a most valuable collection of paintings (admission by personal introduction only). Adjacent is the PAL. GRIMANI of the Lombardi period. Two houses farther on stands the Gothic PAL. BERNARDO, now belonging to Salviati. On either side of the next traghetto (della Madonetta) are two smaller twelfth-century palazzi, with beautiful Byzantine details, the PAL. DONÀ and the PAL. SAIBANTE. Next to a garden is the sixteenth-century Renaissance PAL. PAPADOPOLI (formerly Tiepolo), surmounted by two obelisks. At the farther corner of the rio stands the PAL. BUSINELLI with some interesting Byzantine windows. Next but one is the PAL. MENGALDO, referred to in the "Stones of Venice" as the "terraced house." It has a beautiful Byzantine portal, and arches of the same style are visible in the older part of the building. Just beyond the S. Silvestre Pier is the site of the old palace of the Patriarchs of Grado and Venice. Little of interest meets us until we reach the PONTE DI RIALTO, which replaced a wooden drawbridge similar to that represented in Carpaccio's picture. It was built (1588-92) by Antonio da Ponte from a design by Boldù. Many famous Renaissance architects had at various periods offered designs, among others Michael Angelo, who, when living on the Giudecca, was invited by Doge Gritti to submit a drawing, but this "most rich and rare invention" met the fate of the rest—it was set aside as too costly. An Annunciation is sculptured on the hither side of the bridge: Gabriel and the Virgin on the spandrils; the dove on the keystone.

By the farther side stands the PAL. DEI CAMERLENGHI (1525-28) by Guglielmo Bergamasco, once adorned with pictures by Bonifazio, for the offices of the three Lords of the Treasury. We pass the vegetable and fish-markets. Behind the latter, the last house before reaching the Ponte Pescaria was the old PAL. QUERINI, known as the Stallone, with the two large Gothic portals of the old shambles (p. 109). It became the poultry-market after the fall of the Republic. A new fish-market is, however, projected, and the old palace will probably be incorporated in the new building. A few houses farther on is the Gothic PAL. MOROSINI; yet farther the lofty PAL. CORNER DELLA REGINA (now the municipal pawn-office). It was erected in 1724 by

Rossi, the architect of S. Eustacchio, on the site of a palace occupied by the Queen of Cyprus. The huge assertive PAL. PESARO by Longhena, 1679, now comes into view. It is highly praised by Fergusson.

GRAND CANAL—PALAZZI REZZONICO AND FOSCARI.

GRAND CANAL, WITH THE RIVA DEL CARBON AND RIALTO BRIDGE

CA' D'ORO

The church of S. EUSTACCHIO (S. Stae), 1709, with its *baroque* façade will be easily recognised. The bust of the ill-fated Ant. Foscarini will be found in the third chapel L. of entrance, the higher of the two busts to the R. of the chapel. (The church is rarely open and will be more conveniently visited in connection with S. M., Mater Domini, whose sacristan has the key.) At the farther corner of the campo is the PAL. PRIULI, with an early transitional Gothic arcade. At the near corner of the rio Tron is the PAL. TRON, sixteenth-century Renaissance; at the farther corner, the PAL. BATTAGGIA by Longhena. The building adjacent is one of the old granaries of the Republic, with the outline of the Lion of St Mark still visible on the façade. Interest ends at the restored FONDACO DE' TURCHI (Mart of the Turks) (p. 302).

We cross to the church of S. MARCUOLA (SS. Ermagora and Fortunato), which contains a doubtful Titian (the infant Christ on a pedestal between SS. Catherine and Andrew), thought, however, by Morelli to be a genuine youthful work of the master. Some distance farther on is the PAL. VENDRAMIN by Pietro Lombardi (1481), one of the finest palaces on the canal. The garden wing is by Scamozzi. Next but one is the PAL. ERIZZO, fifteenth-century Gothic. We pass on to the CA' D'ORO, the most exquisite little mansion in Venice. It was built (1424-30) for the Contarini, and being richly gilded, was known as the Ca' d'Oro (the Golden House). The derivation from a supposed Doro family is untenable. The contracts with the Buoni and many another famous *tajapiera* (stone-cutter), and a contract with Mastro Zuan di Franza, Pintor, for the gilding and the painting of the façade with vermilion and ultramarine still exist. The building was profaned by some ill-designed structural alterations and the beautiful wellhead, by Bart. Buono, was sold to a dealer, when the fabric fell into the hands of the ballet-dancer, Taglioni, in 1847. Recently Baron Franchetti has restored it to somewhat of its original form, and the well-head has been recovered.[105] Beyond the Ca' d'Oro Pier is the earlier and simpler Gothic PAL. SAGREDO, now the Ravà College. The small PAL. FOSCARI beyond the Campo S. Sofia has interesting Gothic details. The larger, PAL. MICHIELI DELLE COLONNE, was rebuilt in the seventeenth century. Passing the rio SS. Apostoli we reach the interesting CA' DA MOSTO, twelfth-century Byzantine, but hinting at the coming Gothic. An inscription tells that here was born Alvise da Ca' Mosto, discoverer of the Cape Verde Islands. Set back in a small court (Corte Remera) is a thirteenth-century house with an external stairway and a fine Byzantine portal. It shows admirably the pointed arch asserting itself in a Byzantine building. Hard by the Rialto bridge is the Fondaco dei Tedeschi (Mart of the Germans), designed in 1505 by Girolamo Tedesco and completed by Scarpagnino. It is now the Central Post Office. The solitary figure that remains of Giorgione's frescoes will be seen high up between two of the top-floor windows. The sculptures on this side the Rialto bridge represent SS. Theodore and Mark.

PALAZZO VENDRAMIN

Beyond the bridge the PAL. MANIN by Sansovino, now Banca d' Italia, was the dwelling-place of the last of the Doges. The PAL. BEMBO at the farther corner of the rio is early fifteenth-century Gothic. A small palace farther on, the ground floor of which is used as a café, is usually pointed out as the house of Doge Enrico Dandolo. The present Gothic building, however, with its cusped arches is obviously two centuries later in style, though the Byzantine medallions incorporated in the façade may have belonged to the original structure. A Latin inscription on the adjacent house prays the wayfarer to bestow a thought on the great Doge Dandolo, and another inscription in the Pal. Farsetti (see below) states that that palace was built for Enrico Dandolo (*volle eretto Enrico Dandolo*) in 1203. All that may be said with certainty is that somewhere on the Riva del Carbon stood the Ca' Dandolo. A few houses farther on is the PAL. LOREDAN with its deep stilted arches, esteemed by Ruskin the most beautiful palace on the Grand Canal. It is twelfth-century Byzantine, restored once in Gothic, again in Renaissance times. It bears on the façade the scutcheon of Peter Lusignan, King of Cyprus, who lodged there in 1363-66. The next edifice is the PAL. FARSETTI, in the same style but simpler. It has a fine staircase with carvings by Canova.

TRAGHETTO AND CAMPO S. SAMUELE

These two buildings are used as the Municipal Offices. At the near corner of the rio S. Luca is Sanmichele's stately Renaissance PAL. GRIMANI, rescued by the Austrian Government from the house-breaker's hands, and used as the Post Office. It is now the Court of Appeal. Ruskin considered this to be the principal type at Venice and the best in Europe of the central style of the Renaissance schools. We may disembark and ascend the noble staircase (the Renaissance masters excelled in the construction of stairways) to the spacious landing and halls on the first floor. At the farther corner of the rio is the PAL. CAVALLINI, so named from the horses' heads on the scutcheons. We pass on to the PAL. CORNER SPINELLI at the farther corner of the rio dell'Albero, another of the works of the Lombardi. Beyond the traghetto S. Angelo we reach the three PALAZZI MOCENIGO, sixteenth-century architecture. The ducal cap and shield still figure on the posts, for the Mocenighi gave seven

Doges to the Republic. Byron lodged in the middle of the three palaces. Another famous heretic, Giordano Bruno, that Ishmaelite of philosophy, was run to earth by the Inquisition in the farther one and taken to Rome to perish at the stake in 1600.[106] The early Renaissance palazzo farther on with shields and torches carved on the façade was another of the CONTARINI mansions subsequently inhabited by the Countess Guiccioli. We pass two small Gothic palaces and the wide PAL. MORO-LIN, sixteenth-century, by Seb. Mazzoni, a Florentine painter and architect, and reach round the bend the PAL. GRASSI (1785), by Massari. At the farther corner of the Campo S. Samuele is the PAL. MALIPIERO, seventeenth-century. At the near corner of the next rio is the CA' DEL DUCA (di Milano), begun for Francesco Sforza when he was the Venetian Captain-General. The construction was vetoed by the Signory at a point easily discernible, when Sforza began to play Carmagnola's game and was outlawed. The late Gothic PAL. CAVALLI beyond the iron bridge has been wholly restored by Baron Franchetti. At the farther corner of the rio dell' Orso is the fourteenth-century Gothic PAL. BARBARO debased by additions. Beyond the traghetto S. Stefano and a garden is the PAL. CORNER DELLA CA' GRANDE now the Prefecture, a stately Renaissance edifice by Sansovino (1532). Past the traghetto S. M. del Giglio are three palaces all more or less restored which form the Grand Hotel. The first, PAL. GRITTI, is fourteenth-century Gothic; the second, PAL. FINI, is by Tremignano (1688); the third, PAL. FERRO, fifteenth-century Gothic. The small PAL. CONTARINI-FASAN is the so-called Desdemona House. The balcony with its rich tracery is unique in Venice. Some distance farther on is the PAL. TIEPOLO, now the Hotel Britannia. The Hotel d' Italia is a new building. The fifteenth-century PAL. GIUSTINIANI is now the Hotel de l' Europe. The next house but one is the old RIDOTTO, the famous Assembly Rooms and Gambling Saloon of the later Republic, in its day the Monte Carlo of Europe. It is still used for bals-masqués at Carnival time. We pass the gardens of the Royal Palace; the Zecca (mint), and the S. end of the Libreria Vecchia, both by Sansovino, and reach the Piazzetta, whence we started. Fortunate are they who have the opportunity of seeing the Grand Canal at the time of a royal visit, or other great occasion when steamer traffic being stopped, the waters regain the placidity we see in old engravings, and the lines of palaces hung with tapestry are mirrored in the sea. The grand bissone (festal gondolas) are brought forth, decked with brilliant colours, some of them manned by a score of gondoliers in gorgeous old Venetian costume, and we then catch a glimpse of what Venice was in her splendour.

The traveller will probably choose an afternoon for his survey of the Grand Canal, and no better rounding-off of the day may be imagined than to ferry across from the Molo to the island of S. Giorgio Maggiore, the ancient Isle of the Cypresses, and, after visiting the church, to ascend the campanile and enjoy the beautiful view from the summit. Northwards is the line of the mainland, fringed with trees and dotted with villages; in the foreground the broad curve of the city of a hundred isles; around, as the eye sweeps the horizon, are the lagoons, studded with islands and marked by the bold strokes of the lidi; farther to the S. is the open Adriatic. As the sun sinks to its setting the vast expanse will glow in a symphony of ravishing colour.

Palladio's beautiful and impressive interior (p. 194) has been little disturbed. Among other works of pictorial interest are two Tintorettos in the choir (R., the Last Supper; L., the Fall of Manna), and five other paintings by the same master, all described at length by Ruskin in the Venetian Index. Noteworthy are the beautiful choir stalls by Albert of Brussels, some of the finest examples of Flemish wood-carving in Italy. Longhena's modern monument and the old Latin epitaph to puissant Doge Dom. Michieli will be found in a passage behind the choir to the R. In the Sala del Conclave, where the Sacred College met in 1800 and elected Pius VII., is a fine Carpaccio, St George and the Dragon, with a predella, four episodes in the life of the saint. The campanile is a late erection (1774) on the model of the old tower of St Mark. The campanile collapsed in February 1773, doing much damage to the conventual buildings and killing one of the monks. All that remains of the rich and vast Benedictine monastery, one of the four most opulent in Italy, is now a barrack, and of the 150 brothers it once housed, some half-dozen are permitted to linger amid the secularised surroundings and tend the sanctuary.

SECTION VI

S. Zulian—S. Maria Formosa—S. Zanipolo (SS. Giovanni e Paolo)—The Colleoni Statue—The Scuola di S. Marco—S. Maria dei Miracoli

FRESH from memories evoked by the mansions of the ruling families of the Republic, we may now fitly turn to the more important of the two great churches of the Friars which together form the Walhalla of Venice. We enter the Merceria from the Piazza, noting the site of the Casa del Morter (p. 109). A few hundred yards down the busy street the ramo S. Zulian on the right leads to the church of that name, which contains two unimportant Veroneses, an interesting Boccaccino, Virgin and Child, SS. Peter, Michael, and the two Johns, first altar left of entrance, and one of Campagna's best works, a group in high relief of the dying Christ, to the left of the altar.

From the Campo della Guerra at the back of the church we proceed E., cross the Ponte della Guerra, and continue along the calle until we reach, L., the Salizzada S. Lio. The second calle, to the R., along the salizzada is the picturesque Calle del Paradiso, which leads to the Ponte Paradiso. As we near the bridge we note a beautiful Gothic gable bearing the arms of the Foscari and the Mocenighi, and a fine fourteenth-century relief of the Virgin and Child and a donor. We cross the modern bridge which has replaced the fine old Ponte Paradiso, turn R., over the Ponte dei Preti, and emerge on the spacious Campo. S. Maria Formosa is one of the earliest of Venetian churches (p. 23) but entirely restored after the earthquake of 1689. Palma Vecchio's grandiose St Barbara, for which his daughter Violante is said to have stood as model, stands over the first altar on the R. It is one of the most insistent of Venetian paintings. The composition is in six compartments. R. and L. are SS. Anthony and Sebastian; above is the Virgin of Mercy between the Baptist and St Dominic. The church has also an early work by Bart. Vivarini, a Pietà by Palma Giovane, and a Last Supper by Bassano.

We traverse the campo in a N.E. direction to the calle Lunga, which we follow to the end. Here we turn L. along the Fondamenta Tetta, cross the bridge and enter the calle of the same name which leads to the Ponte and Calle Ospedaletto; the end of the calle debouches on the Salizzada SS. Giovanni e Paolo. We turn L., noting to the R. the towering brick apse of the huge church of the Preaching Friars, due to the piety of Doge Giacomo Tiepolo (p. 78). The monastery was begun in 1236, the church twelve years later. The conventual buildings (now part of the civic hospital) were finished in 1293, and the church was not ready for consecration until 1430, when it was dedicated to the martyred Roman soldiers SS. John and Paul, and became popularly known as S. Zanipolo. To the L. before we enter are the tombs of

Doge Giacomo Tiepolo (1249)[107] and Doge Lorenzo Tiepolo his brother (1275).

The interior is imposing by reason of its vast size and simple plan; though the dome, the Renaissance monuments and rococo details disturb the symmetry. The Mendicant Orders possessing the right to bury the dead within the precincts of their buildings were able to grant permission to wealthy and influential families, their supporters, to erect family chapels and sepulchral monuments in their churches. In this Dominican temple lie buried in monumental pomp Doges and statesmen, great captains and admirals, side by side with famous painters; for the two Bellini and Palma Giovane rest here. The traveller who remembers his Ruskin will doubtless turn first to the two monuments typical of noble and debased sculpture which are contrasted with such vehement rhetoric in the opening chapter of the "Stones of Venice." He will find the "faithful tender portrait" of Doge Tomaso Mocenigo (1423) in the L. aisle beyond the second altar, recumbent on a beautiful transitional tomb wrought by two Florentine sculptors, Piero di Nicolo and Giov. di Martino. It is the last of the Gothic tombs in Venice and marks the advancing Renaissance. In the choir, L. of the high altar, is the monument, "perfect in workmanship but devoid of thought," of Doge Andrea Vendramin (1478), executed by Aless. Leopardi and one of the Lombardi. To this "culminating point of the Renaissance," Ruskin attained "by the ministry of such ancient ladders as he found in the sacristan's keeping," and discerned that the figure of the old Doge had but one hand, and that the "wretched effigy was a mere block on the inner side, ... the artist staying his hand as he reached the bend of the grey forehead." The sculptor of "this lying monument to a dishonoured Doge," adds the passionate critic, "was banished from Venice for forgery in 1478." The tomb is, however, a fine example of early Renaissance work, in Burckhardt's opinion "the most beautiful of all the tombs of the Doges." Two inferior figures of St Catherine and the Virgin at the base are not by Leopardi; they were substituted for the admirable statues of Adam and Eve by Leopardi's colleague, which were transferred to the Pal. Vendramin. To the L. of the choir is the early Gothic tomb of Doge Marco Corner (1368), a beautiful and simple monument, probably by the Massegne. Opposite is the "richest monument of the Gothic period in Venice," the tomb of Michele Morosini (1382). The strongly marked features of the dead Doge, "resolute, thoughtful, serene and full of beauty" are wrought in masterly style. These are the tombs referred to by Ruskin: the former as noble Gothic; the latter is furnishing the exactly intermediate condition in style between the pure Gothic and its final renaissance corruption. L. of this is the monument to Doge Leonardo Loredan (1521) with allegorical figures, late Renaissance, executed in 1572. The statue of the Doge is an early work by Campagna.

Beyond the sacristy door is the fine Renaissance monument of Doge Pasquale Malipiero (1462) by a Florentine of the fifteenth century. In the arcade under the next monument (in the N. aisle) is the recumbent figure of Doge Michel Steno (pp. 124, 139) (1414). The inscription tells that he was a lover of righteousness, peace and plenty. At the end of the aisle against the entrance wall is the monument of Doge Giovanni Mocenigo (1485), a typical and early Renaissance work by Tullio and Ant. Lombardo. Over the main portal are the huge monuments of Doge Alvise Mocenigo (1577), his wife Loredana Marcella, and Doge Giovanni Bembo (1618). Against the entrance wall south aisle is another imposing monument by the Lombardi to Doge Pietro Mocenigo (1476). The growing pride of dominion is clearly seen in these sumptuous mausoleums. Pietro's tomb wrought from the spoils of his enemies, as the inscription tells, is adorned with two reliefs boasting of his exploits in war. "The Vendramin Statue," says Ruskin, "is the last which shows the recumbent figure laid in death. A few years later the idea became disagreeable to polite minds, the figures raised themselves on their elbows and began to look about them.[108] ...But the statue soon rose up and presented itself as an actor on the stage in the front of his tomb, surrounded by every circumstance of pomp and symbol of adulation that flattery could suggest or insolence claim." The development of the sepulchral monument from the simple sarcophagus of the early Doges, as in the Tiepolo tombs on the west front to its culmination in the fourteenth and fifteenth century monuments; its subsequent decline and then its utter degradation in the eighteenth century Bertucci mausoleum, may be traced in this church. In the S. aisle a stone with reliefs of Christ between two angels recalls the memory of Doge Renier Zen (1268). Between the first and second altars is the monument to Marc' Antonio Brigadin, hero of the defence of Famagosta. Beyond the side chapel is the colossal monument, 60 feet in length, of Bertuccio (1658) and Silvestre Valier (1700), and the latter's wife Elisabetta, executed by Baratta and other followers of Bernini. This elaborate specimen of rococo art is denounced by Ruskin as exhibiting every condition of false taste and feeble conception.

Among the paintings we note the St Augustine by Bart. Vivarini, one of the master's greatest works; an altar-piece, The Apotheosis of S. Antonino of Florence, by Lotto; one of Rocco Marconi's best works, Christ with SS. Andrew and Peter; Alvise Vivarini's Christ bearing the Cross, highly praised by Mr Berenson; and Bissolo's Madonna and saints.

The famous monument of Colleoni, in the Campo outside the Church is the finest equestrian statue in Europe. The great stalwart condottiero in full armour sits erect in his saddle, indomitable will and forceful capacity marked in every line of his stern, clean-cut features. The *"vista superba*, the deep-set eyes, piercing and terrible," are rendered with supreme art. The statue was designed by Da Vinci's master Verrocchio, a Florentine sculptor, who, however, died of a cold caught at the casting, and Aless. Leopardi was charged by the Republic to complete the work. The conception and the modelling of horse and rider are due to the Florentine sculptor; the finishing of it and the design and execution of the pedestal to the Venetian. Colleoni left his fortune to the Republic on condition that his statue should be placed in St Mark's Square. This the laws forbade, but there being a *scuola* of St Mark with a spacious campo before it the Senate decided to erect the statue there and accept the inheritance.

STATUE OF BARTOLOMEO COLLEONI

On the N. side of the campo is the Scuola di S. Marco now the city hospital. This, in Ruskin's estimation, is one of the two most refined buildings in Venice by the Lombardi. It was designed in 1485 by Martino, the decorations are due to Pietro. The beautiful lunette over the doorway is probably by Bart. Buon, the lions and the two fine reliefs—the healing of the Cobbler Anianus and St Mark baptising a convert—are by Tullio Lombardo. The second of the buildings referred to by Ruskin, S. Maria dei Miracoli, may be easily reached by crossing the Ponte del Cavallo, and following the calle opposite the west front of S. Zanipolo. This exquisite gem of Renaissance architecture (1480-89) was designed by Pietro Lombardo. To Tullio are due the half figures of the Annunciation on the top of the choir steps and the best of the charming arabesque decorations in the interior. The St Francis and St Clare are by Campagna.

SCUOLA DI SAN MARCO AND STATUE OF COLLEONI.

SECTION VII

The Frari—The Scuola and Church of S. Rocco

IN the "Speculum Perfectionis" is told how that St Francis on coming to Assisi to hold the Chapter of the Order found there a great edifice of stone and mortar, built by the citizens for the meeting place of the brothers, instead of the rude wattle and daub barn in which they were wont to assemble. And the saint, fearing lest the brothers might be tempted to have similar great houses erected where they sojourned, climbed to the roof with his companions, and began to strip off the tiles and cast them to the ground, being minded to destroy the building to the very foundation, nor did he desist until the soldiers forbade him, declaring it to be the property of the town. Up to Doge Giacomo Tiepolo's time, as we have seen, the friars minor had no monastery in Venice, but here, as elsewhere, the Franciscans were unable to resist that unquenchable impulse in devoted human souls to raise temples made with hands to the glory of God, and about 1230 or 1240 the great monastery and church of Our Glorious Lady of the Friars were begun. The church was opened for service in 1280, and rebuilt during the second half of the fourteenth century. Santa Maria Gloriosa de'Frari may be reached from the S. Tomà Pier on the Grand Canal. It is the largest church in Venice, and one of the finest Gothic churches in Italy. Vasari attributes the design to Nicolo Pisano. The campanile (1361-1396) was erected by the Massegne. From the tracery of the lower windows in the apse, Ruskin derives the tracery of the arcade in the Ducal Palace, the circle of the quatrefoil falling between the arches when it had to support the wall. Over the Porta de'Frari, leading to the left aisle, is a beautiful relief of the Virgin and two angels and kneeling donors by the Massegne.

The nobility and simplicity of the vast interior remind us of the great friars' churches in Tuscany and Umbria. Few Doges are buried here, the monuments inside being chiefly to famous soldiers, admirals, statesmen and artists. In the R. aisle is the Titian monument executed in 1852, and on the third altar a fine statue of St Jerome by Aless. Vittoria, said to have been modelled from the figure of Titian when he was 98 years old. On the R. wall of R. transept is the tomb of Jacopo Marcelle (1484) in the style of the Lombardi. To the R. of entrance to the sacristy is the beautiful late Gothic tomb, wrought by a Florentine sculptor, of the Franciscan S. Pacifico (1437), under whom the church was completed.

In the second chapel, R. of the choir, R. wall, is the tomb of the Florentine ambassador, Duccio degli Alberti (1336) by a Tuscan sculptor, noted by Ruskin as the first monument in Venice in which images of the Virtues appear; L. wall, the noble and simple fourteenth-century tomb of an unknown knight, "perfect Gothic form." In the choir are two important works attributed to Ant. Riccio. R. wall, the ornate monument of Doge Francesco Foscari (pp. 141, 151) (1457); L. wall, the mausoleum of Doge Nicolo Tron (1473). The transition of Gothic to Renaissance is admirably illustrated in these two works. Titian's Assumption stood formerly over the high altar. L. aisle beyond the baptistery is the Renaissance tomb of Jacopo Pesare (1547). The inscription states that the buried bishop conquered the Turks in war, and was transported from a noble family among the Venetians to a nobler among the angels. The monstrous pile of masonry beyond the Titian altar-piece (p. 195), erected to Doge Giovanni Pesaro (1659) by Melchior Barthel (a German) and Longhena, qualified by Ruskin as a huge accumulation of theatrical scenery in marble, will illustrate even more clearly than the Valier tomb in S. Zanipolo the depths of bad taste to which monumental art had fallen in the seventeenth century.

Turning to the pictures, we note two altar-pieces (1474) by Bart. Vivarini, St Mark enthroned, and a Virgin and Child with Saints. In the third chapel L. of the choir is Alvise's Apotheosis of St Ambrose. Within the sacristy is treasured Giov. Bellini's altar-piece, the Virgin and Child with four saints (L., St Nicholas and another; R., SS. Benedict and Bernadine), and two of the most exquisitely charming angels in Venetian art. All the master's qualities are here in their highest manifestation—maternal tenderness; fervent, grave and virile piety; and the joy of childhood. The picture makes a direct appeal to our finer emotions and the traveller will prefer to remain in silent and reverent appreciation without further intrusion of guide or critic. The Titian altar-piece in the choir screen aisle, painted for Bishop Jacopo Pesaro, affords an admirable contrast to the Bellini. Progress even in art must be paid for. Although perfect in technique, grand in composition, rich in colour, it yet lacks the atmosphere of tranquil devotion of the earlier master. The doughty bishop, who is seen kneeling to the left, had the picture painted to commemorate a small naval victory that he gained when in charge of a papal fleet over the Turks (p. 164). Above is the Virgin and Child to whom St Francis commends the kneeling Pesaro family. At the Virgin's feet sits St Peter who turns from his reading to look on the donor below. Behind the latter stands a knight in full armour holding in his right hand the papal standard crowned by a sprig of laurel, and grasping in his left hand two Turkish captives in chains. The portraits of the Pesari are in Titian's most perfect manner. This was a favourite of Sir Joshua Reynolds who describes it at length in "The Journey to Flanders and Holland." Crossing the bridge opposite the main portal and turning L. we reach the great Monastery now the Record Office of Venice (Archivio Centrale). It contains the most famous collection of state documents in the world. The custodian will admit the traveller to the noble double cloisters. We return to the Porta dei Frari and further to the W. find the Scuola and church of S. Rocco.

Towards the end of the thirteenth century a young noble of Montpellier found himself the master of great possessions, and following the injunctions of Christ sold all that he had and gave it to the poor. He set forth as a pilgrim to Rome and on his way passed plague-stricken cities where he devoted himself to the service of the hospitals and by his tenderness, sympathy and fervent prayers wrought many wondrous cures. At length on his return from Rome he was stricken himself at Piacenza and a horrible ulcer broke out on his thigh. Wishing to spare his fellow-sufferers the sound of his groans he dragged himself to a ruined hut in a deserted place hard by, where angels tended his sores and a dog brought him daily bread. When healed he went back to his native city but arrived so changed by suffering that he was arrested as a spy and cast into prison. One morning after he had languished there for five years the jailer on entering his dungeon saw it flooded with a bright light, the prisoner dead, and a writing which promised healing to all stricken by plague who should call on his name. In 1485 some Venetians disguised as pilgrims carried off the saint's body to Venice; the Church of S. Rocco was erected to contain it and a guild founded in his name for the tending of the sick and the burial of the dead. The church, entrusted to Bart. Buon of Bergamo, was built in the fifteenth century. The Scuola was begun about the same time (1490) by the same architect, carried on by the Lombardi and Scarpagnino (1524-37) and completed about 1550. Here during eighteen years Tintoretto worked on the stupendous series of paintings which decorate the interior. They are fully described and vigorously appreciated and depreciated by Ruskin in the Venetian Index. The Adoration of the Magi, in the lower hall, facing the entrance, he esteems to be "the most finished picture in the Scuola except the Crucifixion."

SCUOLA DI S. ROCCA.

From the first landing as we ascend the stairs may be seen to the L. an early Annunciation by Titian, refreshing in its repose and simplicity; R. is Tintoretto's Visitation.

On the walls of the upper hall are continued the scenes of New Testament history begun in the lower. They are unequal in merit, and include, according to Ruskin, two of the worst Tintorettos in Venice: The Last Supper and the altar-piece, S. Rocco in Glory. The ceiling, decorated with scenes from Old Testament history, is painted with all the master's force and decorative science.

The Crucifixion in the Guest-Chamber on the same floor is justly esteemed as Tintoretto's greatest work. On it he concentrated all his art and all his majestic power. It was his favourite work, and when Carracci's plate was brought to him for approval he fell on the engraver's neck and kissed him. Opposite the Crucifixion is the Christ before Pilate; over the door, an Ecce Homo. The series closes with the Christ bearing His Cross. The ceiling is decorated with the Apotheosis of S. Rocco (p. 210) and other allegorical figures. The choir stalls in the large hall are beautifully carved with scenes from the life, of S. Rocco by Giovanni Marchiori. In the small room to R. of entrance is an early Titian, Ecce Homo, and the death-mask of Doge Alvise Mocenigo with his ducal cap.

CHURCH OF S. ROCCO.

Tintoretto has here dealt with the story of the saint in his most unequal fashion. Not all his art can make the scenes of disease and death envisaged in so realistic a manner other than disagreeable. We turn from their contemplation with relief to the noble and stately SS. Christopher and Martin by Pordenone and to the latest of miracle-working pictures, Christ led to Execution, by Titian, in the chapel to the R. of the choir. In the vestibule of the sacristy is Pordenone's fresco, St Sebastian.

SECTION VIII

S. Zaccaria—S. Giorgio degli Schiavoni—S. Francesco della Vigna

WE pass the N. portal of St Mark's, follow the Calle di Canonica, turn R., and first observing the beautiful façade of the Palazzo Trevisan, associated with the memory of the notorious Bianca Cappello,[109] cross the Ponte di Canonica. We continue E., cross the Ponte S. Provolo, pass under a Gothic portal with a restored relief in the lunette of the Virgin and Child, the Baptist and St Mark, and reach the Campo and church of S. Zaccaria, once the chapel of the oldest, richest and most extensive nunnery in Venice (now a barrack), and the burial-place of the early Doges. The present church dates from the second half of the fifteenth century. The visitor will infallibly be drawn to the altar on the L. where stands Giovanni Bellini's Virgin and Child with four saints. R. of the enthroned Virgin stand SS. Lucy and Jerome: L., SS. Catherine of Alexandria and Peter. Though imperfectly preserved and ill seen its charm is indescribable. Feminine tenderness and virile strength, fervent piety and dignity are expressed with all the lucidity and winning grace of the master. It was painted in 1505 when he was seventy-nine years of age.

The nuns' choir, entered by a door on the right, has some fine choir stalls by Marco da Vicenza, and some pictures, among them a doubtful Palma Vecchio and a badly-preserved Tintoretto—the Birth of the Baptist. The sacristan will open the chapel of S. Tarasius (p. 31) which contains three gilded, carved altar-pieces of wood with paintings by Giovanni Alemano and Antonio Vivarini. Each altar-piece is inscribed with the name of the donatrix. The expert in the iconography of the saints will find scope for his science in the interpretation of the various symbols. The tomb of Alessandro Vittoria is in the L. aisle.

We return to the Campo S. Provolo and make our way N.E. to the little oratory of S. Giorgio degli Schiavoni (Dalmatians), belonging to the lay foundation (1451) of that name and built (1551) by Zuane Zon, master mason of the arsenal. The foundation is still under Austrian jurisdiction, and a rather poor endowment is helped by a yearly contribution of two lire each from some hundred brethren, the Emperor of Austria assisting by an annual subscription. Three Dalmatian priests serve the chapel. St George's Day, when high mass is sung and the upper chamber is filled by the brethren and their friends, is a great festival. During six years, 1502-8, Carpaccio was employed in decorating the hall with scenes from the lives of three great Dalmatian saints, SS. George, Tryphonius and Jerome. These charming and naïve paintings, happily still in their original setting, have been described by Ruskin in "St Mark's Rest."

L. of the entrance are two panels with scenes from the life of St George. (1) The fight with the dragon; the young princess looks on with clasped hands. The remains of the monster's victims are a somewhat gruesome detail. (2) The victor drags the slain beast, its head transfixed by a dagger, into the city. The gorgeous dresses of the pagan king, the princess and the oriental spectators, the quaint attempts at local colour, and at investing the dragon with some degree of fearsomeness, make the picture one of the most attractive of the series. The story is concluded on the wall L. of the altar. (3) The saint baptises the king and his daughter, carefully holding his cloak lest it be spoiled by the water. This composition is rich in delightfully conceived details of Eastern splendour. R. of the altar-piece (The Virgin and Child by Catena) is a scene from the life of St Tryphonius. He is portrayed as a lad subduing the basilisk which devastated Albania. On the R. wall are the Agony in the Garden and the Calling of Matthew. Then follow three scenes from the life of St Jerome. (1) The terror of the monks at the sight of the lion; (2) death of the saint; (3) the saint in his study translating the Scriptures. The furniture and surroundings in this last, painted with loving care, betray the refined taste of a Venetian scholar. A shelf of books, some manuscripts, an orrery, works of art, objects of devotion, and, a homely detail—the typical Venetian pet dog. The whole scene is pervaded with an atmosphere of calm and studious retirement.

In a northerly direction, towards the Fondamente Nuove, is the great church of S. Francesco della Vigna, whose site is associated with one of the earliest legends of St Mark (p. 17). The land—one of the most extensive vineyards in Venice—was bequeathed to the Franciscans in 1253 by Marco, son of Doge Pietro Ziani. The church was rebuilt (1534-62) by Sansovino, modified subsequently by Palladio, who designed the imposing façade. In a chapel to the R. in the S. transept is a Virgin and Child by Negroponte. The figures are drawn with great fulness and beauty, and, though much repainted, the picture, executed in 1450, is a remarkable example of the Paduan master's art. The church contains seven ducal monuments; among them, L. of the choir, the tomb of Andrea Gritti (1538). But of greater interest are the beautiful reliefs by Tullio, Ant., and Sante Lombardi in the Giustiniani chapel, L. of the choir, of the prophets and Evangelists, and eighteen scenes from New Testament history. The church also contains two paintings by the Bergamasque artists Franc. and Girolamo di Santa Croce (1500-50); a Holy Family and a Resurrection by Veronese; and, in the chapel on the way to the old cloisters, a Virgin and Child with four saints and donor by Giov. Bellini, debased by re-painting.

SECTION IX

The Riva degli Schiavoni—S. Maria della Pietà—Petrarch's House—S. Giovanni in Bragora—S. Martino—The Arsenal—The Public Gardens—S. Pietro in Castello

TURNING S. from the Piazza we pass the Libreria Vecchia, designed by Sansovino to contain the books left to the Republic by Petrarch and Cardinal Bessarione and reach the two columns of grim memories, where Browning delighted to

"observe
The swallows soaring their eternal curve
'Twixt Theodore and Mark."

VENICE FROM THE PUBLIC GARDENS

N.E

To the W., on the site of the present royal gardens, stood the old granaries of the Republic. We turn E., cross the Ponte della Paglia (straw) where the barges laden with straw used to unload, and reach the *Riva degli Schiavoni*, in olden times the most bustling quarter of Venice. Here lived the Schiavoni (Dalmatian sailors), who manned the galleons and argosies of the Republic. Here was the starting-point for the galleys bound for the Holy Land. On the site of the present prison, John the Englishman, in the fourteenth century, kept "The Dragon," a hostelry, with stables, much patronised by English pilgrims, for horses were then almost as common in Venice as in other mediæval towns. Several of the Doges had the finest stables in Italy, and horses and mules were largely used by the Venetians. There was no wide

Riva[110] in those days, only a narrow fondamenta beyond the Molo, which was then a projecting quay, the chief landing-stage of Venice. The Riva is the favourite promenade of the Venetian *popolani*, and affords an ever-changing scene of local colour for the stranger. We cross two bridges to S. Maria della Pietà, which contains a masterpiece (Christ in the House of the Pharisee) by Moretto, the Brescian painter (1498-1560), in the upper choir at the S. end. Just over the next bridge (del Sepolcro, so called because the pilgrims to and from the Holy Sepulchre at Jerusalem lodged near), is the site of the house given by the Republic to Petrarch. Here he lived with his married daughter, entertained Boccaccio, and had a disputation with a notorious atheist of Venice, whom he failed to convert, and ejected from the house.

We turn N., beyond the house, by the calle del Dose, and reach the church of S. Giovanni in Bragora (the marshes). Here we shall find one of the finest Cimas in Venice (The Baptism of Christ), unhappily difficult to see as a whole, owing to its position behind the high altar. It was painted in 1491. On a pillar, R. of the choir, is another work by the same master—SS. Helena and Constantine; on a pillar to the L. is Alvise Vivarini's Resurrection, painted in 1498. The Virgin and Child in the second chapel R. of the entrance is generally given to Alvise, though by some critics attributed to Giov. Bellini. On the L. wall is a Virgin and Child with the Baptist and St Andrew by Bartolomeo Vivarini, painted in the same year. Beneath are three predelle by Cima, with scenes from the Invention of the Cross. The church contains also a doubtful Bissolo between the first and second chapels in the R. nave, and a Last Supper by Paris Bordone, utterly disfigured by restoration, in the L. nave.

On leaving, we turn again E. to the church of S. Martino, with a Bocca del Leone (p. 248) in the façade. Just beyond the church we sight the main portal of the great arsenal, once fortified with twelve watch-towers and walls two miles in extent, paced night and day by sentinels. The portal is flanked by the four Greek lions in marble brought from the Porta Leoni at Athens by Francesco Morosini, and surmounted by the Lion of St Mark and a statue of St Giustina by Campagna, to commemorate the victory of Lepanto. The museum contains on the first floor, among other objects of interest, models of Venetian ships and galleys of all kinds, a small carved panel from an old Bucintoro, and a fragment of a mast, all that remains of the last Bucintoro which Goethe saw and described as not over-loaded with decoration, since it was all decoration. A model of this gorgeous vessel may be seen in the room. On the second floor is a collection of weapons and spoils of war. The simple, noble statue of Vittor Pisani faces us as we ascend the staircase. A striking contrast is afforded by Canova's sentimental monument to Angelo Emo. In the room are preserved the armour of Doge Seb. Ziani, with closed visor and bearing a crest on the cuirass, and of Seb. Venier, with open visor, and crest on cuirass; of Henry IV. of France, and of the condottiero Gattamelata. We cross the iron bridge to the L. of the portal of the arsenal, and return to the Riva. We may now proceed past the church of S. Biagio to the Public Gardens.

SECTION X

S. Salvatore—Corte del Milione—S. Giovanni Grisostomo

S. FOSCA AND PALAZZO GIOVANNELLI.

We take our way along the Merceria, past the church of S. Zulian, until we come in sight of the tall apse of S. Salvatore. We enter from the Merceria by the door of the L. aisle. S. Salvatore is one of the most important examples of ecclesiastical Renaissance architecture in Venice. Spavento, four of the Lombardi, Sansovino, Scamozzi and Longhena all contributed at various periods to the building and decoration, not to speak of more modern restorers. Here in the R. transept is the massive memorial to unhappy Queen Catherine Cornaro by Bernardini Contino. A finer specimen of monumental art is Sansovino's tomb of Doge Franc. Venier (1556), beyond the second altar in the R. aisle. The figures of Faith and Charity, the former said to have been almost wholly carved by the master in his eightieth year, are among the greatest achievements of later Renaissance sculpture. Over the third altar is Titian's Annunciation and at the high altar his Transfiguration, both painted when he was approaching ninety years of age; the latter, however, by some critics is depreciated to a school painting. In the chapel L. of choir is a most interesting, Christ at Emmaus, generally attributed to Giovanni Bellini, but by Crowe and Cavalcaselle confidently assigned to Carpaccio. Another critic (Molmenti) is convinced it is by no other hand than that of Benedetto Diana.

Leaving by the front entrance we find ourselves on the Campo S. Salvatore, where in olden times stood a water trough, and a fig tree to which horses were tied, after the law of 1287 forbade equestrian traffic along the Merceria. We turn R. by the new Merceria due Aprile, pass the Goldoni statue, and cross the Ponte dell' Olio to the church of S. Giovanni Grisostomo. Before we enter, a slight deviation by the calle Ufficio della Seta and the calle del Teatro (over a fruiterer's shop will be seen the inscription: PROVISORES SIRICI, p. 117) will bring us on the R. to the entrance to the Corte Milione. On the N. side of this court stood the house of the Polo family which Marco, then a lad of seventeen, left in 1271, with his uncles Nicolo and Maffeo, for the East. A quarter of a century later three travel-stained wanderers, dressed in coarse garb of Tartar cut and speaking broken Venetian with a Tartar accent, were at first refused admission by their kinsmen. The three, to warm the affection of their relatives, invited them to a sumptuous banquet, and when all were seated entered arrayed in flowing crimson robes of satin. Having washed their hands, they retired and returned clothed in crimson damask, and ordered the first dresses to be cut up and distributed among the servants. After a few dishes a similar change was made into crimson velvet and similarly disposed of. Again they changed into dresses of ordinary fashion. When the nine suits had been divided among the servants, Marco rose, went to his chamber, and appeared with the old Tartar coats, and ripping them open with a knife, showered on the table before his amazed guests a glittering and inestimable treasure of jewels and precious stones. The thirteenth century arched doorway and various fragments of sculptured stonework imbedded in the walls of the neighbouring houses almost certainly formed part of the original Polo mansion (p. 99).

WELL-HEAD: CAMPO S. GIOVANNI GRISOSTOMO.

THE RIALTO BRIDGE

We return to the church of S. Giov. Grisostomo by Tullio or Moro Lombardo. The finely proportioned interior holds one of the most precious of Venetian paintings—the altar-piece by Giov. Bellini, over the first chapel to the R., SS. Jerome, Christopher, and Augustine, dated 1513. It is the last of his signed works, and was painted three years before his death. At the high altar is Sebastiano del Piombo's sensuous painting of the patron saint, with the Baptist, SS. Augustine, Liberale, Catherine of Alexandria, Agnes, and the Magdalen. Over the second altar, L., is a fine relief by Tullio Lombardo. We note the fine Renaissance well-head in the Campo, and retrace our steps to the foot of the Rialto bridge and the pier on the Rio del Carbon.

SECTION XI

S. Moisè—S. Stefano—Site of the Aldine Press—Il Bovolo—S. Vitale—S. Vio—The Salute—The Seminario

FROM the S.W. angle of the Piazza a bustling street leads W. past S. Moisè, a late seventeenth century church by A. Tremignan, whose amazing façade was once thought beautiful. Traversing the Campi S. Maria Zobenigo and S. Maurizio, we reach the large Campo Franc. Morosini. At the N. end of the campo is the fine Gothic brick church of S. Stefano (1294-1320). The principal portal and the windows of the W. front are by the Massegne. The spacious interior contains several good Renaissance monuments, the best being that of Jac. Suriano, L. of entrance; P. Lombardo's statues of SS. Jerome and Paul stand either side of the third altar, L. aisle; those of the Baptist and St Anthony at either side of the altar in the sacristy. The last is one of the master's most perfect works in Venice. Near these statues are Bart. Vivarini's SS. Nicholas and Lawrence. Morosini's tomb is on the pavement of the nave. We quit the church by the L. aisle, and enter the cloister, with some fragmentary remains of Pordenone's frescoes.

Crossing the cloister we emerge on the Campo S. Angelo, which we traverse and walk along the Calle della Mandola to the Campo Manin, at the farther end of which is the *Cassa di Risparmio* (Savings Bank), on the site of the old Aldine Press.

We retrace our steps, and before leaving the campo turn L. by the Calle della Vida, again to the L., and on the R. down the Calle and Corte Contarini del Bovolo reach a beautiful early Renaissance spiral staircase and a Byzantine well-head. We return to the Campo Morosini, at the farther end of which, on the R., is the church of S. Vitale (Vidal), which has a late Carpaccio, S. Vitale on horseback, accompanied by Valeria his wife, his sons Gervasius and Protasius, and other saints. We cross the Grand Canal by the iron bridge, leave the Accademia to the R., turn E. by the calle Nuova S. Agnese, and, after crossing a bridge, reach the church of S. Vio, demolished in 1813 and rebuilt in 1864. A few of the fragments of Tiepolo's house were incorporated in the new building (p. 109). The church is only open once a year, S. Vio's day, but admission at other times may be obtained by applying at the stone mason's, next door. The Campo S. Vio is associated with one of the most charming legends of Venice. Here lived the blessed Contessa Tagliapietra, whose insistent devotion and frequent visits to a priest at S. Maurizio, on the opposite side of the Grand Canal, were deemed unseemly by her family. Entreaties proving vain, the ferrymen were forbidden to row her across;

whereupon the Countess took a thread, laid it upon the waters, and crossed to her devotions without human aid.

PALAZZO CONTARINI, WITH SPIRAL STAIRCASE AND BYZANTINE WELL-HEAD

S. MARIA DELLA SALUTE

We continue E. and after some turning of corners, pass a picturesque little shrine at the end of the calle Barbaro. We cross the Ponte S. Gregorio and at length reach the great plague church of the Salute. The interior contains over the third altar L., Titian's somewhat faded but still beautiful Descent of the Holy Ghost. The Virgin is drawn from the same model as that of the Assumption in the Accademia. The small ceiling medallions behind the high altar, the four Evangelists and four Fathers of the Church are also by Titian. The St Matthew is the artist's own portrait. Over the altar of the sacristy is Titian's St Mark enthroned, attended by SS. Sebastian, Roch, Cosimo, and Damian (1513), sadly spoilt by restoration. The ceiling paintings—the Death of Abel, Abraham's Sacrifice (Isaac is a lovely child), and David and Goliath are in Titian's later manner (1543). The space between the windows on the R. wall is covered by Tintoretto's Marriage at Cana. It is described at length by Ruskin in the Venetian index and is esteemed by the great critic to be "perhaps the most perfect example which human art has produced of the utmost possible force and sharpness of shadow united with richness of local colour." In the sacristy are also a St Sebastian by Paris Bordone, and two small oval paintings to the R. of the altar, SS. Augustine and Nicholas, usually assigned to Ant. and Bart. Vivarini, attributed, however, by Mr Berenson to Giambono. In the ante-sacristy is a fifteenth century pietà in relief and an early painting (1339), The Virgin and Child with the kneeling donors, Doge Francesco Dandolo, and the Dogeressa Elisabetta, with their name saints.

E. of the Salute is the Seminario with a small collection of sculpture and pictures. Ascending Longhena's noble staircase we enter the Galleria Manfredini, which contains works by Filippino Lippi and Veronese, and Giorgione's Apollo and Daphne (p. 202), probably painted for the panel of a *cassone* (bridal chest). The ferry from the Salute or the Dogana point will land us near the Piazza.

SECTION XII

SS. Apostoli-Palazzo Falier—I Gesuiti—I Crociferi—S. Caterina—S. Maria dell' Orto—S. Marziale—Palazzo Giovanelli. (Admission to this last by application to the British Consul, traghetto S. Felice, Grand Canal.)

FROM the Ca' d'Oro Pier on the Grand Canal a narrow calle leads into the broad Corso Vitt. Emanuele, which we follow to the R. and reach the church of the SS. Apostoli. Admirers of Tiepolo will find his St Lucy receiving the Sacrament before her Martyrdom, at the altar of the Cappella Corner to R. of entrance where are also two family monuments in the best style of the Lombardi school. A Veronese school painting, the Fall of Manna, is at the L. of the choir. The remains of Marino Falier's house are incorporated in the palazzo over the Ponte SS. Apostoli opposite the church.

N.E. from the campo stands the church of the Gesuiti, built (1715) on the site of the ruined church of the Crociferi in the base style of the age. The interior, lavishly decorated with marble and inlay of *verde antico*, is incredibly vulgar in taste and contains, first chapel L., Titian's martyrdom of St Lawrence, painted in 1558 when the old painter was under Michael Angelo's influence. The work, which was generally esteemed one of the most rare and remarkable of his creations, is now so darkened by time as to be barely legible. The church possesses also an Assumption by Tintoretto.

Nearly opposite the Gesuiti is the oratory of the Crociferi, with Palma Giovane's, Doge Cigogna visiting the Oratory, and six other paintings in the artist's best style. The room contains also a Flagellation by Tintoretto and a ceiling painting, the Assumption, by Titian. The large monastery buildings opposite, still bearing the device of the order (three crosses), are now a barrack. We retrace our steps across the campo. About a hundred yards along the fondamenta Zen is the entrance to the little church of S. Caterina, which contains Veronese's admirably preserved Marriage of St Catherine (p. 211). The church has works by Palma Giovane and the inevitable Tintoretto, but we have eyes alone for the St Catherine, one of the most satisfying examples of the later glories of the Venetian school.

In an outlying part of the city to the N.W. is the church of S. Maria dell' Orto. Cima's Baptist with SS. Peter, Mark, Jerome and Paul, in a marble setting by Leopardi (p. 200) stands over the first altar, R. aisle. In the third chapel L., is Tintoretto's Presentation at the Temple, and in the Cappella Contarini, the same master's St Agnes. Both have been freely restored, the former, says Ruskin, "has been so daubed as to be a ghastly ruin and a disgrace to modern Venice." We turn to the choir, R. and L. of which are Tintoretto's huge canvases, the Last Judgment, and the Worship of the Golden Calf. These are very highly appreciated by Ruskin but "demand resolute study if the traveller is to derive any pleasure from them." Vasari, who saw them shortly after they were painted, was impressed by the terrible yet capricious invention displayed in the Last Judgment, but lamented the lack of care and diligence which marred what might have been a stupendous creation. Closely scrutinised, however, both seemed to him painted *da burla* (in jest). The first chapel L. of entrance has (R. wall) a Pietà by Lorenzo Lotto, and over the altar an early Virgin and Child by Giov. Bellini disastrously repainted. Over the sacristy door is a miracle-working half-figure of the Virgin and Child (restored), which was discovered in a garden in 1577 and gave the present name to the church (Our Lady of the Garden). Verocchio, Leopardi and Tintoretto were buried in the sacristy, but most of the tombs were defaced or destroyed by the Austrians when the church was used as a military magazine in 1855.

Making our way southward we reach the church of S. Marziale, which contains Titian's Tobias, and Tintoretto's last work, the Patron Saint with SS. Peter and Paul. From the Campo S. Marziale we cross the Ponte Zancani and the Ponte S. Fosca, noting the marble footmarks on the crown (p. 305), and pass the statue of Paolo Sarpi erected near the spot where the friar was stabbed. We continue our way by the church, and a short distance to the L. along the Corso Vitt. Emanuele is the Palazzo Giovanelli, one of the best examples of a restored patrician mansion of the period of the Ducal Palace. The interior is sumptuously decorated, and contains the most precious Giorgione in Venice, the so-called Family of Giorgione (p. 202), referred to by a late contemporary as "a stormy landscape with a gipsy and soldier." Vasari complained that Giorgione's subjects were difficult to characterise by a phrase. In the foreground on the L., with the characteristic Giorgione pose, stands a figure in the flower of manhood holding a staff. The dress, suggesting both knight and peasant, seems to typify the defender and sustainer of maternity symbolised by the young mother sitting, to the R., on a sloping, sunlit meadow, giving suck to her babe, both modelled with perfect naturalness and beauty. Through the centre of the picture flows a mountain stream crossed by a rustic bridge. In the background of the landscape, with its graceful trees, rises the walled city of Castelfranco, Giorgione's birthplace, darkened by storm clouds rent by a flash of lightning. The sunny foreground and the louring sky seem to tell of the vicissitudes of human existence. A classic remain with two broken columns adds to the pathetic beauty of this, one of the earliest paintings in which landscape is transfused with human emotion and poetic sentiment.

Among other attractions the gallery possesses a portrait by Antonello, a Santa Conversazione by Paris Bordone, a battle scene by Tintoretto, a portrait by Titian, and a doubtful Giovanni Bellini, attributed by Mr Berenson to Catena. In the ballroom are some very fine Venetian mirrors.

RIO S. CASSIANO.

PALAZZO GIOVANELLI—GIPSY AND SOLDIER By Giorgione

SECTION XIII

The Rialto—S. Giacomo di Rialto—S. Giovanni Elemosinario—S. Cassiano—S. Maria Mater Domini—Museo Civico

WE cross the Rialto bridge, and in the campo on the farther side find the little church of S. Giacomo di Rialto, according to tradition (p. 6) the oldest in Venice. This spot, Shakespeare's Rialto, was the focus of the commercial life of the old Republic. The colonnade was covered with frescoes, and possessed the famous planisphere or *mappa mondo* showing the routes of Venetian commerce over the world. Here the patricians were wont to meet before noon to discourse together of private and public affairs. The church, rebuilt and altered more than once, no longer stands on its original site. It was removed in 1322, when the Rialto was enlarged and a loggia made, that the merchants might meet under cover. The beautiful relief of the Virgin and Child over the portico is fourteenth-century work. The six columns of the nave are the sole remains of the eleventh-century church, rebuilt by Doge Dom. Selvo. On the exterior of the apse will be found the (Latin) inscription whose discovery so delighted Ruskin: AROUND THIS TEMPLE LET THE MERCHANT'S LAW BE JUST, HIS WEIGHT TRUE, AND HIS COVENANTS FAITHFUL.[111]

EDICT STONE, RIALTO.

On the farther side of the campo, opposite the W. front, is the Hunchback of the Rialto (Il Gobbo di Rialto), restored in 1892, whence in olden times the decrees of the Republic were promulgated. Beyond the market is the church of S. Giovanni Elemosinario, early sixteenth century, by Scarpagnino. The picturesque campanile has an interesting relief below the cella of the bells. The high altar painting is by Titian, the Patron Saint (St John the Almsgiver). In the chapel to the R. is an altar-piece by Pordenone, SS. Sebastian, Roch and Mary Magdalen. Above on the L. wall is a quaint relief, saved from the fire which destroyed the old eleventh-century church.

We follow the hand pointing to the Museo Civico, and soon reach S. Cassiano, containing three Tintorettos. The Crucifixion, held by Ruskin to be one of the finest paintings in Europe by the master, is a most remarkable and original treatment of the subject—a great and solemn picture in excellent condition. The church has an altar-piece by Palma Vecchio, The Baptist and four saints, said to be the first painted by him at Venice, and three paintings by L. Bassano.

Following the indicator, we reach the little church of S. Maria Mater Domini by one of the Lombardi: the façade by Sansovino. It is situated in an interesting campo, where may be seen a few early Gothic houses with some beautiful Byzantine reliefs and crosses. The church possesses, second altar to the R., Catena's S. Cristina. The angel to the left holding the millstone is one of the most sweet and guileless of the master's creations (p. 201). In the R. transept is Tintoretto's Invention of the Cross. Opposite is a Last Supper attributed to Bonifazio.

We at length reach the Museo Civico in the restored Fondaco de' Turchi. The original palace, the Ca' Pesaro, was built for Giac. Palmieri, a rich Guelf refugee from Pesaro, about 1230. In 1861 it was an imposing and picturesque ruin, with a cherry tree growing and fruiting on one of the turrets. In 1869 it was wholly restored (*Guasto e profanato*, says Boni), all the beautiful capitals and columns were recut and scraped, and subsequently anointed with oil to bring out the veining.

BYZANTINE CROSSES—CAMPO S. MARIA MATER DOMINI

In the court are some fine examples of Venetian well-heads. 2nd Floor, Room I. contains a collection of arms and banners, some of them captured from the Turks, and fine standards of the Republic. In Room II. are:—31, A late work by Carpaccio, The Visitation; 41, Lotto, The Virgin and Child with SS. George and Jerome and kneeling donor; and a number of characteristic scenes of Venetian life by Longhi and Guardi. Rooms III., IV., V., VI. are wholly dominated by Francesco Morosini and contain spoils of war, personal relics, among which are a book of hours (concealing a pistol), a bust, a portrait, costumes, pictures of his victories, models of galleys. Room VII. has an interesting and complete set of oselle,[112] beginning (2200) from Doge Ant. Grimani to (2716) Doge Ludovico Manin. Venetian coins, among which are cases of gold Zecchini with a unique Marïn Falier, and medals of the Carraresi. Rooms VIII. and IX. display some beautiful Venetian lace and rich stuffs; costumes, fans, stilted shoes, and miniatures, a diagram showing the method of electing a Doge, and a remarkable fifteenth-century wooden staircase. Room X., besides some furniture, has, No. 14, a portrait of Goldoni, and some paintings by Longhi. Room XI. has a miscellaneous collection of reliefs from the burnt chapel of the Rosary at S. Zanipolo; bronze works and ornaments. Room XII. contains a fine collection of majolica ware and porcelain, and some glass, among which, 912, is a deep blue wedding goblet by the famous Berovieri of Murano. Room XIV. has a precious collection of illuminated MSS. No. 70 (fifteenth century), (Leggenda dell' apparizione di S. Marco) shows the pillar near St Clement's altar from which the hand of the saint is said to have protruded. Here are also a number of Mariegole or guild statutes, one of which (9) shows the Master of the Carpet-makers submitting the statutes to Doge Foscari. A specimen of the manufacture which has been presented to the Doge according to usage is hanging on the balcony; 166 is a portrait of Paolo Sarpi and the dagger with which he was stabbed. Room XV., 43, Basaiti, Virgin and Child with donor. 35, Jac. Bellini, Crucifixion. Room XVI., 2, Alvise Vivarini, St Anthony of Padua. 5, Carpaccio,[113] Two Courtezans with their pets: the stilted shoes then worn by ladies are seen in this picture.[114] Four early works by Giov. Bellini, (6) a Transfiguration, (3) a Pietà with a forged signature of Dürer; (8) a Crucifixion, and (II) Christ mourned by Three Angels. Portraits of Doge Giov. Mocenigo (16) by Gentile Bellini and (19) a Bellini school painting of Doge Franc. Foscari.

The curious old church of S. Giacomo dall' Orio stands S. of the Museo Civico. The timber coved roof dates from the fourteenth century. On the wall R. of the entrance is a fine picture (1511) SS. Sebastian, Lawrence and Roch by Giov. Buonconsiglio, a Vicenzian painter of the early sixteenth century, sometimes known as Marescalco. In the R. aisle is a richly carved and gilded vaulted frieze beneath which is Franc. Bassano's Preaching of the Baptist, one of his most beautiful works: opposite is an Ionic column of *verde antico* of wonderful size and beauty, one of the "jewel shafts"[115] referred to by Ruskin. In a chapel in the L. aisle is a Lorenzo Lotto, Coronation of the Virgin with SS. Andrew, James, Cosimo and Damian (1546). The picture, which has been much restored, brought the artist 130 gold ducats.

SECTION XIV

S. Sebastiano—S. M. del Carmine—S. Pantaleone—The Cobblers' Guildhall—S. Polo—S. Apollinare

WE follow the route (Section XI.) to the Campo Morosini and turn R. by the church of S. Vitale along the Campiello Loredan. After crossing two bridges and turning an angle to the L., we reach the Campo S. Samuele. The ferry across the Grand Canal will land us at the Calle del Traghetto, which we follow to the Campo S. Barnabà. Crossing the Campo obliquely we reach on the R. the Ponte dei Pugni, as its name implies, one of the bridges where the faction fights between the Castellani and Nicolotti used to take place. The former were distinguished by red, the latter by black caps and scarves. These contests were favoured by the Signory, in order, it is believed, to foster a warlike spirit among the people, and were continued until 1705, when a peculiarly bloody affray in which stones and knives were used, led to their abolition.[116] If the traveller will mount to the crown of the bridge he will see two footmarks in stone let into the paving on either side. Victory smiled on that faction which could thrust their adversaries beyond the line marked by the feet. The bridge then had no parapets and in the course of the struggle many a champion fell into the canal. We resume our way along the Fondamenta as far as the Ponte delle Pazienze. A turning opposite, to the L., brings us to the Calle Lunga, which we follow to the R. direct to the church of S. Sebastiano. No admirer of Veronese should leave this church unvisited. Here the painter, when he came, a young man of twenty seven, to try his fortune at Venice, received his first commission to decorate the sacristy, owing to the influence of his uncle the prior of the monastery. Veronese has made the walls of this temple glorious with some of his greatest creations. Here he desired to be buried, and his two sons and his brother (all fellow artists) piously gave effect to his wishes, and a slab of marble on the pavement, with an inscription, marks his resting-place under his bust to the R. of the organ. A year after his work on the ceiling of the sacristy (the Coronation of the Virgin and the Four Evangelists), he painted in 1556 the ceiling of the church with scenes from the Book of Esther. People crowded to see these novel and daring compositions. At one flight he rose to the highest plane of artistic excellence, to rank with the veteran Titian, and with Tintoretto in the height of his fame. In these creations the Veronese of the Ducal Palace is already revealed with his daring perspective, the grand and victorious sweep of his powerful brush, the pulsating life and movement of his figures. In the plenitude of his genius he subsequently decorated the walls of the choir with two scenes from the martyrdom of SS. Sebastiano, Marco and Marcellino (all three victims of the Diocletian persecution), and the high altar with a Virgin and Child with the Baptist, SS. Sebastian, Peter and

Francis, John the Baptist and Elizabeth. In the composition L. of the choir, St Sebastian in armour clasping a banner is seen exhorting SS. Marco and Marcellino to be faithful unto death, while their mothers at the top of the steps entreat them to recant and live. Below, kneeling wives and children add their supplications. This is esteemed by some the masterpiece of the artist, who has painted his own portrait in the figure of St Sebastian. To the R. of the choir is the Martyrdom of St Sebastian.

Veronese designed also the decorations of the organ and painted the panels, (outside) the Purification of the Virgin, (inside) the Pool of Bethesda. The church possesses three altar-pieces by the master (the first altar has a St Nicholas by Titian), and the wall paintings in fresco in the upper choir.

We retrace our steps to the Ponte delle Pazienze, which we cross, and quickly reach the long basilica of S. Maria del Carmine, elaborately renovated in the seventeenth century. The church contains a somewhat faded Cima, Birth of Christ, with a characteristic landscape; an early Tintoretto, the Purification of the Virgin; Lorenzo Lotto's Apotheosis of St Nicholas, with the Baptist, St Lucy, and angels bearing the bishop's mitre and crook. In a landscape to R. is seen St George slaying the dragon; in the centre the Princess near a city by the sea; L. are some peasants—a noble and poetic creation.

N.ERICHSEN

DOORWAY WITH COLOURED RELIEF OF SS. MARK AND
ANIANUS: COBBLERS' GUILD HOUSE, CAMPO S. TOMÀ

We leave by the door of the L. aisle, and make our way through the long Campo S. Margarita to the church of S. Pantaleone, which we visit for the sake of the fine altar-piece, a Coronation of the Virgin, by Giov. Alemano and Antonio Vivarini in the chapel L. of the choir. What art was able to accomplish four centuries later we may see by lifting our eyes to the ceiling of the church over which expatiate Fumiani's paintings of the Martyrdom and Apotheosis of the patron-saint.

We leave the church on our left, and continue N.E. to the Campo S. Tomà. Here we shall find the old Guild Hall of the Cobblers (*Scuola dei Calerghi*) with a relief by Pietro Lombardo, St Mark healing the cobbler. The quaint signs of the craft over the portal and Pietro's sculpture bear traces of the original colouring. We make our way E., passing the fourteenth-century Campanile of S. Polo, one of the finest at Venice. At the base are carved in stone two lions, one of which has a serpent coiled round its neck, the other holds a human head in its claws. They are popularly supposed to symbolise the fate that overtook Marin Faliero. We note on the L. the fine old Gothic S. portal of the church, and emerge into the broad Campo S. Polo.

From the S.E. angle of the campo a way leads along the Calle della Madonetta, and by the Calle del Perdon to the Campo S. Apollinare. On the L., just before we emerge into the campo, are an inscription and a medallion of Pope Alexander III., which mark his legendary resting-place (p. 50). (Another tradition, however, indicates the portico of the old church of S. Salvatore in the Merceria as the spot where he lay.) S. from the campo a way leads to the S. Silvestro Pier on the Grand Canal.

TIMBER BOATS.

SECTION XV

Giudecca—The Redentore—S. Trovaso

A STEAMER leaves the Riva degli Schiavoni every hour for the S. Croce Pier on the island of the Giudecca where stands Palladio's masterpiece, the plague church of the Redentore de' Cappucini. The island, formerly known as Spinalunga was assigned (*giudicata*) in the ninth century as a place of banishment to certain of the nobles implicated in the murder of Doge Tradenico. Hence according to some authorities its name: by others it is believed to have been the ancient Jewry.

The fine proportion and symmetry make the interior of the church even more impressive than that of S. Giorgio Maggiore. In the sacristy are three early Venetian paintings once assigned to Giov. Bellini, now generally attributed: (1) Virgin with the Sleeping Jesus attended by two Angels to Alvise Vivarini (p. 196); (2) Virgin and Child with SS. John and Catherine and (3) Virgin and Child with SS. Mark and Francis to Bissolo. The last is by some critics attributed to Pasqualino, a feeble imitator of Giov. Bellini.

We may return by the steamer that crosses every few minutes to the fondamenta of the Zattere (rafts) so called because here the great rafts of timber from the Alps were and still are landed, and follow the rio di S. Trovaso, on which is a most picturesque *squero* (boat builder's) purchased by the municipality of Venice to save it from destruction, to the church of S. Trovaso. The church contains two Tintorettos of interest. At the high altar is his Temptation of St Anthony. "A small and very carefully finished picture, marvellously temperate and quiet in treatment," says Ruskin, who describes the painting in the Venetian Index. There is little tranquillity in the other picture, the Last Supper, in the L. transept. The whole scene is full of "bustle and tumult" and in nearly all its details the composition is coarse and irreverent. The moment chosen is when Christ has uttered the words, "One of you shall betray Me." An overturned rush-bottom chair is in the foreground. One of the Apostles is leaning down to fill his glass from a large fiasco of wine on the floor; another is in the act of lifting the lid of a soup kettle; a cat is lapping up some of the soup. The solemn scene is degraded to the level of a vulgar beanfeast.

SECTION XVI

Palazzo Labia—S. Giobbe—The Ghetti—Gli Scalzi

FROM the S. Geremia Pier on the Grand Canal we turn along the W. bank of the Cannareggio and quickly reach the Pal. Labia. A hall on the first floor is decorated by the finest of Tiepolo's work existing in Venice. We continue along the fondamenta and at length reach the grass-grown campo, opposite the Ponte Tre Archi, on which stands the Franciscan church of S. Giobbe attributed to Pietro Lombardo. The chief pictures of interest are in the sacristy: the portrait of Doge Cristoforo Moro with a careful representation of a ducal cap is a Bellini school painting; a well-preserved Marriage of St Catherine is by Previtati in the master's most suave and gracious manner; there is also a not very convincing tryptich by Ant. Vivarini. In the Ante-Sacristy is a much-restored Savoldo, the Birth of Christ. Moro's tomb is on the ground before the altar in the beautiful chapel erected by the Doge to his personal friend S. Bernardino. The chapel is a fine example of Pietro Lombardo's decorative genius and power.

FISHING BOATS ON THE GIUDECCA.

CANNAREGGIO.

The Ghetto Vecchio and the Ghetto Nuovo may be reached by crossing the Ponte Tre Archi and following the E. bank of the Cannareggio to a portico which gives access to the Jewry of Venice. The term Ghetto is said to have originated from the fact that here were located the old and new foundries for casting (*gettando*) the ordnance of the Republic. The sites of the old and the new foundries (the Ghetto Vecchio and the Ghetto Nuovo) were in 1516 assigned to the Jews for their quarter. Little that is characteristic now remains. On the L. as we enter the quarter is an inscription declaring the "firm intention of the magistrates of the Republic to severely repress the sin of blasphemy whether committed by Jews or converted Jews. They therefore have ordered this proclamation to be carved in stone in the most frequented part of the Ghetti, and threaten with the cord, stocks, whip, galleys or prisons all who are guilty of blasphemy. Their Excellencies offer to receive secret denunciations and to reward informers by a sum of a hundred ducats to be taken from the property of the offender on conviction."

We return to the fondamenta and pursue our way to the fine bridge on the R. which spans the Cannareggio and leads to the railway station. We cross the bridge and reach the church of S. Maria agli Scalzi (1648-89), designed by Longhena. The façade by Sardi was restored by the Austrians in 1853-62. The interior is condemned by Ruskin as a vulgar abuse of marble in every way. The ceiling is frescoed by Tiepolo in his most flamboyant style. This heavily decorated edifice (p. 195) was erected, as its name implies, for Our Lady of the Shoeless Friars. Behind the high altar is a doubtful Giov. Bellini. The last of the Doges, Ludovico Manin, lies in this church.

SECTION XVII

Titian's House—S. Michele in Isola—Murano

FEW parts of Venice have suffered more from the disfigurement wrought by national decadence, poverty and insensibility than that now bounded by the *Fondamente nuove*. In the sixteenth century this was one of the most charming quarters of the city. Here stood the smaller pleasure palaces of the patricians, with delicious gardens sloping down to the sea, whither they could retire after the business of the day to refresh themselves and entertain their friends. The gardens gave on that exquisite prospect where:—

"the hoar
And aëry Alps towards the north appeared
Thro' mist an heaven-sustaining bulwark reared
Between the east and west; and half the sky
Was roofed with clouds of rich emblazonry."

At evening over the face of the waters, fanned by the cooling breezes of the north, glided the "black Tritons" of the lagoons, graced by the wit and fashion and beauty of Venice. Salutation and repartee were winged with laughter from mouth to mouth, and stanza alternating with stanza of Tasso's noble verse answered each other in song over the rippling sea. Titian's palace,[117] where the master entertained all who were celebrated in art and literature, stood near the present Fondamenta. While the tables were being laid the guests were taken to see his great collection of pictures, then for a stroll about his beautiful gardens. The banquet was arranged with delightful art; tables were loaded with the most delicate viands and the most precious wines; music of sweet voices and many instruments accompanied the feast. Pleasures and amusements followed, suited to the season and the guests, until midnight closed the revelry.

MURANO

There was no brick wall then fencing about the fair island of S. Michele with its beautiful churches, cloisters and gardens; no cloud of coal smoke fouling the atmosphere of Murano, it too adorned with palaces and lovely pleasaunces.

We make our way to the ferry steamer for Murano, which leaves the Fondamente Nuove every quarter of an hour. How has the glory of Murano departed—*Muranum delitiae et voluptas civium Venetorum!* Its palaces and pleasure grounds are said by an anonymous writer of the seventeenth century[118] to be beautiful beyond description. Spacious chambers and banqueting halls were hung with tapestry wrought with scenes from the Punic wars, and furnished with the most precious and ornate productions of Venetian craftsmen. Delicious gardens were traversed by artfully designed paths and provided with arbours of interlaced foliage; fountains, fish-ponds, cool grottos adorned with coral and shells in charming taste, pastures gay with the manifold colours of flowers, and trees bearing choicest fruits. Classic peristyles and *exedræ*, decorated with paintings and arabesques, afforded shelter from the heat of the sun or from rain, and invited to quiet converse.

On gaining the island of Murano we follow the Fondamenta Vetrai and soon reach the church of S. Pietro Martire, which possesses Giov. Bellini's altar-piece (1488), the Virgin and Child, to whom St Mark presents Doge Agostino Barbarigo. Notwithstanding the clumsiness of restorers this remains one of the most precious of Venetian paintings.

We continue along the Fondamenta, and cross the Ponte Vivarini to the ancient basilica of SS. Mary and Donatus. Legend tells of the Emperor Otho I. caught in a fearful storm, and vowing, if saved, to build a church to the Virgin, who appeared to him in a vision and indicated this very triangular space, bright with a mass of red lilies, as the chosen spot. To the basilica of S. Maria here erected, Doge Dom. Michele gave in 1125 the body of S. Donatus and the bones of the slain dragon, which are still suspended over the high altar. The story of the saint, as related by the worthy sacristan of the church with dramatic gestures, is as follows:—A terrible dragon once devastated Cephalonia, devouring the inhabitants and poisoning the waters of the river up which it swam. The good bishop Donatus determined to rid the land of the monster, and, accompanied by his clergy, went towards the river to confront it. On its appearance the clergy fled, but the saint boldly advanced alone and spat at the beast, which at once fell dead. Donatus then took a cup, and drinking of the water of the river, found it pure and sweet, called back his clergy and showed them the dead monster.

The exterior of the apse, with its masterly decoration of coloured brick and marble so lovingly described by Ruskin in the "Stones of Venice," is one of the most interesting examples of twelfth century Lombard architecture in North Italy.

We enter and note the rare and precious pavement of the church which is finer even than that of St Mark's. Much of it has been broken up and reset, but enough has remained undisturbed to rejoice the eye of the traveller. The quaint designs are wrought of opus Alexandrinum, porphyry, *verde antico* and mosaic. A favourite subject is that of two cocks bearing between them a fox with feet bound—the triumph of watchfulness over cunning. The date, September 1, 1140, may still be read on the pavement in the middle of the nave near the main entrance. The tall, solitary figure of the Virgin in the act of blessing in the apse is a twelfth-century mosaic. An example of Sebastiani's work—Virgin and Child with the Baptist, St Donatus and the donor (1484)—will be found in the L. aisle.

The local museum possesses a unique collection of Venetian glass of the finest period by the Berovieri family and the Dalmatian Zorzi il Ballerin, some of the ancient luminous red glass contrasted with a modern imitation, and a Libro d'Oro with genealogies of members of this, the closest of the guilds of Venice (p. 213). Descendants of the Berovieri still work for Salviati.

SECTION XVIII

Torcello—S. Francesco del Deserto

THE poor and almost desolate island of Torcello lies N.E. of Murano and may be reached by steamer, or by gondola with two rowers.

The ride by gondola is a delightful experience. As we are urged along the channels by the stalwart gondoliers with rhythmic strokes, lagoons, islands and mainland villages unfold themselves to our sight. A little group of cottages amid some poplars to the N.W. is all that remains of the once great and rich Roman city of Altinum. To the N.E., among the islands and groups of trees that seem to float mysteriously poised in the soft grey vaporous atmosphere, is S. Francesco del Deserto, with its cypress groves and solitary stone pine, where St Francis bade his little sisters the birds keep silence while he prayed (p. 73).

The tall, square campanile of Torcello has long been in view. We pass St James of the Marshes (S. Giacomo della Palude), now a powder magazine, then Burano, and at length enter a canal, pass under a decayed bridge,[119] and are landed at the edge of a sloping plot of grass, once the busy market-place of an important city. The cathedral of S. Maria has been twice restored or rebuilt (864 and 1088), but much of the material and probably the apse of the original basilica still survive in the actual fabric. Less than fifteen years since could be seen the old episcopal throne and semi-circular tiers of seats worn by generations of Christian pastors[120] as they sat amid their clergy facing the people. But the seats have been rebuilt and the throne partly restored with ill-fitting slabs of cheap Carrara marble. We remember visiting the cathedral shortly after the renewal with a young Italian architect, who, to our expression of pained surprise, replied, *Ma signore, era in disordine* (but, sir, it was so untidy). There is no *disordine* now in the scraped and restored interior. Many of the original marbles, with beautiful and virile designs, however, still remain in the chancel; and in the facings of the pulpit stairs, hewn into blocks and placed in position by the old builders with small regard for continuity of design, we may perhaps gaze on the very stones brought from the mainland at the time of the great migration under Bishop Paul. The restored thirteenth-century mosaic of the Last Judgment on the W. wall, with its ingenuous realism and grim humour, is unrelated in style to anything in St Mark's, and is the analogue of many a sculptured Gothic west front in northern Europe. The mosaic in the apse, the Virgin and the Twelve Apostles, with an Annunciation on the spandrils, is Byzantine in style, and believed by Saccardo to be late seventh-century work.

We note the old stone shutters of the windows as we pass to the campanile, which lost one-third of its height by a lightning stroke in 1640. A magnificent view of the lagoons and the mainland is obtained from the summit. The remarkable little church of S. Fosca, with its picturesque portico round the apse, is Byzantine in plan, and was in existence before 1011. It was restored in 1247 and again later. The cupola has disappeared and is replaced by a low tiled roof, but the four arches which carried the old dome still remain. A rudely-carved font of alabaster is worth notice. On our way back we may touch at the island of S. Francesco del Deserto. The friars give a gracious welcome, but true followers of the *poverello* that they are, will accept no gifts in return save reverence and courtesy. A little church and monastery were built around the spot where St Francis prayed, and a small brotherhood have for seven centuries kept unbroken the traditions of their gentle father.

SECTION XIX

S. Nicolo del Lido

FROM the Riva degli Schiavoni, and from any pier on the Grand Canal, steamers at frequent intervals will carry the traveller to the *Lido di Malamocco*, popularly known as *the* lido, one of the narrow sandbanks which, aided by the wit and industry of man, have preserved Venice from destruction by the patiently eroding, and at times, fiercely aggressive waves of the Adriatic. In earliest times it was covered with pine forest, and many an ancient Doge went hawking there. The Adriatic side, a line of bare, desolate sand dunes, visited only by a few lone fishermen when Byron used to take his daily rides on horseback to and fro between the fort and Malamocco, is now the most frequented bathing-station in North Italy. Along the shore "more barren than the billows of the ocean," Byron and Shelley rode one evening, and as the sun was sinking held that pregnant talk

"Concerning God, Freewill and Destiny,"

which is immortalised in *Julian and Maddalo.*

As the vessel steams along St Mark's Channel, will be seen on the left the once fair island of S. Elena, where the ashes of the mother of Constantine, the discoverer of the True Cross, are reputed to rest, and where many famous scions of the Giustiniani and Loredano families lie buried. But Vulcan has now laid his sooty hand upon it. The old monastery walls with their romantic investure of the *erba della Madonna* and other mural plants, the cloister with its gardens and tangle of rose-bushes, are now demolished to give place to an iron-foundry; the church, once so magnificent within that it seemed a miracle of sumptuous decoration,[121] is now a machine-room (*magazzino da macchine*) and tall smoke-stacks smirch the sky.

VENICE FROM THE LIDO.

The wanderer who cares for the more silent and intimate charm of Venice will, on the arrival of the steamer, turn aside from the thronged and dusty road to the bathing pavilion, follow to the N.E. the Via S. Nicolo, and walk[122] along the shore by meadows bright in spring-time with blue salvia and the star of Bethlehem to the restored eleventh-century church of S. Nicolo inside the fort. The tomb of the founder (Doge Dom. Contarini) stands over the portal, and in a small chamber in the L. transept, now used as a lumber room, a short inscription of a dozen words tells that there lie the ashes of the stout old Imperial Vicar, "Famous Taurello Salinguerra, sole i' the world,"[123] who for seven months held Ferrara (p. 77) for his master, the great Frederick, against the allied forces of the Venetians and of the Lombard League. Here in olden times the galleys and argosies of the Republic called to take in sweet water for the voyage and to pray for protection to the mariners' patron saint, and here stood a fair and costly lighthouse. We retrace our steps to the Jewish cemetery and turn L. down a country lane which we follow as far as the Villa la Favorita; we turn again L. and reach the shore of the open Adriatic, saturated with indescribable tones of blue, from palest turquoise to deepest ultramarine, and dotted with the rich yellow and orange sails of fishing craft.

The walk may be pursued along the grass-grown ramparts of the old Austrian fort to the left, or we may turn to the more material seductions of the Stabilimento dei Bagni to the right.

SECTION XX

Chioggia

VENICE FROM THE SOUTH

A STILL finer view of the Lidi is obtained by a voyage to Chioggia and back on the steamers which start from the Riva some half-dozen times daily, and if the voyager happen on a sunny, vaporous day he will enjoy a feast of gorgeous colour almost cloying in its richness.

On loosing from the Riva we steam along the canal Orfano, the legendary scene of the slaughter of the Franks and pass the islands of S. Servolo (now the lunatic asylum), S. Lazzaro with the Armenian convent and printing-press, S. Spirito and Poveglia. Beyond the porto of Malamocco on the lido of Pellestrina, a few hundred yards to the south of S. Pietro in Volta, stands the little village of Porto Secco on the filled-up porto of Albiola, where the first stand was made against Pepin and his host (p. 16). The beautiful lines of the low-lying Euganean hills have long been in sight, and the richly coloured sails of the Chioggian fishing craft. We pass the porto of Chioggia and enter the harbour. It is said that the old Venetians were wont to distinguish each of the porti by the colour of the water that flowed through: Tre Porti on the N., which gives on the Torcello and Burano group of islands, being yellow; S. Erasmo (now filled up), blue; Lido, red; Malamocco, green; Chioggia, purple. Chioggia, to the jaded sightseer, has the inestimable advantage of offering nothing of interest save the descendants of a fine and stalwart race of islanders still retaining some of their old characteristic traits of costume and language. The admirable view of Venice as we return in the evening, gradually rising with her domes and towers from the sea, is not the least delightful part of a restful and charming excursion.

L'ENVOI

"THE word *Venetia*," says Francesco Sansovino, "is interpreted by some to mean VENI ETIAM, which is to say, 'Come again and again'; for how many times soever thou shalt come, new things and new beauties thou shalt see."

APPENDIX I

LIST OF DOGES

- Paolo Anafesta, A.D. 697-717.
- Marcello Tegaliano, 717-726.
- Orso Ipato, 726-737.
- Six Mastro Miles, 737-742.
- Orso Diodato, 742-755.
- Galla Gaulo, 755-756.
- Domenico Monegaro, 756-765.
- Maurizio Galbaio, 764-787.
- Giovanni Galbaio, 787-804.
- Obelerio de' Antenori, 804-809.
- Angelo Participazio, 809-827.
- Giustiniano Participazio, 827-829.
- Giovanni Participazio I., 829-836.
- Pietro Tradenico, 836-864.
- Orso Participazio I., 864-881.
- Giovanni Participazio II., 881-887.
- Pietro Candiano I., 887-888.
- Pietro Tribuno, 888-912.
- Orso Participazio II., 912-932.
- Pietro Candiano II., 932-939.
- Pietro Participazio, 939-942.
- Pietro Candiano III., 942-959.
- Pietro Candiano IV., 959-976.
- Pietro Orseolo I., 976-977.
- Vitali Candiano, 977-978.

- Pietro Memo, 978-991.
- Pietro Orseolo II., 991-1008.
- Otho Orseolo, 1008-1025.
- Domenico Centranico, 1026-1032.
- Domenico Flabianico, 1032-1043.
- Domenico Contarini, 1043-1071.
- Domenico Selvo, 1071-1084.
- Vitale Falier, 1085-1096.
- Vitale Michieli I., 1096-1102.
- Ordelafo Falier, 1102-1117.
- Domenico Michieli, 1117-1130.
- Pietro Polani, 1130-1148.
- Domenico Morosini, 1148-1156.
- Vitale Michieli II., 1156-1172.
- Sebastiano Ziani, 1173-1178.
- Orio Malipiero, 1178-1192.
- Enrico Dandolo, 1193-1205.
- Pietro Ziani, 1205-1229.
- Giacomo Tiepolo, 1229-1249.
- Marin Morosini, 1249-1252.
- Renier Zeno, 1253-1268.
- Lorenzo Tiepolo, 1268-1275.
- Jacopo Contarini, 1275-1280.
- Giovanni Dandolo, 1280-1289.
- Pietro Gradenigo, 1289-1311.
- Giorgio Marin, 1311-1312.
- Giovanni Soranzo, 1312-1328.
- Francesco Dandolo, 1329-1339.

- Bartolomeo Gradenigo, 1339-1342.

- Andrea Dandolo, 1343-1354.

- Marin Faliero, 1354-1355.

- Giovanni Gradenigo, 1355-1356.

- Giovanni Dolfino, 1356-1361.

- Lorenzo Celsi, 1361-1365.

- Marco Cornaro, 1365-1368.

- Andrea Contarini, 1368-1382.

- Michele Morosini, 1382.

- Antonio Venier, 1382-1400.

- Michel Steno, 1400-1413.

- Tomaso Mocenigo, 1414-1423.

- Francesco Foscari, 1423-1457.

- Pasquale Malipiero, 1457-1462.

- Cristoforo Moro, 1462-1471.

- Nicolo Tron, 1471-1473.

- Nicolo Marcello, 1473-1474.

- Pietro Mocenigo, 1474-1476.

- Andrea Vendramin, 1476-1478.

- Giovanni Mocenigo, 1478-1485.

- Marco Barbarigo, 1485-1486.

- Agostino Barbarigo, 1486-1501.

- Leonardo Loredano, 1501-1521.

- Antonio Grimani, 1521-1523.

- Andrea Gritti, 1523-1539.

- Pietro Lando, 1539-1545.

- Francesco Donato, 1545-1553.

- Marc'antonio Trevisano, 1553-1554.

- Francesco Venier, 1554-1556.
- Lorenzo Priuli, 1556-1559.
- Girolamo Priuli, 1559-1567.
- Pietro Loredano, 1567-1570.
- Luigi Mocenigo, 1570-1577.
- Sebastiano Venier, 1577-1578.
- Nicolo da Ponte, 1578-1585.
- Pasquale Cicogna, 1585-1595.
- Marin Grimani, 1595-1606.
- Leonardo Donato, 1606-1612.
- Marc'antonio Memo, 1612-1615.
- Giovanni Bembo, 1615-1618.
- Nicolo Donato, 1618.
- Antonio Priuli, 1618-1623.
- Francesco Contarini, 1623-1624.
- Giovanni Cornare, 1624-1630.
- Nicolo Contarini, 1630-1631.
- Francesco Erizzo, 1631-1646.
- Francesco Molini, 1646-1655.
- Carlo Contarini, 1655-1656.
- Francesco Cornaro, 1656.
- Bertuccio Valieri, 1656-1658.
- Giovanni Pesaro, 1658-1659.
- Domenico Contarini, 1659-1674.
- Nicolo Sagredo, 1674-1676.
- Luigi Contarini, 1676-1683.
- Marc'antonio Giustiniani, 1683-1688.
- Francesco Morosini, 1688-1694.

- Silvestre Valier, 1694-1700.

- Luigi Mocenigo, 1700-1709.

- Giovanni Cornaro, 1709-1722.

- Sebastiano Mocenigo, 1722-1732.

- Carlo Ruzzini, 1732-1735.

- Luigi Pisani, 1735-1741.

- Pietro Grimani, 1741-1752.

- Francesco Loredano, 1752-1762.

- Marco Foscarini, 1762-1763.

- Luigi Mocenigo, 1763-1779.

- Paolo Renier, 1779-1789.

- Ludovico Manin, 1789-1797.

APPENDIX II

BIBLIOGRAPHY

General Histories.

BROWN, H. R. F.—"Venice: A Historical Sketch of the Republic." London. 1893.

"   "   "Venice" in the Cambridge Modern History. Vol. i. Cambridge. 1902.

"   "   "The Venetian Republic." Temple Primers. London. 1902.

DARU, P.—"Histoire de la République de Venise." 8 Vols. Paris. 1821.

FILIASI, G.—"Memorie storiche dei Veneti." 7 Vols. Padua. 1811-14.

FOUGASSES, T. DE—"Generall Historie of the Magnificent State of Venice." Translated by Shute, W. London. 1612.

HAZLITT, W. C.—"The Venetian Republic." 2 Vols. London. 1900.

HODGSON, F.—"The Early History of Venice." London. 1901.

MICHELET, J.—"Histoire de France. Vol. x. 1879.

PEARS, E.—"The Fall of Constantinople." London. 1885.

ROMANIN, S.—"Storia documentata di Venezia." 10 Vols. Venice. 1853.

Chronicles.

ALTINATE, CRONACA, and CANALE, M. DE.—"La Cronica dei Veneziani. Archivio Storico Italiano." Vol. viii. Florence. 1842.

COMINES, P. DE.—"Les Mémoires." Lyons. 1559.

MALIPIERO, D.—"Annali Veneti. Archivio Storico Italiano." Vol. vii. Florence. 1842.

ROMUALDI II.—"Archiepiscopo Salernatini Chronicon. Muratori." Rer. Ital. Script. Vol. vii.

SANUDO, M.—"Diarii di." (In course of publication.) Venice. 1879-1902.

"   "Vite de' Duchi de Venezia." Muratori. Rer. Ital. Script. Vol. xxii.

"   "Ragguali sulla Vita e sulle Opere di." Brown, R. 2 Vols. Venice. 1837.

"Venetian Calendar of State Papers." 10 Vols. London. 1864-1900.

VILLEHARDOUIN, G. DE.—"La Conquête de Constantinople." Edited by Bouchet, E. 2 Vols. Paris. 1891.

Art.

"Architecture, Dictionary of." London. 1892.

BERENSON, B.—"Lorenzo Lotto." London. 1901.

"   "Study and Criticism of Italian Art." London. 1901.

"   "Venetian Painters of the Renaissance." London. 1899.

BURCKHARDT, J.—"Der Cicerone." Edited by Bode, W. 2 Vols. Leipzig. 1884.

CROWE and CAVALCASELLE.—"A History of Painting in N. Italy." 2 Vols. London. 1871.

"   "   "Life and Times of Titian." 2 Vols. London. 1881.

JAMESON, Mrs.—"Sacred and Legendary Art." 2 Vols. London. 1890.

KUGLER.—"Handbook of Painting." Edited by Layard, A. H. London. 1887.

LAFENESTRE, G.—"La Peinture en Europe—Venise." Paris.

LEVI, C. A.—"I Campanili." Venice. 1870.

LUDWIG, G.—"Jahrbuch der königlich-preussichen Kunstsammlungen." Vols. xxii. and xxiii. Berlin. 1901-1902.

MELANI, A.—"Architettura italiana." Milan. 4a edizione.

MORELLI, G.—"Italian Masters in German Galleries." Translated by Richter, L. M. London. 1883.

MORELLI, G.—"Italian Painters." Translated by Foulkes, C. F. London. 1892.

PAOLETTI, P.—"Catalogo delle R. R. Gallerie di Venezia." Venice. 1903.

RUSKIN, J.—"The Stones of Venice." 3 Vols. Orpington. 1886.

"   "St Mark's Rest." 1 Vol. Orpington. 1884.

"   "A Guide to the Principal Pictures in the Academy of Fine Arts at Venice." Venice. 1887.

SACCARDO, P.—"Les Mosaïques de S. Marc à Venise." Venice. 1897.

SANSOVINO, F.—"Venezia Città nobilissima." Venice. 1580.

VASARI, G.—"Le Vite dei più excellenti Pittori," etc. Edited by Milanesi, G. 1878.

"   "Lives," etc. Translated by Hinds, A. B. Temple Classics. London. 1900.

ZANOTTO, F.—"Il Palazzo ducale." Venice. 1841-61.

WOODS, J.—"Letters of an Architect." Vol. i. London. 1828.

Miscellaneous.

BROWN, H. R. F.—"Life in the Lagoons." London. 1900.

CENTELLI, A.—"Caterina Cornare e il suo Regno." Venice. 1892.

CORONELLI, P.—"Armi Blasoni," etc. Venice. 1700.

DIDOT, F.—"Aide Manuce." Paris. 1875.

GOZZI, C.—"Memoirs." Translated by J. A. Symonds. 1889.

HOWELL, J.—"Familiar Letters." Temple Classics. London. 1903.

MIDDLETON, J. H., and YRIATE, C.—"Venice"; Encyclopædia Britannica. 1888.

MOLMENTI, P.—"Calli e Canali di Venezia." Venice. 1890.

    "   "Venezia: Nuovi Studi di Storia e d' Arte." Florence. 1897.

    "   "Studi e Ricerche di Storia e d' Arte." Turin. 1892.

MORYSON, FYNES.—"Itinerary." London. 1617.

ROBERTSON, A.—"The Bible of St Mark." London. 1898.

SYMONDS, J. A.—"Bergamo and Bart. Colleoni: Sketches and Studies in Southern Europe." Vol. ii. New York. 1880.

TASSINI, A.—"Curiosità Veneziane." Venice. 1897.

VORAGINE, J. DE—"The Golden Legend." Englished by William Caxton. Temple Classics. London. 1900.

YRIATE, C.—"La Vie d'un Patricien de Venise." Venice. 1886.

ZANOTTO, F.—"I Pozzi ed i Piombi, antiche Prigioni di Stato della Repubblica di Venezia." Venice. 1876.

FOOTNOTES:

[1] See Appendix II. An exhaustive bibliography will be found in "The Cambridge Modern History," Vol. I.

[2] Rimini, Pesaro, Fano, Sinigaglia and Ancona.

[3] A method of disposing of a political enemy, so common in Italy, in the middle ages, that it was expressed by a word *abbacinare*, from the *bacino* or red hot basin of brass fixed before the eyes of the victim.

[4] See "Archæologia," vol. xliv. p. 128. This curious inscription purports to have been interpreted in 1202 by Marin Dandolo, Procurator of St Mark, from the Latin of an old and decayed parchment written by Orso Hypato of Heraclea.

[5] So late as 1428 a Russian female slave was sold by one friar to another for 52 sequins, with "right to dispose of her body and soul in perpetuity." The contract is quoted by Filiasi. In 1492 a Saracen slave, 15 years old, fetched 25 sequins.

[6] The original Malamocco, destroyed by flood in the twelfth century, was a fortified place girt with walls and towers, whose precise locality is not now known. It was situated on the open Adriatic, not far from the present Malamocco. Filiasi, writing about 1800, says the ruins used to be seen at low tide about a good stone's throw from the *lido*.

[7] The Greek Emperor at Constantinople.

[8] Pietro in his two years of office could have done little more than repair the old St Mark's. Recent researches have proved that the present structure was begun in 1061 under Doge Contarini. Part of the ducal palace was pulled down to extend the basilica southwards, and part of the Church of St Theodore incorporated on the north. When the wall which separated the Chapel of St Isidore from the north transept was stripped of its marble casing in 1887 it showed a bare surface of brick blackened by exposure to the weather and one of the windows which lighted the north aisle of old St Theodore's.

[9] In 1456 the See of Castello and the Patriarchate of Grado were united, and S. Lorenzo Giustiniano was made first Patriarch of Venice.

[10] Writing about 1500-1520.

[11] The memorable triumph of the Papacy when the Emperor was made to stand barefoot in the bitter January cold outside the castle of Canossa for three days before Pope Gregory VII. would admit and absolve him.

[12] Two-thirds of the people were said to have perished.

[13] As in the arsenal of the Venetians, the sticky pitch boils in winter to daub their leaky ships which they cannot sail, and instead, one builds his ship anew, another caulks the ribs of that which many voyages hath made. One hammers at the prow and one at the poop: another makes oars: another twists the ropes: another mends the jib and mainsail.—"Inferno," xxi. 7-15.

[14] The Emperor complained much of the mosquitoes and other less volatile vermin at Chioggia. Dare we assume that these irritants were not without effect in hastening the conclusion?

[15] "*Ante cujus atrium.*" The scene is described by the Archbishop of Salerno who was present. See "Muratori, Rer. Ital.," Scrip. vii.

[16] A similar story is however told of the raising of the great obelisk at Rome.

[17] Actually one is of red, the other of grey marble.

[18] It was to join the standard of this renowned knight that St Francis, fired by stories of his prowess, set forth in 1204 and saw at Spoleto that vision which determined him to return to Assisi and devote himself to the service of another Lord.

[19] See "The Fall of Constantinople," by Edwin Pears, p. 263. This allegation is, however, much canvassed by authorities.

[20] The alleged blindness of Dandolo is one of the enigmas of history. The chroniclers are hopelessly at variance. Villehardouin, his constant associate, says he *ne voit goutte* (couldn't see a bit). Others ignore the blindness, and it is difficult to explain his career on that theory.

[21] Probably from his attempt to convert the Sultan in 1219-1220. See Sabatier's "Vie de St François, p. 271." The story of the birds is obviously an echo of the *Fioretti*.

[22] Experts in heresy.

[23] According to the archives of the Holy Office only six cases are found of the death penalty, drowning or strangling (never burning), being inflicted for heresy in Venice.

[24] Hollow balls of wax were first used, afterwards the thirty were made of gold and the others of silver.

[25] "Christ conquereth; Christ reigneth; Christ ruleth. Salvation, honour, long life and victory to our lord, Lorenzo Tiepolo, by the grace of God renowned Doge of Venice, Dalmatia and Croatia, Dominator of one-fourth and a half of the Empire of Romania. O St Mark, lend him thine aid!"

[26] Purgatorio, iii. 115.

[27] The details of the victory are inscribed in St Matthew's, the private church of the Doria family, at Genoa. Hapless Dandolo, rather than figure in a Genoese triumph, dashed out his brains against the mast of the ship that bore him away.

[28] The supreme legal authority.

[29] Birdwood, Report on the old records of the India Office.

[30] The value of a ducat is estimated by Col. Yule at about 9s. 6d. of English money.

[31] The tune sung by sailors to-day as they lift the anchor is the same as that sung a thousand years ago by the Venetians as they manned their oars or spread their sails.

[32] Lindsay's "History of Merchant Shipping."

[33] The name adopted by the Participazii at the end of the ninth century.

[34] "And a certain woman cast a piece of a millstone upon Abimelech's head, and all to brake his skull."—JUDGES ix. 53.

[35] The Quirini house is now incorporated in the new Fish Market.

[36] The column is now in the Museo Civico.

[37] The Ten could act promptly too. In 1484, one of the *Capi* crossing the Piazza saw a priest and two soldiers set upon a man with drawn weapons. He ordered their arrest. The same evening the three were hanged by torchlight between the columns.

[38] I pozzi e i piombi. Venice, 1876.

[39] Not the present *Scala dei Giganti*, built two centuries later in a different position.

[40] "*I'vo gridando pace, pace, pace!*" *Canzone all'Italia.*

[41] The hero's statue and a Latin inscription from his tomb in the demolished church of S. Antonio are now in the Museum of the Arsenal.

[42] By an unhappy misprint (*ne* for *non*) in Muratori's ed. of Sanudo Morosini has been grievously calumniated and accused of speculating on his country's misfortune. See Romanin, iii., p. 310, and Muratori, *Rerum Ital. Scriptores*, xxii. 743.

[43] The last of the Scalas died a few years ago, a poor cobbler, at Verona.

[44] The ordinary method of putting to the "question" was to tie the victim's hands behind him and swing him by the wrists over a pulley.

[45] Sanudo gives the population in 1422 as 190,000 souls, about equal to that of Cardiff to-day.

[46] In 1347, a Flanders galley, after a voyage of eight months and seven days, made a profit of 10,000 ducats.

[47] In the reign of Francesco Dandolo.

[48] The Doge uses the familiar *tu*. Jacopo the formal *voi*.

[49] Ruskin, by a curious misunderstanding of Rawdon Brown, has confused this Doge (who, according to a contemporary was a short-statured squint-eyed creature) with the original of Shakespeare's "Othello," and the error has since been repeated. Rawdon Brown's ingenious identification of the Moor of Venice with one Cristoforo Moro, refers to another Venetian of that name who lived a generation later and was a prominent official in the service of the Republic during the wars of the League of Cambrai. *Cf.* Ruskin, "Stones of Venice," vol. ii. p. 302, note, with Rawdon Brown's "Ragguali sulla vita e sulle opere di M. Sanuto," Parte I. pp. 229-235.

[50] Met to deal with the situation created by the attempt of the famous Venetian Condottiero Colleoni to win the duchy of Milan in collusion with the Florentine exiles.

[51] In 1483 the Flanders galleys were attacked by a famous Spanish privateer; 130 Venetians were killed, 300 wounded, and an enormous booty was taken. The Signory demanded satisfaction from the Emperor Charles VII., which was refused on the plea that Venice was under the ban of the Church. A certain Christopher Columbus was serving among the Spaniards.

[52] The firm, resolute features of this grand old Pontiff look out to us from Raphael's portrait of him in the National Gallery of London.

[53] Our own Henry VIII. was an important piece in the game. "You are all rascals" (*ribaldi*), exclaimed Pope Julius II. to the English ambassador in 1510.

[54] The words of this oft-misquoted phrase are: *"De toutes choses ne n'est demeuré que l'honneur et la vie qui est sauve."*

[55] Sir Thomas More was the English envoy.

[56] Girolamo Diedo's story of the famous battle is published in the *Biblioteca Diamante*, for twenty *centesimi* (twopence).

[57] By the interdict the Venetian clergy were forbidden to exercise any of the functions of the Church. By excommunication the Government and citizens of Venice were excluded from the communion of the faithful.

[58] Sir Henry Wotton told the Doge that the blow was struck by a Scotchman, who used to hang about the English embassy.

[59] The writer of the "History of the Council of Trent" is placed by Ranke second to Macchaevelli alone as an Italian historian. Mazzini, in an essay published in vol. iv. of his collected works, claims that Sarpi was the real discoverer of the circulation of the blood.

[60] So indelible an impression was made by the long struggle on the popular mind, that the locution, a *vera guerra di Candia*, to express bitter personal enmity was common in Byron's time.

[61] The incidents of this, a nobler chapter than any of the foregoing in Venetian history, may be read in Mr Bolton King's "History of United Italy," 2 vols., Nisbet, 1899.

[62] Macigno is a hard sandstone.

[63] Later researches have brought into prominence the name of Pietro Basseggio, who is now believed to have designed the earlier S. façade of the Palace.

[64] Il Palazzo Ducale di Venezia.

[65] In early times architecture, sculpture, and engineering were branches of the same profession. Michel Angelo worked for six months at San Miniato on the fortifications of Florence.

[66] *Arch. Stor. Ital.* vol. vii. p. 674.

[67] Now assigned to Marc' Antonio Gambello and Moro Coducci.

[68] The present façade is the result of alterations by Scamozzi in 1610.

[69] See Plate 72 in the Dream of Poliphilus, called the Hypnerotomachia, published in Venice by Aldus, 1499, reproduced by the Science and Art Department, South Kensington, 1888.

[70] See Berenson's "Lorenzo Lotto," chap. ii., sec. vii., revised ed., 1901.

[71] The Pietà, and the Transfiguration in the Correr Museum.

[72] The ivy-leaved toadflax.

[73] It has again been exalted to a prominent position in Room X.

[74] Morelli, however, classes it among Titian's early productions.

[75] See "XIXth Century and After," 1902, p. 156, where H. Cook gives reasons for believing the painter to have been but 86 years of age at his death in 1576.

[76] Morelli, *Italian Masters in German Galleries*, translated by Mrs Richter, pp. 184-94.

[77] *Jahrbuch der Königlich Preussischen Kunstsammlungen.* Berlin, vols. xxii. and xxiii., 1901-1902.

[78] "Marietta or the Maid of Venice."

[79] Goldoni's grandfather was a native of Modena: *Il Burbero Benefico* was first performed at Paris and subsequently translated into Italian.

[80] Now assigned to Moro Coducci of Bergamo.

[81] The Ducal Palace is not built on piles, but rests on a stratum of stiff clay.

[82] Sanudo.

[83] *Italiæ brevis Descriptio*, Ultrajecti, 1650.

[84] "Letters of an Architect from France, Italy and Greece," by Joseph Woods, 1828, vol. i., p. 256, *et seq.*

[85] Unhappily most of the old Greek marbles have been replaced by inferior Carrara. It was once proposed by the restorers to varnish and smoke the S. façade, to imitate the rich colours which the mellowing effect of time has given to the original incrustations.

[86] Left of the spectator.

[87] No. 567 in the Accademia.

[88] The traveller who is acquainted with Burne-Jones' Days of Creation will note the influence of these mosaics on the English master's work.

[89] In 1682 the slab of this tomb was accidentally discovered embedded in the wall of the Ducal Palace. In 1810 the French ordered the carving to be defaced, but the mason evaded the command by setting the stone face downwards, and in 1839 Rawdon Brown secured it and sent it to England.

[90] The figure may still be discerned in the great mosque when the light is favourable.

[91] "Devastated," says Saccardo.

[92] Reproduced in Parker's "Introduction to Gothic Architecture," ninth Edition, p. 296.

[93] During the excavations made in 1903 round the foundations of the fallen Campanile the old brick paving was clearly seen.

[94] On free days the entrance is by the farther Scala dei Censori.

[95] "The most terrific brain that ever applied itself to painting" (Vasari).

[96] (1) The Carità, (2) S. Giovanni Evangelista, (3) The Misericordia, (4) S. Marco, (5) S. Rocco, (6) S. Teodoro.

[97] Four pictures were painted for the Guild of St Mark. Two, the Carrying of the Body of St Mark from Alexandria, and St Mark saving a Saracen, are in the Royal Palace of Venice; the fourth is in the Brera at Milan.

[98] Said in the official catalogue to represent Henry VIII. and Anne Boleyn respectively!

[99] 283, SS. Mark and Vincent, is interesting from the fact that the latter saint was originally the beardless St Lawrence, which was painted over by Tintoretto to represent a full-bearded magistrate, and became St Vincent. The original painting was by Michele Parrhasio, a wealthy dilettante working in Bonifazio's atelier, who used to treat his critics to sweets and wine.

[100] Now promoted to Room X.

[101] *Quando del ver si sogna* (when dreams are true).—INFERNO, xxvi. 7.

[102] The eminent critic and scholar, 1706-78.

[103] More probably Vice or Slander.

[104] We retain the modern appellation. The old Venetians were content with Ca' (Casa) House.

[105] See *Venezia: Nuovi Studi*, etc., p. 37, by P. Molmenti.

[106] Grave reasons for doubting whether Bruno suffered death by order of the Inquisition have, however, been adduced by Théophile Desdouits, who believes the whole story to be a fabrication. See *La Légende tragique de Jordano Bruno*, 1885.

[107] Date of death.

[108] As in Jacopo Pesaro's tomb in the Frari.

[109] A rich heiress who, when fifteen years of age, eloped to Florence with a poor bookkeeper and married him. She there became the mistress, then the wife, of Francesco de' Medici, Duke of Tuscany, who was implicated in the assassination of her first husband. Notwithstanding her scandalous past and condemnation by the laws of Venice, the Signory, on her second marriage, took her under their protection for political reasons, and proclaimed her the "true and particular daughter of the Republic." She and the Grand Duke died within a day of each other in 1587, not without suspicion of poison. The Ca' Trevisan was bought by Bianca in 1577, and given to her brother, Vittore Cappello. Francesco Sansovino dedicated his *Venezia Città Nobilissima* to her.

[110] The widening was effected at the end of the eighteenth century.

[111] "Hoc circa templum sit jus mercatoribus aequm: pondera ne vergant nec sit conventio prava."

[112] It was the custom of the early Doges to make a coronation present of wild ducks to each of the nobles in Venice. Owing to the difficulty of finding sufficient game in the lagoons Doge Celsi in 1361 gave a sum of money instead. In 1521 the number of recipients had so increased that the Grand Council permitted Doge Ant. Grimani to substitute a silver medal which was called an *osella*, the Venetian for bird. The custom survived till the end of the Republic.

[113] In the sixteenth century a catalogue was published *de tutte le principali e più onorate cortigiane de Venetia.*

[114] How wayward are Ruskin's judgments at times may be illustrated by this poor work on which he lavishes the most ecstatic eulogy in the "Shrine of the Slaves," p. 38, where it is referred to as the finest picture in the world, superior even to the Bellinis in the Frari and in S. Zaccaria.

[115] From Franc. Sansovino's description of it as being reputed a jewel rather than a stone.

[116] The factions were formally reconciled in 1848.

[117] Now hidden by workmen's dwellings.

[118] *Italiae brevis descriptio.* Ultrajecti, 1650.

[119] Painted in Walter Crane's "Bridge of Life."

[120] In primitive times the bishop sat in the centre of the apse facing the congregation, just as the judge had done in the law-courts, which served as models for the first Christian churches.

[121] *Italiæ Brevis Descriptio.*

[122] The walk may be shortened by taking the direct steamer to S. Nicolo which leaves the Riva hourly.

[123] See Browning's "Sordello," *passim.*